The Science of Biometrics

The Science of Biometrics: Security Technology for Identity Verification covers the technical aspects of iris and facial recognition, focusing primarily on the mathematical and statistical algorithms that run the verification and identification processes in these two modalities.

Each chapter begins with a review of the technologies, examining how they work, their advantages and disadvantages, as well as some of their established market applications. Numerous approaches are examined. Facial recognition is much more of an emerging biometric technology than iris recognition; therefore, there are more algorithms that are currently being developed in that area. After this review, numerous applications of these two modalities are covered as well, some of which have just been commercially deployed while others are under research and development. Chapters 3 and 4 conclude with case studies to provide further application review.

This book is directed to security managers, electronic security system designers, consultants, and system integrators, as well as electronic security system manufacturers working in access control and biometrics.

Ravindra Das is a technical writer for BN.Net, Inc.™, a leading technical communications company based in Chicago, IL. He has written two books, as well as the online course content for numerous certification exams. He has been published extensively worldwide, and holds an MBA in Management Information Systems from Bowling Green State University.

The Science of Biometrics

Security Technology for Identity Verification

Ravindra Das

Routledge
Taylor & Francis Group

NEW YORK AND LONDON

First published 2019
by Routledge
711 Third Avenue, New York, NY 10017

and by Routledge
2 Park Square, Milton Park, Abingdon, Oxon, OX14 4RN

Routledge is an imprint of the Taylor & Francis Group, an informa business

© 2019 Taylor & Francis

Library of Congress Cataloging-in-Publication Data
Names: Das, Ravindra, author.
Title: The science of biometrics : security technology for
identity verification / Ravindra Das.
Description: New York, NY : Routledge, 2018. |
Includes bibliographical references and index.
Identifiers: LCCN 2018004825 (print) | LCCN 2018012109 (ebook) |
ISBN 9780429487583 (master) | ISBN 9781138594425 (hbk) |
ISBN 9781498761246 (pbk) | ISBN 9780429487583 (ebk)
Subjects: LCSH: Biometric identification.
Classification: LCC TK7882.B56 (ebook) | LCC TK7882.B56
D3725 2018 (print) | DDC 006.2/48–dc23
LC record available at https://lccn.loc.gov/2018004825

ISBN: 978-1-138-59442-5 (hbk)
ISBN: 978-1-498-76124-6 (pbk)
ISBN: 978-0-429-48758-3 (ebk)

Typeset in Optima
by Out of House Publishing

This book first and foremost is dedicated to my Lord and Savior, Jesus Christ.

This book is also dedicated in loving memory to my parents, Dr. Gopal Das and Mrs. Kunda Das.

This book is also lovingly dedicated to Anita Das, Mary Hanlon, Jaya Chandra, Satish Chandra, Robert Rodriguez, Pastor So Young Kim (and the entire congregation at the First United Methodist Church of Bensenville, IL), Dennis Johnting, Carolyn Johnson, Arun Bhalla, Jane Andrew, Asha Genna, David Genna, David Genna, Jr., Kevin Genna, and Adam and Bree Szafranski.

Contents

Chapter 1   **Introduction**   1

Overview of *Biometric Technology: Authentication,*
   Biocryptography, and Cloud-Based Architecture   1

Overview of *Adopting Biometric*
   Technologies: Challenges and Solutions   12

Chapter 2   **Review of Biometrics**   41

Two Components of Biometric Technology – A
   Review of the Technical and Social Impacts   41

The Social Implications   43

The Technical Implications   52

   A Formal Definition of Biometrics   52

   The Difference Between Physiological and
      Behavioral-Based Biometrics   55

   What is Recognition?   58

   Physical Biometrics   60

   Behavioral Biometrics   61

   Understanding the Biometric Template   63

   The Mathematical Files of the Biometric Templates   64

   The Important Biometric Metrics and Key Performance
      Indicators   66

The Major Market Applications of the Biometric
   Technologies   70

   Physical Access Control   71

   Time and Attendance   72

Logical Access Control	73
Mobile and Wireless	74
Mobile and E-Commerce	75
Surveillance	76
A Technical Review of the Major Biometric Modalities	78
Physical Biometrics – Hand Geometry Recognition	79
Physical Biometrics – Vein Pattern Recognition	81
Physical Biometrics – Facial Recognition	82
Physical Biometrics – Voice Recognition	83
Physical Biometrics – Iris Recognition	84
Physical Biometrics – Fingerprint Recognition	85
Behavioral Biometrics – Signature Recognition	87
Behavioral Biometrics – Keystroke Recognition	88
Chapter 3 Iris Recognition	90
Physical and Behavioral Biometrics	90
The Differences Between Physical Biometrics and Behavioral Biometrics	90
The Eye: The Iris and the Retina	92
The Retina	92
The Physiology of the Retina	94
The Process of Retinal Recognition	95
The Advantages and Disadvantages of Retinal Recognition	97
The Iris	100
The Physiological Structure of the Iris	101
How Iris Recognition Works: The Mathematical Algorithms	104
The "Father" of Iris Recognition – Dr. John Daugman	104
The Theoretical Framework of Iris Recognition – Tarawneh and Thunibat	106
Reducing the Effects of Pupil Dilation and Constriction – Proenca and Neves	115
Reducing the Effects of Eyelids and Eyelashes – Lin et al. and Zhou and Sun	120
Reducing the Signal Noise in the Eye Image – Shivani and Sharma	124

The Applications of Iris Recognition | 128
Overview of the Major Applications | 129
Spoofing – Print Attacks – Gupta et al. | 131
Wireless Networks – Ibrahim et al. | 139
Fuzzy Neural Networks – Karthikeyan | 147
Biocryptography | 153
Introduction to Cryptography | 155
Message Scrambling and Descrambling | 156
Encryption and Decryption | 156
Ciphertexts | 157
Symmetric Key Systems and Asymmetric Key Systems | 158
The Mathematical Algorithms with Symmetric
    Cryptography | 158
Asymmetric Key Cryptography | 159
Keys and Public Private Keys | 160
The Differences Between Asymmetric and Symmetric
    Cryptography | 161
The Mathematical Algorithms of Asymmetric
    Cryptography | 162
An Introduction to Biocryptography | 164
The Cipher Biometric Template | 165
Biocryptography Keys | 166
A Review of How Biocryptography Can Be Used to
    Further Protect Iris Templates | 167
Case Study: "The Afghan Girl – Sharbat Gula" | 174

Chapter 4   **Facial Recognition** | 179
Which One to Use? Iris Recognition or Facial
    Recognition? | 179
An Introduction to Facial Recognition | 181
Facial Recognition: How it Works | 182
Defining the Effectiveness of a Facial
    Recognition System | 184
The Techniques of Facial Recognition | 186
Facial Recognition: The Advantages and the
    Disadvantages | 188
An Overview of the Facial Recognition
    Methodologies | 190

Contents

The Various Approaches to Facial Recognition 191
The Geometry-Based Approach 191
The Template-Based Approach 192
The Bit by Bit Approach 193
The Appearance/Model-Based Approach 193
The Neural Network Approach 194
The Statistical Algorithms of Facial Recognition 195
An Overview of Facial Recognition Template Matching 195
Principal Component Analysis 197
Discrete Cosine Transform 202
Linear Discriminant Analysis 203
Locality-Preserving Projections 203
Gabor Wavelets 204
Independent Component Analysis 205
The Kernel PCA 206
The Mathematical Algorithms 206
Eigenfaces 207
Fisherfaces 213
Local Binary Pattern Histograms (LBPH) 215
Neural Networks 217
Neural Networks with Gabor Filters 221
Neural Networks with Hidden Markov Models 223
Fuzzy Neural Networks 224
Convolutional Neural Networks 225
The Applications of Facial Recognition 233
The Use of a Facial Makeup-Detection System in Facial
   Recognition – Chen et al. 234
Thermal Face Recognition for Human-Robot
   Interactions – Hermosilla et al. 245
The Use of Facial Recognition in Forensics – Ali et al. 251
The Limitations of Facial Recognition 258
Illumination 259
Pose 260
Occlusion 262
Optical Technology 262
Expression 263
Mathematical/Statistical Algorithmic Evaluations 263

The Applications of Facial Recognition 264
*Case Study: Razko Security Adds Face Recognition
Technology to Video Surveillance Systems* 265

Chapter 5 Final Conclusions 269

Index 293

Introduction

Overview of *Biometric Technology: Authentication, Biocryptography, and Cloud-Based Architecture*

So far in this sequence on biometric technology, we have published two books. The first one is entitled *Biometric Technology: Authentication, Biocryptography, and Cloud-Based Architecture* and the second book is entitled *Adopting Biometric Technology: Challenges and Solutions.*

Both of these works examine the use of Biometric Technology from both a technical and social perspective. Obviously, if two books can be written and created upon this security tool, it must have a huge impact on society in general, and especially upon the citizens here in the United States.

As I have suggested in both pieces of works, if one were to critically examine biometric technology on a spectrum in comparison with the other security mechanisms which are available upon to us today, it would rank very high (if not the highest) in terms of curiosity, understanding, and social impacts. To illustrate this point, consider your everyday lifestyle.

You get up at a certain time to go to work, you perform your job functions according to a daily schedule, you return home, spend time with your family, and get ready yet once again for the next work day. Then there are of course the weekends, which are available to us to catch up on personal matters and chores around our household.

From the moment that we get up, we are faced with security. When we take a shower, we can lock the bathroom door, and when we leave our place of residence, we make sure that the main doors are locked and made secure as well.

We unlock our cars, and when arrive at our place of employment we often have to prove our identity. This can be done merely by showing our identification badge, or, if the business or organization is sophisticated enough as well, they might employ a smart-card-based system.

With this technology, our personal information and data are stored in the memory bank of the smart card, and this is all confirmed by the smart card reader as we swipe it into the electromagnetic slide at the turnstile.

When we arrive at our workstation, we have yet another barrier of security to go through. This is primarily done by entering our username and password combination on our computer. This of course just gives us authority to access resources at the local level.

If we need to access confidential and proprietary information at a more granular level (for instance, gaining access to a particular network drive), we then have to establish and enter a whole new suite of usernames and passwords.

This goes on the entire workday. If we have to conduct virtual meetings and the like, there are yet more usernames and passwords to be entered. Then as the workday comes to an end, we walk to our car, and unlock it. As we proceed to step out and enter our respective homes, there is yet another layer of security we have to go through, which is unlocking the door lock.

But, if we choose to implement a multimodal security solution (such as an ADT burglar alarm), we have to quickly remember to disarm it.

Then as the weekend fast approaches, we face yet another host of security to go through as we set out to fulfill our objectives. For example, if we choose to fly to a particular destination, we will have to go through the security mechanisms at the airport, which will involve primarily walking through a magnetometer, and having our driver's license or even passport scrutinized in order to confirm and validate our identity.

Of course, our shoes will have to be scanned as well in order to assure the security officials that we do not have a bomb in them.

But if we choose to stay around our locales for the weekend, we still face security measures to go through as well. For instance, if we go grocery shopping, if we choose to purchase our products with a check, we will have to establish our identity to the cashier by showing our driver's license yet again, or even a state-issued identification card.

Or if we choose to attend a large-scale social event (such as a concert, sports festival, or other type of get-together which involves a lot of people) the chances are high that we will have to show our infamous driver's license yet once again, and even walk through a magnetometer.

Now, in these examples just illustrated assume that the average person is in a non-technology-related job. But, what if this particular individual is in a career which relates to security technology? Obviously then he or she will be involved in installing, deploying, configuring, and even troubleshooting these devices on a daily basis.

For example, this could be having a direct interface with network security items such as firewalls (which inspect for and prohibit malformed data packets entering into the network infrastructure of a place of business or organization); network intrusion devices (these types of technologies sniff out and detect threats occurring in a particular network segment, isolate them, and mitigate the risk or threat), or even routers (these devices route the flow of data packets on a given network trunk securely and safely via the use of mathematically based routing tables).

The point of all this is that, whether it is just the average person or even a certified and educated security professional, we do not even think twice about the security measures we face each and every single day.

For example, as you enter your username and password into your employer's workstation, do you think twice about it (except for the frustration and anger which it will cause if indeed you do forget your password, and have to have it reset again – but this time with a much longer and more complex one)? For sure you do not, it just becomes a routine part of everyday professional life.

Or what about those days in which you go to a grocery store to pay by check and you are asked to show your state-issued identification card ... do you think twice about that? Probably not, other than the fact it is just a pure hassle and perhaps a waste of time, particularly if you are in a rush to be at your next destination.

Or what if you are attending a large social event such as the ones just described, do you ever think twice to ponder about the levels of security which are implemented there? Once again, probably not here either. The only thought that is transpiring in your mind is why is so much security needed, and how soon can I get to my reserved spot?

In terms of the security professional, when dealing with the types of technologies just detailed, they do not even entertain a second thought about it. Why is this so? Well of course, he or she deals with them on a daily basis.

In other words, to them, it is second nature, and no extra thought is needed or required. In reality though, the only other thought that would enter his or her mind is if the layers of security which they have been deployed and implemented will be enough to thwart any cyber-related threats to the business or organization by which they are employed.

Then why is it when we compare all of these typical scenarios with that of biometric technology, it gets the highest level of scrutinization? Well, as these two books have examined and explained as well, when we register ourselves with a particular biometric system, it is a piece or a snapshot of our individual selves which is being captured, in order to help confirm our identity at a later point in time.

For example, from the standpoint of physiologically based biometric technologies (which are also known simply as physical biometrics), it could be an image of our fingerprint, vein pattern, face, eyes (in particular either the retina or the iris), hand shape, or even our voice which is being captured.

From the standpoint of behaviorally based biometric technologies (which are also known simply as behavioral biometrics), it could be mannerisms in the way we sign our name or even type on a computer which could be captured.

If you take some time to think about it, no other type of security technology does this – not even firewalls, network intrusion devices or even routers. it is only biometric technology which does this. This is one of the major reasons why we are so intrigued by it, fascinated by it, or even scared by it.

We have no control over those images which are being captured or even recorded upon us.

What compounds this fear even more is that once the raw image (this specific term has been used in both books – it merely refers to the physiological or behavioral image which is being captured by the Biometric system) is captured, we have no idea as to how it will be processed, computed, and even stored into a database.

It is this latter situation which causes one of the highest levels of apprehension.

For instance, we do not know by what methods the biometric templates (these are the mathematical files which are computed from the raw images) will be stored, how they will be protected from cyber-attacks, or even, worst yet, if they will be used maliciously by some third party, such as the Federal Government, when it comes to purposes of practicing high levels of law enforcement.

Also, when compared to the other types of security technologies which are available today (once again, routers, firewalls, and the network intrusion devices), there is a fundamental lack of understanding of what biometric technology is truly all about.

Of course, this same type of hypothesis could be very easily extended as well to the network security technologies just described, but yet once again it is biometric technology which gets picked at over and over again.

Also, then there comes the issue of the societal impacts which biometric technology has upon the citizens of the world. Truth be told, as was examined in the second book, many nations and their respective governments are actually quite accepting and even exuberant when it comes time to deploying and implementing a biometrics-based infrastructure for their country, whether it is for e-passports, e-voting, border security, a national ID card scheme, or even to fortify the existing wide area network (WAN) or even a local area network (LAN).

This trend appears to be occurring quite heavily and rapidly in the developing nations. This is primarily due to the fact that the use of biometric technology gives the citizens of these developing nations a sense of self-worth, fulfillment, and most importantly, knowing that they are actually recognized as unique and single citizens in the eyes of their own government, especially when it comes to receiving their particular allotted government entitlements and benefits.

But, in the developed nations, such as those of Europe, Australia, and the United States in particular, the societal impacts are much stronger, and also very negative. As also examined in quite a bit of detail in the second book, the primary reason for this is that as citizens of the United States, we are endowed with certain inalienable rights which are guaranteed to us by our very own Constitution.

For example, some of these include the rights to privacy, freedom, the ability to vote for whom we choose at the time of elections, and to pretty much lead our lives the way we want to as long as it does not intrude upon the rights or the welfare of our fellow citizens. Because of this fact, we can claim that using biometric technology intrudes upon our said rights and freedoms.

In other words, we can lay the foundation for the argument that biometric technology is a sheer intrusion upon our civil liberties and privacy rights. This stands in stark opposition to the citizens of the developing nations, where such freedoms and rights have no guarantee or place in those respective societies.

Thus, this the primary reason that the social acceptance of biometric technology in these specific geographic regions is so high – because it helps to give these citizens such cherished rights as we enjoy here in the United States.

But, because we are already guaranteed all of this by our Constitution, we can totally decry the use of biometric technology with a great margin of comfort, still knowing that there are certain mechanisms in place which will guarantee us that no matter what, we will still be counted as unique and single citizens by our own Federal Government, and that no matter what events transpire in our life (of course to a certain degree), we will still be able to claim and receive our entitlements and benefits.

And if we do not receive them in a timely manner, there are certain legal recourses established for us by which we can still receive them, albeit at a later point in time.

As mentioned, although the traditional security technologies (which include those from the standpoint of both physical- and logical-based access) will continue to serve individuals, partnerships, corporations, organizations and businesses worldwide, it will be biometric technology which will come to the forefront in the future. This is primarily due to a number of reasons, which include the following:

- In terms of logical access entry, the use of the username and password combination is also becoming counterproductive to any types of security measures. For example, corporations and businesses are now mandating the use of complex passwords which are very difficult for the end-user to remember. This is so because passwords are now the main targets of covert cyber-attacks, and can be easily guessed in just a matter of seconds with the right hacking technologies. And with much longer and more complex passwords, employees are now resorting to writing down these passwords on Post-it notes, and literally attaching these to their workstation monitors. This can be easily seen and detected by others, especially by non-employees of the business or organization, such as contractors, and as a result large-scale cases of identity theft can occur. Even worse, the costs associated with resetting these complex passwords are high for the IT team, and can be as much as $300 per employee. For a small-scale business or organization, these costs and expenses may not be as much, but as the employee numbers grow over time, these costs can become quite steep. As a result, other means are being looked at to replace the traditional username and password combination, and the use of biometric technology is receiving very close attention in this respect.

- In terms of physical access entry, the traditional lock and key methods are often used. While there is no doubt that they provide a decent means of securing a building or even an internal office setting, they can be very easily tampered into. For example, a padlock can be very easily cut off, or picked at enough until it opens up. Even built-in door locks do not provide adequate protection: if a person has enough intent, he or she can even literally take a gun and simply blow it off in just a matter of seconds. Apart from this traditional lock and key approach, there are now much more sophisticated means by which to protect the physical premises of a building. For instance, smart-card technology is now being used as well. As has been mentioned throughout the other two books and at the beginning of this chapter, smart cards look just like a credit card – but with one major difference. A smart card actually consists of a specialized memory bank, and in this all of the information and data about a card bearer can be stored. So, for example, in order to confirm the identity of a particular individual, all he or she has to do is merely either flash their smart card (which is really their work-related identification card) in front of a smart-card reader, or swipe it in a turnstile as he or she walks through it. If the information and data which are stored in the memory bank of the smart card match and correspond to what is stored in the employee database of the business or organization, then that particular employee is of course allowed entrance. If these credentials do not match up, then obviously, he or she is not allowed to gain access. But here too, there are inherent security weaknesses. For example, what if the employee loses their smart-card-based ID badge? It can be very easily picked up by a person not affiliated with the business or organization, and unless the security guard actually compares the picture on the ID badge with the face of the person, this impostor could get inside a business or organization quite easily. Or worse yet, if the hacker is covert and sophisticated enough, he or she could make use of a network sniffer and actually intercept the information and data which reside upon the memory bank of the smart card. From here, the cyber-attacker could then create a legitimate- and authentic-looking smart card ID badge, and import the intercepted information and data into the memory bank of this faked ID badge, and gain easy and quick access to the business or organization. The primary reason why this can happen is that when smart cards are read by a particular smart-card reader, the communication between the two is based upon a wireless protocol known specifically as "near field communications," or "NFC" for short. This form of communication is unencrypted, thus the information and data which reside in the memory back of the Smart Card can be intercepted as plain text, without any sort of deciphering required on the part of the hacker. Because of these security weaknesses with both the traditional lock and key as well as smart-card technology, the use of the various biometric modalities is also being called upon quite heavily in this market segment as well.

- With regard to time and attendance applications, in most places of businesses and in most organizations the traditional timecard is still used. Given the recent advances in technology, this method may seem to be very archaic as well as rudimentary, but people are resistant to change, and still continue to use the time card as the primary means by which to record the hours their employees have worked. But, this method poses not only an administrative headache, but a huge security threat as well. For instance, with the timecard, the time as it is recorded by the time clock and punched onto the timecard has to be entered manually into a spreadsheet of sorts. This is not only time-consuming and laborious, but many clerical-related errors can be introduced into the spreadsheet, and hiring the administrative staff to enter all of these hours can be quite costly for any place of business or organization. Also, one must consider, what if the corporation is hit with either a manmade or natural disaster? What will happen to all of these timecard records? Obviously, there is no easy way to electronically back them up, and if this particular scenario were to actually happen, once again, it would be very laborious and costly to scan in each and every timecard as set forth by the security policies of the place of business or organization. In terms of the latter point, probably the greatest potential threat is the phenomenon known as "buddy punching." For example, in this particular scenario, an employee calls in sick, and instead has his or her friend (who is another employee of the business or organization) punch in and punch out their timecard. So, in other words, the "sick" employee still gets paid even when they are not actually "sick." This problem is probably not so much the case with a small business, as each and every employee can be seen working and accounted for. But this is not the case with a much larger corporation. Given the much greater employee pool, each and every one cannot be accounted for and their work rotations observed with the naked eye. Thus, in this regard, the use of biometric technology is also being looked at very closely – not only to help automate and keep the administrative costs associated with time-keeping down, but also to eliminate the security threat of "buddy punching" altogether.

- In terms of security documents, driver's licenses and even the paper passports have been widely used in order to confirm the actual identity of a particular individual. The former is used mostly at the local and state levels, and the latter is used mostly as a means of identification at the federal level (such as proving one's identity at the major international airports, or when an individual travels overseas). Although these types of security documents have literally stood the test of time, they too have a major security vulnerability. That is, given the advances in technology, a driver's license or even the traditional paper passport can be quite easily spoofed and even replicated. One again, smart-card technology has been used here as well to circumvent this particular security threat, but the information and data can also be easily intercepted here as well, primarily through the use of a network sniffer. Once again, it is the near-field communications wireless protocol which is being used, and this offers no means of encryption whatsoever. So, in order to prevent the threats of easy replication of these types of security documents, as well as the easy interception of the information and data which reside in the memory bank of a smart card, the use of the biometric technology has been called upon in this market segment as well.

Given these reasons as to why biometric technology will now become one of the predominant security technologies to come into the marketplace, both the technical and the social issues surrounding the use of biometric technology will still continue to persist and evolve even more. It is therefore very important to make an attempt to resolve these particular issues (both technical and social), so that the adoption rate of biometric technology can continue to grow in the developed nations (versus the developing nations), especially here in the United States.

But, it is important to remember that the social and technical issues which surround biometric technology are complex ones; in other words, there is no easy solution to them. Perhaps one of the best ways the developed nations like the United States can learn how to actually embrace biometric technology and adopt it properly into mainstream society is to examine closely the developing nations (such as those in Africa, Asia, and Eastern Europe) that have taken to using the various biometric modalities which are now available.

For example, it has long baffled social science scholars as to why the developing nations around the world can quickly embrace new technologies such as the various biometric modalities, and why the developed nations of the world (in particular the United States) cannot.

It really appears as a paradox, for example, that the developing geographic regions really do not possess a strong enough information-technology infrastructure to support the most sophisticated means of security.

But for some reason or another, the governments of these nations are able to quickly and to some degree easily and efficiently create a national ID card system, an e-passport infrastructure, and very strong levels of border security, and even create and deploy an infrastructure to thwart any cyber-attacks with regard to the logical-based assets of that particular developing nation.

If you take a moment to think about it, you do not hear much of these developing nations as being a primary victim of a cyber-based attack or threat; rather, it is all targeted towards the developed nations.

Now take the example of the developed nations, in particular Australia, the United States, and those in Europe as well. Here, the most modern technological infrastructures are present, and one would think that it would be very easy to deploy a biometric system, without any problems at all. But still, this problem persists.

There is huge resistance not just to deploying a biometrics-based infrastructure in any way, shape or form, but there is also a strong reluctance to incorporate any type of national ID card system or an e-passport infrastructure, or even to adopt a non-biometric means by which to secure the critical information-technology infrastructure.

Now, when in comparison to the developing nations, it is the United States which has been one of the prime targets of cyber-attacks and threats, mostly stemming from the developing regions, such as North Korea and eastern Russia. Why do these sharp differences exist between the developing nations and the developed nations? Once again, it is a question of the standard of living and the constitutional rights which we are afforded.

For example, in the developing nations, the standard of living is obviously very low when compared to Western standards of living. Thus, the citizens of these nations yearn for every opportunity for a better life and to be counted as citizens in the eyes of their own government, even if it means using the various biometric modalities to achieve this particular goal.

But in stark comparison, especially here in the United States, we take our standard of living for granted, thus we can afford to have a "nay saying" attitude towards those particular technologies which would give us a better life, even if it means using biometric technology.

In other words, we know that our standard of living will continue to be the same regardless of the choices we make in securing both our professional and personal environments and ways of living. Social science scholars often point to this flaw and weakness in our thinking as American Society, as to why we always tend to be the prime target of cyber-based attacks and threats.

So as one can see, changing the overall mindset of the American public (as well as those of the other developed nations around the world) into adopting and using biometric technology will take an entire generation, if not a lifetime, to conquer.

In other words, do not expect the adoption rate of biometric technology to pick up all at once here in the United States; rather it will take very many little steps to achieve this gargantuan purpose and objective. But in the end, perhaps very small steps towards a positive rate of adoption are far superior to no steps at all being taken.

Overview of *Adopting Biometric Technologies: Challenges and Solutions*

The goal of our second book, *Adopting Biometric Technologies: Challenges and Solutions*, was to take both a critical and exhaustive look and review as to why the adoption rate of biometric technology is so low here in the United States when compared to the rest of the world.

The second chapter of this book examines this at a microscopic level, and starts with a serious discussion as to why the American public is very often exposed to the "bad news and stories," as opposed to hearing the "good news and stories" surrounding the use of biometric technology. In this regard, the media and press here in the United States are primarily to blame.

Probably one of the best examples of this is right after the tragic and horrible incidents of "9/11." Just after these terrorist attacks, the use of biometric technology was acclaimed by the American press as the ultimate security tool which would thwart any future, potential terrorist attacks. The biometric modality which got the most attention in this regard was facial recognition.

In fact, because of all of this media attention, the stock market price of many of the publicly traded biometric companies also skyrocketed. It almost felt like the internet boom of the late 1990s once again.

But after a brief period of time, after facial recognition failed to live up to all of the hype and expectations laid down before it, the American press totally decried the use of it, and made claims that it was a technology which would never prove its worth in securing and fortifying American borders.

As a result of this, the American public's already poor perception of biometric technology was only fueled further by these negative stories and reports by the American Press and Media. But if truth be told, facial recognition never failed to live up to its expectations in the technical and scientific sense.

For instance, at that particular point in time, facial recognition was still a biometric technology in its infancy, which was totally ignored by the American press, and as a result went totally unnoticed to the American public. Facial recognition merely failed to live up to the test and scrutinization of the American media.

The rest of Chapter 2 examined in very close detail the social factors which have impeded the adoption and growth rate of biometric technology here in the United States. The following fundamental reasons were explicitly cited:

* The issue of privacy rights:

  Once again, this concern or problem is a recurring one which occurs almost on a daily basis with biometric technology. This subject was also covered in the first book. But in the second book, the concept of privacy rights was more critically explored, and a specific definition was provided for it as well. It was further suggested that there are three main components of privacy rights, and they are as follows:

- Anonymity;
- Tracking/surveillance;
- Profiling.

  The first one deals more with the civil liberties groups, the second takes issue with the Federal Government (the fear of "Big Brother" watching), and the last one deals primarily with law enforcement. In reality though, it is this last issue which arouses the most fear of biometrics in the American public, especially with the recent news stories about law enforcement across all levels (federal, state, and local). This fear of law enforcement officials misusing the various biometric modalities also extends to various age groups, especially senior citizens, the younger age group, and even especially the religious groups in the United States, making claims of the "Mark of The Beast." In fact, in the second book, an entire section is dedicated to reviewing a specific scientific study which was conducted which examined the perception of biometric technology amongst various age groups. It was also noted that the United States Constitution offers indirect provisions for the protection of privacy rights amongst United States citizens as well as foreign nationals. According to social science scholars, these specific provisions have been one of the main trigger points for the controversy of privacy rights and civil liberties violations surrounding the use of biometric technology here in the United States.

- The fear of identity theft:

  There is no question that identity theft (ID theft) is one of the most prevalent forms of cyber-attacks and threats today. This happens when an important piece of information and data about a particular individual is stolen in a very covert fashion. As a result, the identity theft victim may not actually realize what has happened to him or her until literally years later. By then, the damage has already been done, and it is then often too late for the victim to rebuild his or her own identity once again. In many of these cases, it is very often the credit card number which is hijacked or intercepted, and used either for making large-scale purchases or as a vehicle through which to assume the total identity of the victim. A brief history of identity theft was reviewed, as well as how the major attacks occur today in the digital era. This fear of identity theft has passed into the biometrics industry as well. This fear is triggered in many citizens of the United States because one's physiological or behavioral self cannot be changed if the associated biometric template has been hijacked. This stands in stark contrast to the username/password or credit card number. For example, if any bits of these types of data or information were to be intercepted, hijacked, or even stolen, they can be easily reset and issued once again. However, this is not the case with regard to biometric templates. If they are ever hijacked or intercepted, there is nothing that can be done about it. As was reviewed in this specific section, a biometric template is nothing but a mathematical file. For instance, a fingerprint-recognition-based biometric template is represented as a binary mathematical file – just a series of zeros and ones (for example, 1010100001111101010). If this mathematical file were to be hijacked, there is nothing that a hacker can do with it. For instance, it is not the same as having your credit card number stolen and being used to make a massive number of purchases. To date, there have been no actual cases of identity theft occurring by a biometric template being hijacked or covertly intercepted. But, as was also reviewed in the second book, there have been cases where latent fingerprint images have been left behind on an optical-based fingerprint recognition sensor. Scientific studies have shown that these latent images can actually be used to reconstruct the actual raw image of the fingerprint, from which the unique features can be extracted and new biometric templates created.

- The overall perception of biometric technology:

  With this issue, it is not the social belief about biometric technology that is impacted, but rather it is what the American public thinks about biometric technology if they were to see an actual biometric modality or device. For example, if a particular individual were to see for the first time a fingerprint recognition device, or an iris recognition device, or even a facial recognition device, what will his or her initial perceptions about it be? There is no doubt that there will be some wonderment about it, but for the most part there will be a lot of apprehension and perhaps even grave fear about having to use it. As this section explained, the American public simply does not understand what biometric technology is all about, or what it can do. In large part, it is the biometrics industry which is to blame for this, for their lack of taking the much-needed initiative to launch training and education programs for the American public to understand truly the concepts of biometric technology. Now, this is not to say that the average American citizen has to understand in great technical detail how a facial recognition system actually works, but there should be enough knowledge prevalent so that the average American citizen can have an appreciation of the levels of enhanced security that the various biometric modalities bring to the marketplace, as well as for the benefits and the strategic advantages they bring. Instead, the American public views the differing biometric modalities as a "James Bond" type of technology, or, simply put, the "garbage in garbage out" phenomenon. To a certain degree this is understandable, because once we submit our physiological or behavioral samples to a particular system, we have no control over how it will be processed or even stored. The latter is the major concern, because many business entities (even our United States Federal Government) do not disclose how biometric templates are stored, or what security measures are afforded to make sure that they are not the prime target of a cyber-based attack or threat. In order to help calm these fears and anxieties amongst the American public, the biometric vendors here in the United States have now started to make great efforts to make the various biometric modalities available today to possess a strong level of ease of use for the end-user. Another factor which adds to the very poor perception of biometric technology here in the United States is that the processes which are used to develop the biometric devices by every different biometric vendor are proprietary, especially in the mathematical algorithms which are used. For example, the biometric vendors have their own mathematical algorithms which are used to create both the enrollment and verification templates as well as for extracting the unique features from the raw image which is captured. But, this tends to be a gray area, because these algorithms tend to be the main revenue generator (or the "bread and butter") for these biometric vendors. But by the same token, this lack of transparency has also led to a lack of standards and best practices within the biometrics industry. If there was a list which could be easily accessed by the American public, perhaps in the end biometric technology would not be viewed as a so-called "black magic" technology.

• The ergonomic factor in the biometric modalities:

The last section just reviewed now lends itself to this new section. As was discussed in the second book, when the first biometric devices (which were actually the hand geometry scanner and the fingerprint scanner) came out, they were very bulky to deploy and implement. As a result of this, the American public was very hesitant to use them, because of the way these particular modalities literally looked. This is even true for the first retinal recognition device. This too was very bulky as well as very intimidating to use for the American public, because the end-user literally had to place their eye in a receptacle which was very cumbersome and tedious to use as well. This totally discouraged any further use of retinal recognition devices, and today, while it is a very powerful biometric modality to use for physical access entry market applications, in reality it is hardly deployed or implemented any more. Because of this, the biometrics industry here in the United States is now starting to realize that the way a particular biometric device looks to an end-user (from an engineering standpoint) is very important in how it will be subsequently adopted and used later by the specific end-user population. Therefore, there is now a movement from within the biometrics industry here in the United States to make the various biometric modalities very easy and, most importantly, comfortable for the end-user to have their identity either verified or confirmed. Also in this section, a scientific study was examined which further stressed the importance of ergonomic design in the various biometric modalities in order to increase the adoption and acceptance rate of biometrics here in the United States. This particular scientific study also stressed that the biometric device must not look intimidating in the eyes of the American public.

- The phenomenon of function creep:

  As this section describes, biometric technology can be used either in a stand-alone mode (this is an instance where one biometric device is enough to conduct all of the verification transactions of the end-user population – this is primarily used by the very small to medium-sized businesses in corporate America), or the various biometric modalities can be used in conjunction with another (such as a fingerprint recognition device being used with a facial recognition device and even a third biometric modality such as iris recognition), or even be used with other non-biometric security technologies (such as a fingerprint recognition device or even an iris recognition device being used with a router or a firewall as a means of logical access entry). These specific instances of layered security solutions (in other words, biometric device with a biometric device, or a biometric device with a non-biometric device) are also known technically as "multi-modal security solutions." As a result of this, there is a lot of information and data interchange between all of these security devices, and at times it could occur that the information and data collected from one security device could be accidentally picked up by another security device, and used in a non-intentional format. Or it could be the case that the biometric templates in one database could be accidentally transferred to another database containing information and data in another security device. This phenomenon is known as "spillover," or in more technical terms it is also known as "function creep." Although this phenomenon occurs primarily internally within businesses and organizations across corporate America, it has actually become quite transparent to the American public. The primary reason for this is that the United States Federal Government is by far the largest customer for biometric solutions from the biometrics industry, and is also the biggest awarder of contracts (in terms of biometric technology procurement and deployment) to the private sector. It should also be noted as well that the United States Federal Government also maintains some of the world's largest biometric databases, which are primarily used by law enforcement agencies not only here in the United States, but worldwide as well. Because of this, there is great fear and angst amongst the American public as to how the biometric templates which are stored in these respective databases will be used against them. For example, will the biometric templates stored in one database within a different agency of the United States Federal Government be easily accessed by a local law enforcement official if a citizen is pulled over? In other words, the American public wants assurances that the information and data which are stored about them will not be used covertly against them by the United States Federal Government in other areas of their life, due to this "function creep" phenomenon.

- The legal considerations of biometric technology and its uses:

Without a doubt, technology, no matter what purposes it serves or even the specific market segments it delivers solutions to, evolves and moves at a very quick and very rapid pace. Probably one of the best examples is that of wireless technology, especially the smartphone. This is also true of biometric technology. It is also advancing at a very rapid pace to the point now that it is very miniature, and the cost has become so low now the simplest biometric device can be acquired at a local office supply store. But, the legal framework which surrounds the use and deployment of biometric technology moves quite literally at a snail's pace. For example, if a fifth-generation fingerprint recognition device were to come out, the courts here in the United States would still be working upon crafting the legal framework for the first version of this specific fingerprint recognition device. This very slow process of creating legislation around biometric technology has also proved to be a major hindrance for the adoption of biometric technology here in the United States. The following are the specific legal ramifications surrounding the use of biometric technology:

- The legal status of a biometric template:

In this regard, is a biometric template considered to be private or public data? Or should it be classified as "anonymous data"? In this regard, the European Union has made much greater progress than the United States' judicial system in ascertaining and formulating these specific classification schemes as they relate to the biometric templates which are created by the various biometric modalities.

- The storage of biometric templates:

  This has been a topic examined from both a technical and a social perspective in both books. One of the biggest legal issues here is who owns the biometric templates once they are actually stored in a database. For example, is it the individual person, or is it the entity that is responsible for maintaining the database, or is it the Federal Government which owns these specific biometric templates? The other major legal hurdle in this regard is who addresses the security issues for protecting these biometric-based databases. Is it once again the Federal Government, or is it the entity that is responsible for it? Also, how much security is deemed to be enough? Are there any legal precedents which need to be established in this regard?

- The usage of smart card technology:

  As it was mentioned earlier in this chapter, smart cards possess a special memory bank which can hold information and data about the card bearer, including the biometric templates of that particular individual. But, the legal question which arises here is who actually owns these biometric templates. Is it once again the card bearer, or the smart card vendor who actually manufactured the smart card technology being used?

- Can biometric technology be made into a mandatory security mechanism?

  This particular legal framework lends itself to corporate America. For example, what if a place of business or organization has deployed the use of biometric technology in order to confirm the identities of their employees. Can the management team at this place of business or organization force the employees against their will by mandating that their employees have to use the biometric system in place? Or will the place of business or organization be required to offer other means of verification and/or identification if the employee refuses to utilize the biometric system set in place?

- The legal admissibility of biometric templates in a court proceeding/trial:

  As we all know, it took quite a long time for DNA to be recognized as a piece of evidence which can be legally used in a legal case in order to win a guilty verdict or exonerate a convicted individual. The same holds true for biometric templates. At the present time, there is no legal precedence established as to whether a biometric template can be used with absolute certainty in a criminal trial or proceeding. Rather, it is up to the individual judge presiding over these particular legal cases whether a biometric template can be introduced as legal evidence or not. Because of this judgement call, fear resides in the American public and even amongst the legal community concerning the fairness of a criminal trial or proceeding if biometric templates can be introduced as evidence, much in the same way as DNA being used as evidence.

After these impediments or social roadblocks hindering the growth rate of biometric technology here in the United States in Chapter 2, the next two chapters (Chapter 3 and Chapter 4) looked at and examined in very close detail two major market applications of biometric technology: specifically, these were the e-passport infrastructure and the e-voting infrastructure.

In both of these gargantuan market applications, biometric technology is used quite heavily as one of the predominant means of security: in other words, using the various biometric modalities to fully and unquestionably ascertain and confirm the identity of the individual who is either travelling overseas (making use of the e-passport) or voting in an election (making use of an e-voting mechanism in order to have a ballot cast and tallied).

Many countries around the world have now adopted both of these types of infrastructures just described, but once again it is the developing nations of primarily Africa and Asia which have been at the forefront in both of these market segments.

21

For example, the citizens of many of these developing nations simply have not had the means at their disposal to visit a foreign country. But with the possession of an e-passport and now the e-passport infrastructure within their own country, the ability to travel for the citizens of these nations is now possible.

The same also holds true for the e-voting infrastructure. Once again, in many of these developing nations, the citizens have never been officially recognized by their respective governments as unique and single individuals. As a result, these people did not have the ability to cast their ballots in the elections held in their countries.

Even if they had the chance of casting a ballot, it was done by the traditional method of using an old-style paper ballot (this is also reviewed quite extensively in Chapter 3 of the second book). With these old methods, the government and election officials who were monitoring a particular voting precinct could quite literally throw away a paper ballot, or even further succumb to bribery and financial temptation in order to deliberately sway the outcome of a particular election.

But with an e-voting infrastructure which makes use of biometric technology, the citizens of these developing nations are now afforded the liberty of not only being counted as individual and unique citizens in the eyes of their own, respective governments, but now they also possess the right to vote, which is a right they never enjoyed before.

With the use of the biometric modalities in the e-voting infrastructure, not only will an individual's vote and ballot be counted, but there is now an irrefutable audit trail which will have been created of this vote and stored permanently in the e-voting infrastructure's various types of databases.

Thus, if there are any charges of corruption or voter fraud in any given election, there is now an irrefutable electronic audit trail which can be queried and pulled up immediately from the respective databases in order to resolve any disputes or claims of election fraud or corruption.

But once again in stark contrast, it is the developed nations, and in particular the United States, which so far have not adopted either an e-passport infrastructure or even an e-voting infrastructure.

One of the primary reasons for this is that it is our own Constitution which guarantees the right to American citizens that they will be counted as unique individuals in the eyes of the United States Federal Government, and that no matter what, we as the American public will always possess the right to vote and that our ballot will be counted and tallied under any type of negative circumstance which might exist or develop.

In this regard, perhaps social science scholars could even technically find fault with the United States Constitution as being probably the biggest roadblock or impediment for the poor adoption rate of biometric technology here in the United States.

As just previously described, Chapter 3 of the second book reviewed in quite a bit of detail the development of e-passport infrastructure, and how the use of the various biometric modalities is now coming into critical play within it. More specifically, this chapter reviewed the following topics:

- The origins and the history surrounding the evolution and usage of the traditional paper passport:

    This section looked at how the traditional paper passport evolved and all of the stages of growth it went through. This includes such discussions as how it was transformed from the standards set forth by the International Civil Aviation Organization (also known as the ICAO) to being a mechanism which could be read by a machine-based reader (this particular type of paper passport is also known as a machine-readable passport). Also, the different types of traditional passport which are available today were also examined, along with their key and distinct features.

- The transition from the traditional paper passport to the e-passport infrastructure:

    This section of the chapter examined some of the weaknesses which are associated with an e-passport infrastructure, in particular the security risks and threats which are posed to it. The basics of the e-passport infrastructure (from both a technical and a social perspective) were then reviewed, as well as the advantages and the disadvantages it possesses. The legal ramification of the deployment and implementation of an e-passport infrastructure was also reviewed, from the standpoint of both the country of origin and the country of destination, as well as the financial considerations and burdens which also must be taken into consideration by the government of a country that is considering the deployment and implementation of an e-passport infrastructure within their own borders.

- The mechanics and the engineering design behind the e-passport:

  This particular section of the third chapter examined in very close detail the processes which are involved in actually creating an e-passport-based infrastructure. The following topics were then further analyzed:

  - The software for the IT structure:

    Such ramifications as the software tools needed for the capture of the respective biometric information and data; performing the needed quality control checks, as well as the software needed to house the biometric databases were examined.

  - The hardware for the IT structure:

    Such concepts as the contactless integrated circuit (IC) smart-card-based microchip and the e-passport reader (which essentially reads the information and the data stored in the memory banks in the e-passport) were also looked at. The usage of a PKI (public key infrastructure) structure to help secure and fortify an e-passport infrastructure as well as the issues of the storage and processing of biometric templates (and their associated pieces of information and data) and the placement of the microchip within an e-passport as well as a scientific study which examined the effectiveness of the RFID protocol in an e-passport infrastructure were also critically reviewed.

- The security vulnerabilities and weaknesses associated with the e-passport:

  Just like the traditional paper passport, the e-passport infrastructure suffers from a set of security weaknesses and vulnerabilities, especially those which are cyber- or wireless-based. In particular, the following security threats and attacks which can affect an e-passport infrastructure were examined:

- Cloning attacks;
- Eavesdropping attacks;
- Adversary attacks;
- Weak entropy of the basic access control keys;
- Lack of access rules;
- Once valid readers;
- Denial of service attacks;
- Leakage of biometric data;
- A weak encryption key;
- Man in the middle attacks;
- No key revocation.

Also, a traceability attack posed to a particular e-passport infrastructure was also examined, from the standpoint of a scientific study.

- The social impacts of the e-passport infrastructure:

Since biometric technology is now widely employed in the various e-passport infrastructures around the world, it too now has many and great social implications. This section of Chapter 3 carefully examined the following social issues surrounding the deployment and implementation of a particular e-passport infrastructure:

- How the biometric templates (and their corresponding pieces of information and data) will be stored and used by the respective governments of country of origin and the country of destination;
- The issues of privacy rights and civil liberties violations in a macro sense, which includes all of the countries around the world that have adopted and deployed an e-passport infrastructure;
- The severe lack of understanding of citizens around the world of the benefits and strategic advantages that an e-passport infrastructure brings to the government of a country;
- Once again, the issue not only of the storage of biometric templates in the e- passport itself, but also of how these biometric templates will be stored and used in both the country of origin and the country of destination;

- The ergonomic design considerations of the biometric modalities which need to be taken into account by the government in the country of origin that is issuing the e-passport to a citizen;

- The health and safety considerations when a citizen has to visit the e-passport office in their country in order to have their biometric template processed so that it can be placed not only in the microchip of the e-passport itself, but also in the biometric databases which are located in both the country of origin and the country of destination;

- The varying and differing cultural and social beliefs which are held amongst citizens around the world regarding the usage of an e-passport infrastructure;

- Specific strategies and recommendations were also reviewed to ascertain what the governments around the world can do to help increase the acceptance rate of the usage of e-passports and their associated infrastructures amongst their own citizens.

Finally, at the end of this chapter, an actual case study was reviewed which examined the procurement, deployment, and implementation of an e-passport infrastructure in the country of Senegal.

As was discussed not only in this last chapter but elsewhere in the second book as well, both the e-passport infrastructure and the e-voting infrastructure can be viewed as symbols of establishment and embodiment for those countries which deploy and implement such types of technologies.

For example, with the e-passport infrastructure, to many nations this represents a certain way of life and prestige in which their citizens can travel abroad and bring their experiences back with them, and perhaps use that to launch a business or an organization to help stimulate their respective economies.

With the e-voting infrastructure, this gives nations around the world, especially the developing ones, a sense that their election processes have now become fair and free of corruption and bribery, and that they are also transparent to the rest of the world.

For instance, once again, in many of the developing nations, the governments have been heavily criticized by the governments of the developed nations that far too often their elections are rigged and are very much prone to bribery and corruption.

But as mentioned previously, with an e-voting infrastructure in place making use of the various biometric modalities which are available today, there is now not only fairness in these types of elections, but each and every citizen is now counted in the eyes of their respective governments, and are now finally given an equal opportunity to cast their ballot for the candidate(s) of their choice.

And if there are any questions of unfairness in the election processes of these developing nations, as also discussed in this chapter, there is now an irrefutable audit trail which can resolve any discrepancies very quickly.

But quite interestingly again, just like the e-passport infrastructure, the United States has still not yet totally adopted an e-voting infrastructure, for the reasons cited before.

According to the social science scholars, this is quite a contradiction when compared to the rest of the developing nations who have adopted, deployed, and implemented an e-voting infrastructure, and are, in fact, using it quite effectively, efficiently, as well as successfully.

The fourth chapter of the second book examines as well in extremely close detail the e-voting infrastructure. The following topics were covered and analyzed:

- The history of voting:

  In this section of the chapter, a critical look was taken at how the traditional methods of voting evolved. For example, the history of the voting process was looked at in a couple of countries, but the main focus was on the United States. The pitfalls and the setbacks which voters faced were examined, such as the use of property and religion to either allow or deny an individual the fundamental right to vote, as well as the passage of the various constitutional amendments which were required in order to bring equality and fairness to all citizens in the United States. Also, a timeline was provided which characterized the major social movements in the history of the United States' voting system since its evolution.

- The traditional methods of voting:

  This portion of the chapter examined in very close detail the inception as well as the evolution of the traditional voting mechanisms which have been utilized in the history of voting in the United States, dating all the way back to the early 1700s. Throughout this unique and rich growth, five primary stages of the traditional methods also evolved, and were covered in detail as well. It should be noted here as well that the first voting methods were based upon the "open outcry" system, and that by the late 1800s the first true mechanical voting machines actually came into use. These devices were first invented in the United Kingdom, then made their way to the United States. After the mechanical voting machines were eradicated in the late 1890s, the paper ballot method of voting came into use, then came the punched card method of voting, and finally the optical scanning ballot system was implemented.

- The problems with the traditional methods of voting:

  There is no doubt that the traditional methods of voting had (and even continue to have today) their fair share of security vulnerabilities and threats. This part of the chapter did not examine this particular component, but it took a unique perspective as well in order to determine why the voter turnout in recent elections has been so low (and which is also part of the reason for the very slow adoption rates of an e-voting infrastructure here in the United States). The following are cited as reasons for this:

  - The overall dissatisfaction with the candidates at the time of the election;
  - The economic conditions in the United States current at the time of a particular election;
  - Electoral competitiveness;
  - The type of election which is taking place;
  - The age of the voters in question;
  - The race and ethnicity of the voters;
  - The gender of the voter;
  - Hereditary factors;

- Voter fatigue;
- Cultural factors;
- Institutional factors;
- The level of saliency;
- The ease of voting.
- The transition to e-voting:

  This section of the chapter examined the movement from traditional methods of voting to the much newer methods of the
  e-voting infrastructure. The primary catalyst for this was the great
  closeness of the 2000 presidential election. A formal definition of the
  e-voting infrastructure was provided, as well as the major advantages
  and disadvantages of an e-voting infrastructure if it were to be
  implemented here in the United States. The first type of e-voting infrastructure to be experimented with here in the United States was direct
  recording electronic devices, and its major technical and electronic
  components were reviewed as well in detail, which are as follows:

  - Electronic voter lists;
  - Poll worker interfaces;
  - Interfaces for voting;
  - Special interfaces for disabled voters;
  - Interfaces for displaying the output/results of an election;
  - Result transmission systems;
  - A more modern means of displaying election results;
  - Confirmation code systems.

  The major technological classifications of an e-voting infrastructure
  were also examined, and they are as follows:

  - The direct recording electronic voting machine;
  - The optical mark recognition (OMR) system;
  - The electronic ballot printer system;
  - The internet voting system.

  It should be noted here as well that a particular e-voting infrastructure can be deployed and implemented either in a controlled

environment (where it is being used at a polling station), or in an uncontrolled environmental setting (this is typically where Internet-based voting is utilized). The differences between these two environments as well as their respective advantages and disadvantages were also critically reviewed, as well as the use of open-source software versus the use of closed in creating the electronic-based modules in an e-voting infrastructure.

- The security vulnerabilities of e-voting:
- Just like its traditional voting counterpart, an e-voting infrastructure also possesses its set of security vulnerabilities, as was examined in this section. These vulnerabilities include the following:

  - Voter fraud;
  - Improper security measures on the boxes containing the votes;
  - Election corruption;
  - Voter identity authentication;
  - Adware, malware, and spyware;
  - "Buggy" software;
  - Distributed denial of service (DDoS) attacks;
  - Insider attacks;
  - Spoofing;
  - Man in the middle attacks.

A specific scientific study was reviewed as well which closely examined the security threats posed to an e-voting infrastructure, especially from the client side (this is when Internet-based voting is used and the voter needs to access a special type of graphical user interface from either their computer or a wireless device in order to cast and transmit their ballot).

The use of the principles of cryptography to combat these major security threats and risks which are presented to an e-voting infrastructure was also examined in this section. However, as applied to the e-voting process, a cryptographic-based infrastructure must also meet a set of stringent requirements, which are as follows:

- It must ensure privacy;

- It must preserve the authentication process;
- It must ensure the level of accuracy of the e-voting infrastructure;
- It must maintain the secrecy of the e-voting process;
- Non-coercion by third parties;
- The verifiability of the e-voting process must be established.
- A specific type of application-layer cryptographic protocol which can be used in an e-voting infrastructure was examined; this is known as the "Pynx" software package, and it includes the following components:
- The key principle;
- The service protection;
- The security techniques;
- Restricted computational processing demands;
- The use of audit trails;
- The principal security requirements are met or exceeded;
- Cryptographic hashing functions;
- Encryption keys;
- Digital signatures.

With these principles in mind, the possibilities of using a public key infrastructure in an e-voting process was also examined. This would make use of public keys and private keys, the advanced encryption standard, as well as the digital signature algorithm.

- The use of biometrics with e-voting:

This component of the chapter looked closely at how the various types of biometric modalities (from both the physical biometric and behavioral biometric standpoints) can be incorporated and utilized in an e-voting infrastructure. These modalities can be used from three standpoints:

- Physical access entry;
- Time and attendance;
- Single sign-on solutions.

As was also reviewed, the most common Biometric modalities which are being used in e-voting infrastructures worldwide include finger-print recognition, hand geometry recognition, iris Recognition, and even facial recognition. The various policies and directives being used to create a list of best practices and standards in the creation, deployment, and implementation of an e-voting infrastructure were also carefully examined. These include the following:

- ISO/IEC 7816-11;
- The common biometric exchange format framework;
- The XML common biometric format;
- ANSI B10.8;
- ANSI/NIST ITL 1-2000;
- ESIGN-K;
- DIN V64400;
- The BioAPI;
- The biometric API.

Launching an entire e-voting infrastructure can be a quite a project management endeavor, and many key variables need to be taken into consideration. Some of these specific variables include the following:

- The cost of the biometric modality;
- The metrics of the biometric modalities;
- The false reject rate (also known as the FRR);
- The false accept rate (also known as the FAR);
- The resilience of the biometric system to identity theft attacks;
- The fail-safe component of the biometric system.

The use of the principles of biocryptography in an e-voting infrastructure was examined, and a scientific study which further explored this use of it, and which also looked at the use of a virtual private network, or VPN, was also reviewed. Also, an e-voting infra-structure can make use of either a unimodal biometric system (where just one biometric modality is used, such as fingerprint recognition) or a multimodal biometric system (where two or more biometric modalities are used, such as fingerprint recognition and iris recognition being used sequentially together). Another scientific study was also examined in this regard, which looked at the security vulnerabilities of using just a unimodal biometric system in an e-voting infrastructure. A third scientific study was also reviewed, which examined the benefits and strategic advantages of using a multimodal biometric system in an e-voting infrastructure. It appears that the use of an e-voting infrastructure in an uncontrolled environment (such as with remote, Internet-based voting) will be the trend of the future. Therefore, a cloud-based infrastructure could be used quite easily and effectively here as well (also known as "biometrics as a service," or BaaS for short). In this regard, another scientific study was also closely looked at which examined how an e-Voting infrastructure would actually take place in a virtualized, or cloud-based environment.

Finally, a case study was reviewed which examined the deployment and implementation of an e-passport infrastructure in the country of Mozambique.

As was discussed in this chapter, it is the e-passport infrastructure as well as the e-voting infrastructures which are utilized the most around the world, especially in developing nations such as those in Africa and Asia.

But in the developed nations, such as in Europe and the United States, the evolution and growth of these market applications of biometric technology simply have not yet reached the level where the rest of the world is at.

Numerous reasons and explanations have been cited for this, one of them primarily being the rights and the liberties which are guaranteed to American citizens by the United States Constitution. In fact, it is not just in the areas of e-voting infrastructure and e-passport infrastructures which have been lacking here in the United States, but there are also other market applications which utilize the various biometric modalities which simply have not had a quick adoption rate.

But as was mentioned at the beginning of this chapter, when compared to other security technologies, it is biometric technology which leaves a lasting technical as well as social implication for American society at large. The social science issue of how to increase the adoption rate of biometric technology here in the United States is a very complex one.

For example, not only are the privacy rights and civil liberties which are guaranteed to us by the United States Constitution an impediment to trying to escalate this particular adoption rate, but also what makes this issue such a gray area is that it contains both macro and micro issues as well. For example, in terms of the former, it is the United States Federal Government that is still by far the largest consumer of biometric technology.

The impacts of this can be felt across all industries here in the United States. For instance, whenever we travel, we are now subject to extra means of security at the major international airports, one of them being the so-called body scan. This technology can literally see through the inside of a person, even in the most private of places.

Because of this, the American public has claimed that the use of this body scanning technology is an utter and sheer violation of privacy rights as well as of civil liberties. Because of the negative impacts created by the use of body scanning technology, this has had a negative, ripple effect upon the overall acceptance of biometric technology by the American public.

An example of a micro issue is that now the United States Federal Government has started to introduce and mandate the usage of biometric technology for school lunch programs for the children of families who are living well below the poverty line. With this, a student does not have to pay for their school lunch with cash, rather they can pay for it by registering and enrolling their respective fingerprints in a biometric database.

Therefore, once they enter the line to procure their lunch for the day, all the students have to do is merely have their identity confirmed by the fingerprint recognition system, and from there all the food and the other consumable items are paid for by the Federal Government.

But despite these best intentions, many parents have totally and outright objected to the use of biometric technology (in this case fingerprint recognition) to register their children in these subsidized school meal programs.

The concluding chapter of the second book not only summarized the content covered in the preceding four chapters, but it also examined in a little bit more detail some of these other social and technical issues.

For example, it was pointed out in this concluding chapter that the type of biometric modality which is being used can also have a great impact upon the overall adoption rate of biometric technology here in the United States.

For example, in this regard, the oldest of the biometric modalities such as hand geometry recognition and fingerprint recognition will probably be the most widely accepted for usage by the American public.

This is primarily so because these two types of biometric modalities have been around the longest, and the ergonomic designs of these two particular biometric modalities have also become much more appealing and easy to use, thus helping to increase their adoption rate in the various market segments that they both serve.

But on the contrary side of this, the Biometric modalities of facial recognition and retinal recognition would have a very poor and dismal acceptance rate with the American public. In terms of the former, the nature of this particular biometric technology has always had a negative social connotation attached to it (primarily that of "Big Brother" watching over the shoulders of everyday average American citizens). In terms of the latter, as was discussed in the first book as well, this particular biometric modality is just way too user-invasive to be widely accepted by the American public.

Interestingly enough, a subset of retinal recognition is iris recognition. As a sharp contrast, this particular biometric modality is actually starting now to receive a higher acceptance rate amongst the American public. At one point in time in the last decade iris recognition was also deemed to be just as user-invasive as retinal recognition continues to be today.

But over time, iris recognition technology became much more user friendly and "sleek" in terms of its particular ergonomic design, as well as in terms of its strong level of ease of use. As a result of all of these positive factors, the American public has been more receptive and accepting towards both the adoption and usage of iris recognition.

In terms of the behavioral biometrics, such as keystroke recognition and signature recognition, it is also highly expected that over the course of time they too will have a strong adoption rate here in the United States.

The primary reason for this is that these two particular biometric modalities are not only quite easy to use for the American public, but they can be very easily installed into an existing security-based or IT infrastructure quite easily and quickly as well.

But, the reason why these two behavioral-based biometric modalities will need time to be accepted by American citizens is that when compared to the other physical-based biometric modalities, keystroke recognition and signature recognition are the least deployed, used, and implemented. The first book also examined three potential biometric modalities which currently in the research and development phases. They are as follows:

- Earlobe recognition;
- Gait recognition;
- DNA recognition.

So far, it is gait recognition which holds the most promise of being a valid biometric technology. With this modality, the identity of a particular individual can be confirmed by the way they walk, or their unique strides which they possess. After gait recognition, the next potential biometric modality which holds great promise is DNA recognition.

A particular individual can have their identity confirmed just based solely upon the four unique strands they possess in their DNA (which are adenine, guanine, cytosine, and thymine). But if DNA recognition ever does become a viable biometric technology, it too will be prone to severe claims of privacy rights as well as civil liberties violations.

The primary reason for this is that the usage of DNA is viewed by the American public to be amongst the most private in terms of a physiological or biological snapshot being captured of our individual selves.

However, despite the very negative images which are portrayed here in the United States, there are several growth areas of the usage of biometric technology, and, as the concluding chapter of the second book examines, these particular market segments could be those specific catalysts and triggers which are needed in order to spur the adoption rate of biometric technology here in the United States.

These specific market segments include the following:

- Single-sign-on solutions;
- Time and attendance;
- Mobility and wireless devices.

In terms of the first one, the American public knows all too well of the security vulnerabilities which the username/password combination possesses. It can be easily hacked into, and intercepted as well by a malicious third party. Because of this, corporate America has now literally mandated the use of much more stringent passwords, which are often too long and complex to remember.

Because of this, many employees now write their passwords down on a Post-it note, and literally attach it to their workstation monitor. This has become known as the "Post-it syndrome," and of course defeats all purposes of having a longer and much more complex password to remember.

This phenomenon has also led to an increase in the number of password resets which take place, and this can be an expensive proposition for any type of business or organization. For example, on average, it costs at least $300 per employee per year for each password reset.

As a result of all of this, the use of biometric technology has been called upon.

In this particular market segment, it is fingerprint recognition which is most widely used biometric modality. The optical sensor can be attached within the actual workstation, or be connected to it via a USB cable.

With one swipe of the finger, the employee of the business or organization can be logged into their workstation in just a matter of minutes, hence its name, the "single-sign-on solution." It totally eliminates the need for or usage of the username/password combination.

In terms of the second market application, many business entities here in the United States still utilize the old-fashioned method of the timecard system in order to keep track of employee working hours, and for computing payroll as well.

But as one can see, this old-fashioned method poses a lot of problems and security threats as well. For example, it can take a lot of administrative manpower and time to enter all of the clock-in and clock-out times onto a separate spreadsheet. Also, the phenomenon known as "buddy punching" is also prevalent when using the old-fashioned timecard system.

This occurs when an employee calls in sick, but still has his or her friend at the place of business or organization covertly and secretly punch in and punch out their time for them. The end result is that the employee who fictitiously called in sick will still get paid for the hours in which no productivity occurred whatsoever.

To combat all of this, once again, the use of biometric technology has been called upon as well. In this regard, it is hand geometry recognition and fingerprint recognition which are used the most, with iris recognition coming in a close third. With the usage of these various biometric modalities, there is now irrefutable proof available as to the actual employees who have worked a particular day, as well as their respective punch-in and punch-out times.

Not only is the "buddy punching" security risk totally eradicated, but so is the need to hire extra administrative personnel to record the punch-in and punch-out times onto a spreadsheet and to compute payroll as well. All of this is done automatically and quickly with the biometric modalities just mentioned.

With regard to the last market application, the use of the smartphone has exploded worldwide, including here in the United States. In reality, the Smartphone has become literally an extension of both our personal and professional lives.

We use it to communicate not only by phone, but to send text messages and various email messages as well. We conduct e-commerce transactions on it, and even use it as a calendar to help us keep track of our daily agendas, activities, and meetings.

But, there are two inherent security weaknesses with the smartphone: they can be lost or easily stolen. In any case, it is quite likely that it will fall into the hands of a malicious third party. From here, information and data can be quite easily hijacked, and become the launching pad to launch covert identity theft attacks from.

To help secure their smartphone, the major wireless carriers have long mandated the use of a password or a unique PIN code to help secure them. But as has been illustrated, the use of the password has now become the weakest link in the chain, especially when it comes to securing smartphones.

Therefore, once again, the use of biometric technology has been called upon to help secure the smartphone as well as other types of wireless technologies. In this fashion, fingerprint recognition has been the most widely used biometric modality, as a tiny optical sensor can be placed onto the hardware of the smartphone. The pioneer in this area has been the Apple corporation, with its specialized "Touch ID" fingerprint recognition technology.

Iris recognition and facial recognition have also been used, and in this regard it is the smartphone camera which can be used to capture the image of the iris or the face, respectively. From this point, specialized mobile apps can then be downloaded onto the smartphone which can then take these iris-based or facial-based raw images, extract the unique features, and subsequently create the required enrollment and verification templates.

As the last chapter of the book concluded, the adoption of biometric technology here in the United States will take a very long time to occur. But there is no doubt that one day it will actually happen, given not only the need for more sophisticated versions of security technology, but also to help combat the ever-growing and constant threats of cyber and internet-based attacks and threats.

As also discussed, the first book discussed the technical ramifications of biometric technologies, and the second book discussed the social ramifications of biometric technologies.

However, there is yet another critical, third piece which needs to be examined when it comes to biometrics. That, is the software development and application side of it.

For example, whenever we see an actual biometric device, or view an image of it, we often think that it is all about hardware-related aspects only. Yes, the hardware component (which is the actual biometric device) is a critical piece, after all, this is where the biometric templates can be stored and the respective verification and/or identification transactions actually take place.

But the truth is, many biometric devices can all be interlinked together, and even be connected to a central server.

At this level, the database containing the biometric templates and the verification and/or identification transactions can be stored here.

Therefore, the need to create customized software applications and interfaces becomes important.

At the present time, many biometric vendors offer their own "canned" suite of software applications which an end-user can easily install and use literally straight out of the box. But many different businesses and organizations have their own unique set of requirements when it comes to the software application side of a biometric system implementation.

As a result of this, many of the biometric vendors also offer (along with their "canned" suite of software applications) what are known as software development kits, also known as SDKs for short.

With this, the IT development team at a business or organization can use these various SDKs to build their own customized applications.

However, the software applications which are developed as a result of using these SDKs are often not known to the public, or for that matter even in the IT security and biometrics sectors. In the software development world, there is often a need to have a "best practices" list in order to create the most robust and efficient software code possible, and these particular lists do often exist. However, in the biometrics industry, when it comes to the development of software related applications, no such "best practices" list exists.

2 | Review of Biometrics

Two Components of Biometric Technology – A Review of the Technical and Social Impacts

As described in the last chapter, biometric technology is one of those security tools which possesses what is known as a "double-edged sword." This simply means that as it is being understood, procured, acquired, tested, and ultimately deployed and implemented, there are issues which will be faced for any business leader from two sides of the spectrum: (1) the technical side and (2) the social implications perspective.

For example, although deploying biometric technology can be a very simple task (such as wiring a fingerprint-recognition-based USB device into a wireless device or a tablet as means of a single sign-on solution, which is designed to replace the traditional username/password combination), it can also be very a complex task as well, depending upon the needs of the corporation or organization.

For instance, if a business entity already has legacy security systems in place, these have to be take into serious consideration as the planning for the provisioning of the biometric technology evolves.

Some key factors which need to be taken consideration include how the new biometric technology will interface with the legacy security system(s) currently in place, and if this new technology will actually deliver the multimodal security benefit which it has been promised to deliver by the particular biometrics vendor.

Also, this biometric technology cannot be simply deployed in an "all at once" manner either. It takes a lot of project planning, conducting detailed requirements analysis and design, but, above all, also ensuring that the security needs of the corporation or business are met (or even surpassed).

As a result, a "phased-in approach" is very often used by big businesses, in order to guarantee that not only will the acquired Biometric technology work in terms of providing additional levels of security, but that also it will "behave" or "co-mingle" well with the existing security technologies.

As this new biometric technology is being deployed at the place of business, another very critical, key component which needs to be understood is how well the end-users (such as the employees) will be properly enrolled and verified by the new biometric system.

For example, although there is a very good chance that most of the end-user population will be accepted, there is also a very good chance that a small percentage will not be able to be registered.

For example, if it is a physical biometric technology which is being deployed, the end-user population may have suffered physical injuries to their fingers, hands, or even face which will prevent them from being properly enrolled into the biometric system. This will be the case if hand geometry recognition, fingerprint recognition, or facial recognition technologies are being deployed.

So, in these instance, the business or corporation must give careful consideration as to what the alternative or back-up method will be used to properly register this small percentage of the end-user population. After all, they will have to go through the same level of scrutiny as their peers will have to go through by the biometric system. Anything less, there could be cries of preferential treatment being administered.

These examples merely highlight some of the technical issues which could very well be faced by the corporation or business as they deploy their particular biometric technology. Of course, each technical issue and how they will be respectively solved will be unique and obviously quite different from business to business.

The Social Implications

As these technical issues get resolved, there is another "umbrella of issues" which is still yet to be faced. These are the social ramifications of using biometric technology. As has been stated in the past, when biometric technology is viewed and analyzed across a spectrum of the other security technologies with which it competes, it is most prone to criticism, attack, and even praise.

Simply stated from a different perspective, if a business were to install a series of firewalls or routers at its premises, there are hardly any questions or any issues raised about it, except for the IT staff who have deployed it. As the employees and management of the business log onto their workstations and servers, nobody will notice that there are new pieces of security technology which have just been installed, and there will be no questions asked.

But now, imagine if new biometric technologies (whether physical or behavioral-based) have been deployed by the IT staff at the place of business or organization. Not only will the employees take immediate notice of it, but they will also most likely be the first to raise serious issues and concerns about it. Why is this the case (as opposed to our previous example of the firewall and router)?

Truth to be told, one of the primary reasons why biometric technology arouses so much fear, apprehension, doubt, criticism ands skepticism is that it is a piece of our individual person (whether it is from a physical or a behavioral perspective) which is being captured, recorded, and analyzed by the particular biometric system. In other words, not only do we view this as a fundamental invasion of privacy, but we also lose all sense of control when this happens.

After all, if we need to gain access to the various entry points or network resources which reside at the place of business or organization, we have no choice but to accept this security technology, and comply with the rules and regulations which are set forth with it.

The social implications which are manifested with the deployment and use of biometric technology are very complex, and in fact, were the topic of the book entitled *Adopting Biometric Technologies: Challenges and Solutions*. Because of the grave social complexities which are manifested with biometric technology, there are no clear-cut answers which can be found and utilized. Each social issue is unique amongst the individual, end-user population, and even nations as a whole.

As has also been described, this even holds true for the corporations and business which are trying to deploy it. For example, at the very beginning, after the biometric technology has been installed, the management of the business could very well face stiff resistance as well as opposition to it by their employees in terms of using it.

Some of the issues faced will more than likely involve claims of privacy rights violations (and in extreme cases, cries of civil liberties violations could also proliferate as well), mandatory submissions, and even fears of contracting a serious illness upon directly interfacing with a particular biometric modality. As mentioned, there are no clear-cut solutions which can be easily found and implemented. Rather, the social issue(s) which each employee faces will have to be examined and reviewed on a case by case basis.

Although the social implications which surround biometric technology can never be truly, one hundred percent eradicated, steps can be taken to greatly mitigate them for the business or corporation attempting to deploy it. For example, as the biometric technology is being deployed and implemented, it is very important not to just "surprise" employees about it all at once. This technique will only make employees even more resistant and opposed to using the new technology.

One of the best techniques by which to introduce employees to biometric technology is, once again, a "phased-in approach." This simply means that the management at the corporation or business needs to inform the employees from the very beginning about their intention to use biometric technology as an additional layer of security.

Now, not each and every detail has to be revealed, but just enough to let the employees know that they are deemed to be a very important part of the deployment process, and that their fears, issues, and concerns are being taken seriously.

In this regard, education about the biometric technology will become very important, and could quite literally be the "make or break" difference in the ultimate acceptance by the employees of the newly acquired biometric technology. When it comes to educating the employees, of course they do not need to know every minute, technical detail of the biometric technology. Rather, they need just enough understanding of what biometric technology is all about, and above all, how they and the corporation and the business will benefit from its use. A perfect example of this is the use of biometric technology as a single-sign-on solution. It could be stated in an education program that using passwords not only poses a grave security threat, but they are also difficult and very expensive to maintain as well.

As a result of this, fingerprint recognition (or for that matter, even iris recognition) is going to be deployed. With this, the primary advantages are that an employee will not have to remember a long and complex password any more, and that with one swipe of a fingertip an employee will be able to log on their workstation or access shared network resources within two seconds or less. Also, there will be no more issues of a forgotten or stolen password, because, after all, you carry your fingertip with you, and nobody else can steal it.

From this point onwards, some of the details of fingerprint recognition technology can be explained, such as the enrollment and authentication processes, and how biometric templates are created, what they are, and how they are stored.

Of course, separate education modules will have to be created as well in which employees will be specifically instructed how to use the fingerprint recognition system which will be deployed at their workstation (it would be used for them to login with their fingertip as opposed to the traditional password). Also, various workshops can be held in which the fears and concerns of the employees can be specifically addressed and resolved.

But despite these efforts to mitigate the social issues of using biometric technology with extensive education, it could also very well be the case that a certain percentage of the end-user base will just be totally opposed to using it altogether (such as the case with the fingerprint recognition system).

In these cases, alternative means of authentication will have to be provided such as keeping in place the existing username/password combination. If this were to be the case, another extra layer of security will have to be put in place as well, such as a challenge/response system, which would transpire after the employee has logged into their workstation with their username/password combination.

When an end-user looks at a particular biometric modality (in this regard, the actual industry type or the kind of end-user involved does not matter), very often bewilderment sets into the mind. For example, probably the first question which gets asked is, "What exactly is this thing?"

Once it has been explained to the end-user, in general terms, what the device is, then other questions often follow as to how the biometric modality specifically works, what sort of data are being collected by it, how the data are processed, how the process of verification and authentication works, and how an individual's identity can be actually confirmed.

At this point, the end-user might very well be accepting in terms of using it, other questions might still persist, or there will still be an outright objection in terms of its use. But in reality, these types of questions which have just been outlined can more or less be satisfied with just general answers. In other words, there is no need to get too "deep" with all of the technical detail as to how a particular biometric modality will actually work or perform.

One of the primary reasons for this is that biometric technology is actually becoming much more ergonomically friendly in terms of design and implementation when compared to in the past. For example, take the case of the fingerprint recognition reader.

Probably about a decade ago, this was a very cumbersome device to deploy and implement, and it was not deemed to be aesthetically pleasing in the eyes of the end-user (in this case, the end-user can be viewed as the corporation or business with employees using this fingerprint recognition device).

Because of these factors, the adoption and subsequent usage rates of these fingerprint recognition devices were rather poor, at least here in the United States. But over time, the technology behind fingerprint recognition has greatly improved, thus resulting in a much more acceptable ergonomic design. For example, it has become much smaller, and it now appears to fit seamlessly in the workplace environment.

As has been eluded to earlier in this chapter, fingerprint recognition is now the primary biometric modality which is being used to replace the traditional password. With just one quick and simple scan of a fingerprint, the end-user can be literally logged into their workstation in just a matter of two seconds or less.

The optical sensor which is used can come as a separate USB device (which can be connected to a tablet or wireless device either with a USB cable or wirelessly), or it can be embedded directly into the hardware of the computer. Other typical advances in biometric technologies also include both facial recognition and iris recognition, with the technologies of both of these specific modalities being used in smartphones. For instance, the camera of an iPhone, Samsung Galaxy, or even the Google Android can be used to capture very high-quality and robust images of both the iris and the face.

In order to create the respective biometric templates and to conduct the verification transactions, the end-user of the smartphone will have to download the appropriate mobile app, which in most cases is available from the specific biometric vendor.

On the opposite side of all of these technologies being made with all of these biometric modalities is retinal recognition. This particular biometric is deemed to be, at least from a scientific standpoint, the "ultimate" biometric. The reason for this is that the retina (which is the grouping of blood vessels in the back of the eye) possesses very rich and unique information about the end-user.

The technology for this biometric modality actually evolved back in the late 1960s to the 1970s. Through pioneering the research and development efforts, the first true retinal recognition device came about. The device was very bulky to use, and in fact very difficult to implement as well (our first book entitled *Biometric Technology: Authentication, Biocryptography, and Cloud-Based Architecture* reviews this in great detail).

For example, the end-user had to place their eye in a very ergonomically unfriendly receptacle, and then had to keep utterly still for a period of least five minutes. During this timeframe, an infrared beam of light was shone directly into the eye in a circular fashion. From here, the retina of the end-user was illuminated back into the retinal recognition device, where the unique features were then extracted and the biometric template was created.

Because this device seemed so cumbersome to both use and implement, it was deemed to be very end-user-invasive. Thus, both the adoption and acceptance of retinal recognition were extremely poor, and as a result it never truly made a big "splash" in the market place, as the other Biometric Modalities have.

Even to this day, it is used in only extremely limited physical access applications, such as use at nuclear facilities or other very sensitive Federal Government installations.

Apart from these questions being asked, there is also another misconception, at least with the American public, that all biometric modalities and their respective technologies are hardware-based. In other words, all that the end-user sees when they use a particular biometric modality is the hardware aspect of it.

For instance, if a corporation or business implements a hand geometry scanner at all of the main entry points, the end-user will obviously have to have their hand scanned, and have their identity confirmed by the shape of their hand.

In these cases, if there is a positive match (or in more technical terms, a very close statistical correlation) between the enrollment and verification templates, the hand geometry scanner will transmit a signal to the electromagnetic lock strike to unlock the door. Of course, there are other biometric modalities which can fit the role of physical access entry, and these include fingerprint recognition, iris recognition, facial recognition, and even vein-pattern recognition.

But the point being made here is that although this whole process of having an end-user's identity being confirmed by the shape of their hand, the perception that this Biometrics based Solution is all hardware based still persists in the mind of the end-user for a long time to come. Also contributing to this perception are the images of Biometric Technology which are portrayed by the Vendors themselves.

For example, whenever any literature is distributed to potential new customers or the American media, the only obvious images which are supplied are of the biometric hardware. As a result, very little attention is given to the other components which drive a particular biometric modality.

While there is no doubt that the hardware is a big component of a Biometric modality, there are also other facets of it which are important as well, in order to yield the end result of the successful confirmation of an end-user's identity.

For instance, let us go back to the example of the hand geometry scanner once again. Within this device is the optical scanner which captures the many images of the hand in just a matter of a few seconds or less.

Also housed are the mathematical algorithms which are used to compile the multiple images of the hand into one composite image, to extract the unique features of the hand (specifically, there are at least 96 unique features which can be collected), to create both the enrollment and verification templates, and also to compare and evaluate the closeness of the statistical correlation between the two (if there is enough closeness between the two, the identity of the end-user is then positively confirmed).

Also housed within this hand geometry scanner is the database. This crucial component of the biometric modality contains all of the verification and enrollment templates of all of the end-users who have been registered in this system (profiles of up to 36,000 end-users can be contained), as well as the transaction log of all successful and failed verification and identification attempts.

Even from this point, there are also other special database filters as well as mathematical algorithms contained within the hand geometry scanner which can be used for data warehousing and mining purposes.

In other words, the IT staff within seconds can pull reports by using these specific functionalities in order to get a true gauge of how the hand geometry scanner is functioning, and what areas need improvement.

An analogy which can be made to the hand geometry scanner is the automobile. It too has many moving and complex parts associated with it, and all are needed to operate at peak efficiency in order for it to run from point A to point B. But the scenario just described is just for one hand geometry scanner.

This is also known as known in technical terms is a "stand-alone solution," because only one biometric modality is required to fulfill the security needs of the business or corporation. In fact, all of the biometric modalities which are available today (both physical and behavioral-based) can be used in a "stand-alone mode."

But, now imagine if the corporation or business has much more complex requirements. Suppose that they need a hand geometry Scanner at every point of entry. Given this situation, the number of moving parts and components which are needed will escalate, as a separate hand geometry scanner will now have to be located at each point of entry.

But even in this scenario, all of the new hand geometry scanners which will be deployed can still operate in the so called "stand-alone mode." This simply means that just one hand geometry scanner will be dedicated for each point of entry in order to handle those end-users.

But now, imagine if the requirements of this particular corporation or business have now grown to not only requiring one hundred percent verification in physical access scenarios, but also for time and attendance and single-sign-on applications.

Even at this point, a dedicated hand geometry scanner can be used for each and every application need. But keep in mind as these needs grow, so will the number of hand geometry scanners, as well as other biometric modalities if the business or organization chooses to use them as well. In this situation, not only will it be expensive to procure so many biometric devices, but the network connectivity overhead will also escalate just as much.

So, rather than having a dedicated biometric modality for each type of security requirement, it would be much more efficient as well as productive to have just one biometric modality address these multiple requirements. So, for example, just a single fingerprint recognition device can be used for physical access entry, time and attendance and single-sign-on.

The question often asked at this point is how can one biometric modality address simultaneous security needs and requirements?

Truth be told, multiple biometric devices can literally communicate with each other, and share biometric templates with each other. For example, if biometric device A (which can be used for single-sign-on solutions) needs to receive the biometric templates of an end-user which it does not possess but which biometric device B (which is used for time and attendance) possesses, these two biometric devices can be networked together in order for these biometric templates to be shared.

Having these two biometric devices networked together in such a fashion is not only economical, but it also increases the usage rate of these two biometric devices, as the end-user is not inconvenienced by walking from biometric device A to biometric device B.

Such a design of biometric technologies is also known as a "client-server network topology." This simply means that many and differing biometric modalities are all networked together in order to optimize the verification and/or identification needs of the business or corporation.

This type of network configuration can also be used for very simple biometrics-based deployments, to even the most complex ones which have multiple application requirements. In this type of set up, all of the biometric modalities are connected to a central server (or even more than one). These servers become the central point, as the biometrics-based databases are stored there, and all of the verification and/or identification transactions take place here as well.

But it should be noted that all of the other components which exist in a biometric device in a "stand-alone mode" are now made available at the server level, for ease of administration. For example, as was discussed previously, all of the reports which could be pulled from just one bio-metric device can now be extracted from the central server. Doing it this way has many advantages. First, reports don't have to be pulled from each individual biometric device, they can now be pulled from just one source. Second, an IT administrator can now get an overall view of how the entire business or corporation is functioning from the standpoint of the biometric devices which are being used.

Also, if needed, various database views can also be established if the performance metrics from just one biometric device are required. The biometric vendors realize that in today's security world, software applications will have to be created in order for the business or corpor-ation to manage their client-server based networks.

As a result, they now offer what is known as "canned software" and simply give it to the customer for them to install onto their server in order for them to manage their biometric devices. However, the end-users who make use of a client-server-based network (which in this case would be the corporation or business) often have very specific needs which cannot be met by this "canned software" approach.

In response to this, the biometric vendors have also given the customer an option to procure what is known as a "software development kit," also known as an SDK for short. It can be specifically defined as follows: "A **software development kit** (**SDK** or **devkit**) is typically a set of software development tools that allows the creation of applications for a certain software package, software framework, hardware platform, computer system, video game console, operating system, or similar development platform" [1].

However, creating a software application for a biometric device let alone a client-server-based network can be a very complex task. It can be very costly for a corporation or business to accomplish this task, because it takes a software developer with a special skill set to do this.

Very often, the software application development side of procuring and deploying a biometric system is an overlooked aspect. Many businesses and corporations simply assume that by simply purchasing a biometric Device all of their respective security needs will be met.

But as can be seen, this is far from the truth. The end-user has to give very careful consideration to what implementing a biometric system means, not only from the standpoint of the hardware, but also from the standpoint of the software applications which will be required.

Because of this, the software side of biometric solutions is often viewed as the third "misunderstood" or "unknown" leg (the other two being the technical and social aspects, as reviewed at the beginning of this chapter).

Very often, these particular types of applications can be developed in house, without the need to hire very expensive software developers.

The Technical Implications

A Formal Definition of Biometrics

In order to truly start understanding what biometrics is all about, and the potential advantages it brings to a corporation or business, one must first understand the general definition of it. When people hear this specific term, the world of medicine often comes to mind. It is true that biometrics does indeed a play a very important role in this field.

In this area, biometrics refers to the actual, individual components of the human anatomy. This includes all physiological components ranging from the brain to the heart to the blood vessels all the way down to the most miniscule capillaries and cellular tissue. But how biometrics is used and what it measures in this regard is totally dependent upon the organ which is being examined.

For example, in this field, a popular use of the term biometrics is often associated with the heart. Various biometric components have been created which can examine and analyze the breadth of the heartbeat at much deeper levels than just using a simple stethoscope.

Also, the very complex electrical mechanisms which actually make the heart beat can also be studied in greater depth than can be seen through an echocardiogram or a catherization-based angiogram, with the use of biometrics.

As one can see, a lot of medical developments and breakthroughs are occurring with the use of biometrics, it is not just restricted to the heart alone. This type of technology can also be used on the brain in order to help prevent and mitigate any strokes or other medical mishaps.

The lessons which are being learned from the application of bio-metrics in the medical field are now being applied to other market applications as well.

Probably one of the best examples is in the field of market research. In the past, studies would have to rely upon a survey, conducted via either the telephone or postal mail, in order to ascertain how a select group of potential customers would react when a corporation or a business announced the launch of a new product or service, or if one were actually launched.

Since this was much more of a qualitative-based approach, much time and effort were spent in collecting the results, analyzing them, and interpreting them in order to make a product or service launch more successful.

But with the use of biometrics today, focus group interviews can now be conducted, with a large number of potential customers, and their reactions can now be examined in real time.

For example, the participants in a focus group interview can now be connected to various biometric sensors which can capture the pulse rate, the brain waves, and even the amount of perspiration as advertisements for new products and service launches are presented to them. It is important to note at this point that an advertisement is not just a television commercial, rather, it can any form of content stimuli (such as written, visual, audio, etc.).

Because these reactions from the focus group participants can now be captured in real time, all of the analysis and interpretation of this information and data can happen almost instantaneously, thus making it much more cost-effective than the traditional methods previously described.

Also by using these real-time data, the advertisements can be very finely tuned before they are launched in real time.

To summarize, the examples just portrayed are those which are being used in the medical and market research fields. But, biometrics is also being used for an entirely different purpose, namely that of security.

However, in this regard, biometrics (referred to as "biometric technology" in the remainder of this book) serves just one purpose: to be able to verify or confirm the identity of a particular individual wishing to gain access to certain resources.

At this point, one may very well be asking the question, "What are these resources?" They can be literally anything from gaining access to files which reside on a corporate or government server, to gaining access to a highly secure room from within an office, or even gaining access to the main entry points of a building.

These resources can also include gaining access to an employee's workstation (for example, using a fingerprint in lieu of a password), proprietary and confidential healthcare information and data, and even accessing the time and attendance records of employees after they have clocked in and clocked out.

There are many other resources which can be accessed through the use of biometric technology, but the examples just illustrated are the primary ones which require higher levels of security before access can be granted.

For the purposes of this book and the software applications which are created, biometric technology can be specifically defined as: "The use of computer science technology to extract the unique features of an individual, whether it be physical or behavioral traits in order to positively verify and/or identify the identity of an individual, so that he or she may have access to certain resources" [2].

To further illustrate this example of biometric technology, imagine that this computer science technology as just explored in the above definition is connected either to a main door or to a primary (central) server.

Once the identity of an individual has been confirmed via the technology, that particular individual will then gain instantaneous access to the files which he or she needs, or the door will unlock automatically, via the use of an electromagnetic lock strike.

Obviously, the reverse of all this is true as well. For example, a biometrics-based system could also very well determine that the particular individual is not who he or she claims to be, and thus will be denied access to whatever resources they are attempting to access.

Now that we have provided a formal definition of biometric technology, it is important at this point to review some of the fundamental concepts behind it.

The Difference Between Physiological and Behavioral-Based Biometrics

As the owner of the business or organization decides that they are going to implement a particular biometric modality (after hopefully conducting an exhaustive project management feasibility study analysis and study), the question then very often comes to mind as to what specific tool should be implemented in order to further fortify their lines of defenses (either from a physical access entry or a logical access entry standpoint).

This in itself can be a very difficult to question to answer. As the project management study should point out, there are many further variables and constraints which will come up which need serious consideration. In other words, it is not simply procuring a fingerprint recognition device, installing it, creating a software application for it, and then hoping it will be the answer to all of your security-based nightmares.

The complexity of the variables and constraints which will be revealed in the Project management study will depend primarily upon the physical size of the business or organization. For example, if it is a small business with very few employees, the security needs will be much more simplified in nature.

Either they will require a security-based solution for physical access entry or logical access entry, or perhaps this particular business entity will need a sophisticated tool in order to further streamline their time and attendance systems.

When the security needs are much more simplified, then the choice of the biometric modality to be used is very clear as well. In the cases of physical access entry, perhaps the use of a fingerprint recognition device or even an iris recognition may prove to be quite useful. This situation even holds true for logical access entry applications.

With regard to time and attendance, the choice of using either a hand geometry scanner or even a vein pattern recognition device could prove to be optimal. Now, let us the take the case of a Fortune 500 organization or business.

Obviously, their particular security needs will be much more complex and demanding compared to the much smaller business or organization. This is mainly due to the fact there are much higher numbers of employees, and also the company will have a much greater presence upon the international scene, with multiple offices in different global locations.

With these factors being kept in mind, there will now be multiple security needs which will face the Fortune 500 organization or business. Very often these needs will overlap one another, with the various departments having varying needs. For example, it is quite possible that all three primary security needs will exist and will have to be met. These are of course those dealing with Physical access entry, logical access entry, and time attendance. Of course, there could be other, more specific security needs which will have to be met as well.

With this much more complex security picture now in mind, the type of biometric modalities which will need to be implemented now deserves much more serious consideration. For instance, not just fingerprint recognition will work, but other biometric technologies can be utilized, say for instance for physical access entry.

With this, hand geometry scanners could be used for the main access points into the place of business or organization, and from there iris recognition and even vein pattern recognition could be used to help further secure the private office areas inside the corporation or business.

The biometric templates (which will be further explored later in this chapter) which are stored in the databases for the purposes of physical access entry could also then be transmitted to other biometric modalities which deal with the logical access entry and the time and attendance needs.

As discussed previously in this chapter, all of this would be wired to a central server (or servers) in order to help expedite communications between the various biometric modalities connected to one another, and to make the enrollment and authorization transactions that much more robust as well.

One has to keep in mind also that, with a Fortune 500 business or organization, there will be a legacy security system (or systems) in place as well, and these will have to communicate with the various biometric modalities being used.

As is obvious from the examples just portrayed, truly understanding what biometric modalities (or even modalities) are needed and required and which will best meet the needs of the corporation or business is one of the most important considerations to be undertaken.

When the image of a particular piece of biometric technology comes into mind, the image of either a fingerprint recognition device or an iris recognition device are the first to be conjured up. But the truth is, these two biometric modalities are part of just one category of biometric technology. There are actually two broad categories of biometric technology, and they are as follows:

- The physical-based biometrics modalities;
- The behavioral-based biometric modalities.

In very general terms, with the physical-based biometric modalities it is a snapshot which is taken of the physical parts of our bodies, and then this particular snapshot (usually, more than one snapshot or picture is taken, and these are then aggregated together to form one overall, composite image) is then used to extract the unique features by which our identity will be confirmed. Hence, the term "Physical biometrics" has been coined.

Also in very a broad sense, with the behavioral-based biometric modalities it is our non-physical parts which are being captured. For example, with keystroke recognition, it is our physical selves conducting the motion of typing on the keyboard and signing our name – in particular, our fingers. But, if you were to look at a deeper level, there is no physiological component which is being caught.

Rather, it is the resultant motion of our fingers which is being captured. Let us look at this in a little bit more detail. For example, when typing upon the keypad, there is a unique rhythm to it, especially in terms of how long we hold down the keys, the pattern or stride of our typing, the pressure we put upon the keys, how many times we use the same key, the speed at which we type our text, etc.

But of course, anybody with a physical ailment (such as arthritis of the fingers) will have a much different typing rhythm and pattern, when compared to an individual who does not have arthritis.

And, when we sign our name, it is virtually the same type of behavioral characteristics which are being captured from our fingers.

This also includes the pressure we put upon the pen, the angle at which we sign our name, the speed at which we compose our signature, the type of fluid momentum involved (for example, do we pick up the pen at various intervals, or do we sign our name in one continuous motion, etc.). It is very important to note at this point that the actual uniqueness of the signature does not come into consideration at all here.

After having gained an appreciation for what the overall differences of what physical biometrics and behavioral biometrics are, the next major concept to be understood is that of "recognition."

What is Recognition?

If you really think about it, having the ability to properly and quickly recognize both organic and non-organic objects is a trait and mannerism which most human beings take for granted on an almost daily basis.

For example, when one goes to work, one can remember and recognize where one has parked the car, and can quickly recognize the roads which need to be traveled to get from point A to point B.

Or, if the individual does not possess their own vehicle, then having the ability to quickly recognize the modes of public transportation becomes vital. These forms of recognition very often rely upon using visual-based cues.

But there are also other forms of recognition which are available to the human being, and these include both auditory and olfactory senses. In fact, after using the visual sense of recognition, the nasal sense of recognition is the second most powerful.

In fact, with the sense of smell, many past memories which have been cognitively stored in the brain can be triggered in an instant. But, these resurfacings of memories often happen when we least expect it, from sniffing a particular odor we did not intend to smell.

But this ability to recognize objects and the other daily facets in our lives can be taken away in an instant if a particular individual suddenly suffers from some sort of serious medical mishap, such as a stroke. Then, the ability that was given to us at birth could take very well years to regain.

The bottom line is that having the ability to recognize is a very powerful sense which we possess as human beings, in whatever form that particular recognition takes place (such as visual senses, olfactory senses, memory recognition, cognitive recognition, etc.).

Given this, scientists have spent many years, if not decades, researching how computers can possess the same sense and caliber of recognition which human beings possess. Obviously, a computer will not have much in the way of recognition in terms of the olfactory senses or in other ways, but a computer can actually see and visualize objects quite well, to a certain degree. This is best exemplified by the field known as "computer vision."

It is the sheer hope of scientists and researchers who are involved in this field that one day computers will see just as clearly as the human eye can, and process the visual information which is captured to the level and quickness that the human brain can.

In fact, the concepts of the field of "computer vision" have been applied to other technologies as well, even biometric technology. In fact, this is the primary objective for using Biometric technology:

To have the ability to recognize a particular individual, and to either confirm or not confirm their identity. However, when it comes to attempting to recognize an individual, biometric technology does not get as complex as the field of "computer vision" does.

Rather, biometric technology attempts to recognize and identify a particular individual based upon the unique physiological features or behavioral mannerisms which he or she possesses. Thus, this gives rise to the two main classifications of biometric technologies: physical biometrics and behavioral biometrics (as was discussed in the last section of this chapter).

The breakdown of these modalities and the unique features they use in order to attempt to recognize and identify a particular individual are as follows.

Physical Biometrics

- Fingerprint recognition:

  The breaks and ridges in the whorls and valleys (also known as the "minutiae") of a fingerprint are unique to each individual, and this is what is captured by the system.

- Hand geometry recognition:

  Every individual possesses some sort of unique shape of the hand, and this is what is captured by the system.

- Iris recognition:

  Recent scientific studies have shown that even identical twins have unique and distinct feature sets, which include the ridges, folds, freckles, arches, crypts, and the coronas. This is what is captured by the system.

- Retinal recognition:

  The retina is the grouping of blood vessels in the back of the eye, which lead into the optic nerve which goes into the brain. This particular grouping is so unique that it is deemed to possess the most unique information and data amongst all of the biometric modalities. This is what is captured by the system.

- Facial recognition:

  Scientific studies have also proved that most individuals have different facial structures, in the way that the major features of the face are set apart from one another (for example, the distance from the eye to the lips, the distance from the lips to the nose, etc.). This is what is captured by the system.

- Voice recognition:

  It has also been proved that most individuals possess a unique pitch in their voice when they recite a particular phrase or text. This is what is captured by the system.

- Vein pattern recognition:

  The fingertip and the back of the hand (or the palm) contain a distinct set of blood vessel patterns, especially when comparing veins amongst individuals. This is what is captured by the system.

Behavioral Biometrics

- Keystroke recognition:

  As was reviewed in some detail in the last section, most individuals also possess some sort of unique, rhythmic pattern when they type on a keyboard. This can include how fast the keys are pressed, how long they are held down, how quickly the fingers of a particular individual move from one key to the next, etc. This is what is captured by the system.

- Signature recognition:

  Whenever individuals sign their name, just like keystroke recognition, there is also a unique pattern to it. This can include how long the writing pen is held down, the pressure applied to the pen when the particular signature is signed, how long it takes to compose the signature in question, other types of unique movements of the pen, etc. This is what is captured by the system.

As has been mentioned, in the world of biometric technology there are two specific cases of formal recognition: (1) verification and (2) identification.

Now, turning the first component of recognition, which is verification, the question being asked is: "Am I who I claim to be?" This means that we make a claim to the biometric system of our identity, and in turn the biometric system has to confirm this claim by searching through all of the information and data stored in its database.

So, for example, when we approach a biometric system and present our fingerprint to the sensor or the camera, the unique features will be extracted, and then compared to see if these features are very similar to the features which currently reside in the database of the biometric system.

Once again, this the typical operating mode of most biometric systems today in the corporate world.

With regard to the second component of recognition, which is identification, the primary question being asked is: "Who am I?." This means that we are making no claims of our own, individual identity, rather, we are leaving it up to the biometric system entirely to determine who we actually are.

In other words, it is not known whether our unique information and data are already in existence in the database of the biometric system.

In these situations, the biometric system has to conduct an exhaustive search of its entire database to see if our unique information and data already exist within it. So again, for example, if we present our fingerprint to the sensor or camera, the unique features from it will be extracted, and then used to see if we actually exist in the database of the biometric system.

However, a very important point needs to be made here. One may be wondering at this point why it is that verification is used so much more often than identification. The answer to this is quite simple.

Those applications which make use of verification can confirm the identity of an individual in typically less than one second, and those applications which make use of identification can take much longer, typically minutes or even hours in order to confirm the identity of a particular person.

Also, verification applications consume much less network and bandwidth resources than those applications which make use of identification.

Now that we have explored what recognition means in the world of biometric technology, it is now important to review the vehicle which is used to either verify or identify an individual – the biometric template.

Understanding the Biometric Template

As mentioned in the previous section, the biometric modalities of today recognize and confirm the identity of a particular individual based upon the unique traits and features which he or she possesses, whether it is from either a physical or behavioral perspective.

However, at this point in trying to understand what biometric technology is all about, there is very often a misconception which comes about. That is, that as the specific biometric modality captures the unique features, it is the raw image which is stored and subsequently used to recognize and confirm the identity of the individual in question.

Yes, it is true that this does happen, and in fact it is not just one image which is being captured. The biometric modality, for instance if it is fingerprint recognition which is being used, will collect multiple images of the fingertip which is being captured.

As many as 10 to 12 images could very well be captured, and then all of these images are compiled into one master image, which is known more specifically as the "composite image." The multiple images which are captured before this composite image is created are known specifically as the "raw images."

It is the composite image from which the unique features of the fingertip are extracted (see the last section for which specific unique features are extracted). However, the individual in question is not recognized and confirmed at this point from the unique features which are extracted from the raw image.

Rather, these unique features are converted into what are as known as special types of "forms." Well, there is a specific name for this "form," and it will be used throughout the remainder of this book, especially in the software application chapters.

This form it is known as a "biometric template." The specific definition of a Biometric Template is as follows: "It is a digital representation of the unique features (either physical or behavioral) of the raw image which is captured from the individual in question" [2].

However, biometric templates are a little bit more complex than that. Rather, they are mathematical files, and the exact type of mathematical file depends upon the specific biometric which is being collected, and of course the biometric vendor who developed the exact biometric system being used to collect the raw images.

Let us illustrate this with an example, and again we will turn to the most basic one, the fingerprint. After the minutiae are collected, examined, and extracted, they are then converted into a mathematical file known simply as a "binary" mathematical file.

From the days of high-school mathematics, we all know that binary digits are simply a series of zeros and ones. So, as you can imagine, the fingerprint template now becomes a series of zeros and ones in the biometric system.

After reading this chapter thus far, you will now notice a sequence of events occurring emerging in what can be termed as the "biometric process." This process thus far includes the presentation of the biological and physiological features being captured by the sensor or the camera, from there, multiple images of this feature being captured and converted into one composite image, and from there the unique traits of that feature being captured and analyzed and converted into the biometric template.

The Mathematical Files of the Biometric Templates

It should be noted at this point that it is this biometric template, or mathematical file, which is stored in the biometric system.

The raw images of our physiological and biological features are **never** stored permanently in the biometric system. If they are stored, it is for a very short time only, up to the point when the unique features are extracted, and then these raw images are discarded.

As mentioned, each different biometric technology possesses its own kind of mathematical file. The following is a representative sampling of some of these files:

(1) Fingerprint recognition: binary mathematical files are used;

(2) Hand geometry recognition: binary mathematical files are used;

(3) Iris recognition: traditionally, Gabor wavelet theory mathematics was utilized, but, with the expiration of the original patents of Dr. John Daugman, many other, numerous types of mathematical files have emerged onto the marketplace;

(4) Facial recognition: eigenfaces and eigenvalues have been the traditional mathematical files used, but, with the advance in technology, other types of mathematical files have been used as well (again, this will be explored in much more detail in the next chapter);

(5) Keystroke recognition/signature recognition: since these are behavioral biometrics, there are no physiological or biological characteristics which are captured. Rather, statistical modeling is very often used, and from here statistical profiles are generated which then become the respective biometric templates. The theory of hidden Markov models is used the most frequently.

Even amongst the American public and the corporate sector, there is a common myth which exists about biometric templates. In fact, it is this very myth which triggers the biggest fears about biometrics, and consequently its very slow adoption rate here in the United States.

This myth is the misconception that it is the raw image which is stored, despite the fact it is just the mathematical record which resides in the database of the biometric system.

As a result, the question that gets asked too many times is: "What if my biometric template is stolen? Is that the same as credit card theft?" Well, this is true, but only to a very small degree.

Any type of hacking, whether it is a biometric template or not, is still theft, but it is nowhere near the level of the damage credit card theft can do.

After all, since the biometric templates are just mathematical files (and the algorithms which support them) which are unique to each specific technology and vendor, really, in the end, what can a hacker do with them? Really, nothing in the end.

For example, a hacker cannot take these biometric templates and purchase high-end merchandise, as opposed to accomplishing this task with a stolen credit card.

After a biometric modality or even an entire biometric system has been procured by the corporation or organization, it should be kept in mind that not all biometric technologies operate at the same level. In other words, although the general process of recognition and confirming the identity of a particular individual is the same, the specific degree to which the recognition and identification actually occurs varies greatly. This variance occurs greatly not only between the two classes of biometric technologies (physical-based and behavioral-based) but within these two classifications as well.

For example, the degree to which a fingerprint recognition device recognizes and confirms the identity of a particular individual differs when compared to a keystroke recognition device (a behavioral biometric modality), and even compared to an iris recognition device (a physical biometric modality). This occurs because it is primarily up to the IT administrator of the biometric modality or the biometric system to determine the appropriate security-based thresholds at which these modalities should be set at. Again, this is entirely dependent upon the security requirements of the corporation or the organization.

In order to help determine the appropriate threshold(s) the biometric modality needs to be set at, there are a number of key metrics which need to be looked at, even from the perspective of creating a software application.

These key metrics are now reviewed in the next section.

The Important Biometric Metrics and Key Performance Indicators

It does not relate just to Security, but whenever a corporation or organization procures products and services from an outside entity (such as another vendor, like a manufacturing one, or even a supplier, etc.), the C-level executives who are responsible for making these decisions must look at various performance-based metrics.

In other words, before the actual acquisition of a product or service takes place, the C-level executive(s) must determine how well what they intend to purchase will actually deliver the results which have been promised by the third-party vendor.

The only way that this can be accomplished is by looking at the various performance metrics of the product or service, and see how it compares with the overall industry standard. Obviously, the way to make absolutely certain that a product or service which is intended to be acquired by a corporation or a business is suitable is to do a pilot study of it first, in order to determine how well it will in work in the intended environment.

Simply stated, it is important to take the intended to be acquired product or service, and run it in a test environment before it is permanently placed into a production environment. This example also holds true for the various biometric modalities.

As discussed thus far in this book, a biometric modality (it does not actually matter whether it is a physical or behavioral-based modality) can serve in many types of configurations, which are as follows:

- In a stand-alone mode, where just one biometric device handles all of the verification and/or identification transactions;
- In a peer-to-peer mode, where all of the same biometric devices are connected together and communicate with each other;
- In a peer-to-peer mode, where different biometric devices (such as a fingerprint recognition scanner and an iris recognition scanner) are networked together and communicate with each other;
- In a client-server topology, where all of the same biometric devices are connected together and communicate with each other, but are also connected to a central server which conducts all verification and/or identification transactions;
- In a client-server topology, where different biometric devices (such as a fingerprint recognition scanner, an iris recognition scanner, and even a facial recognition scanner) are connected together and

communicate with each other, but are also connected to a central server which conducts all verification and/or identification transactions;

- All of the biometric devices which are being deployed will operate in tandem with a non-biometric, legacy security system in the corporation or the business.

Given all this multitude of configurations which are possible, it is quite easy to discern that it is best to test the biometric modalities which are intended to be procured and deployed first. Only then, of course depending on how they operate in the test environment, should they be fully implemented in the production or, in this case, the security environment.

Although this is the best-case scenario, it is also equally important to keep in mind that not all corporations and businesses can afford to do these pilot studies and evaluate new products and services at such levels of depth. The bottom line is that even this takes money, and conducting a pilot project was probably not even considered in the overall budget.

Thus, the only other alternative that a corporation or a business has, as mentioned at the beginning of this section, is to evaluate a particular biometric modality based upon the performance metrics it has been given by the respective biometric vendor, and compare it to the prescribed industry standards.

Also, in the world of biometrics, it is very easy to acquire a biometric system just because it looks "good," or is within budget, without even considering the performance metrics (also known as the "key performance indicators," or "KPIs"). Thus now, at this point, it is very important to examine and review some of these performance metrics, which can be described as follows.

The False Acceptance Rate

With regard to the false acceptance rate, this metric reflects the possibility of an illegitimate user, or even an impostor, being accepted by the biometric system. For example, this happens when John Doe who is not registered in the biometric system or even has no affiliation with the place of business, for some reason or another is actually verified by the biometric system, is allowed into the business, and is given access to confidential network files they have no business or reason to have access to.

Yes, the above example actually does happen and, as mentioned previously, biometrics are not infallible, and are prone to faults and errors just like any other technology.

The False Rejection Rate

With respect to the false rejection rate, this metric reflects the statistical probability of an individual who is legitimately enrolled in the biometric system actually being denied by it. In other words, for example, suppose John Doe is a legitimate employee of a particular place of business, and is enrolled in the biometric system. For some reason or another, despite his legitimacy, he is totally rejected by the biometric system, and is denied access to entry or whatever resources he has requested.

The Equal Error Rate

In terms of the equal error rate, this is where the false acceptance rate and the false rejection rate equal each other, and thus is the ideal or optimal setting for any type of biometric system which is to be deployed.

The Ability to Verify Rate

The ability to verify rate describes the overall percentage of a particular population which can actually be legitimately enrolled in the Biometric system. For instance, it does not matter what type the exact population is. It can be the total number of employees in a place of business, or the entire citizenship of a particular country.

All that matters is the total number of people who can be properly enrolled in the biometric system.

In terms of mathematics, the ability to verify rate can be thought of as the union or the combination of the failure to enroll rate and the false rejection rate. Specifically, the formula is:

$$ATV = [(1-FTE) * (1-FRR)]$$

The Failure to Enroll Rate

Finally, the failure to enroll rate statistically describes that percentage of the population which **cannot** be legitimately accepted by the biometric system. This metric can also be thought of as the converse, or the mirror image, of the ability to verify rate.

There are a number of reasons why particular individuals cannot be enrolled in a biometric system, such as arthritis, skin discoloration, blindness, and the sheer lack of physical or biological features.

It is also important to keep in mind that the way in which these performance metrics should be evaluated and analyzed is largely dependent upon the type of market application(s) the intended biometric modality will serve. This is discussed in the next section.

The Major Market Applications of the Biometric Technologies

As we have discussed in this book thus far, biometric technology is one of those tools which encompasses both ends of the spectrum, when compared to the other security technologies which are available today in the marketplace.

This spectrum goes all the way from the technical implications of deployment and implementation to the social impacts affecting the everyday user of the various biometric modalities.

Also unlike the other security technologies, the biometric modalities can also fit in just about every type of industry and market segment as well as the various applications which are associated with them.

The primary reason why this is possible is that all businesses, organizations, and corporations, regardless of their size or financial situation, need to have security. The bottom line is that each and every one of them has tangible property and intellectual assets which need to be protected to the maximum level possible.

For instance, property assets include the actual physical premises of the corporation or business. Included in this category are the assets which are included inside, such as the IT infrastructures, the workspaces of all of the employees, the customer information and data which reside in all of the databases, confidential and proprietary company records, etc.

The intellectual assets are the research and development, the ideas, the process flows, the documentation, the innovativeness, the collaboration, the project management, the testing, the prototyping, and the final development of the products and services which are exclusive to that particular corporation or organization.

In both of these categories, as well as their respective subcategories, biometric technology can be called upon and used in order to provide that extra layer of protection. At this point, it is also very important to keep in mind that although biometric technology can be utilized as a single line of security defense for a corporation or an organization, this is not the ideal situation.

For example, if the above scenario were the actual case, any hacker or attacker could breach this line of defense and cause irreparable damage and harm. Rather, it is highly recommended that biometric technology should be used as tool to create an extra layer of defense for a corporation or an organization.

That way, if the first line of defense were to be penetrated, the other layers of security will provide that extra protection. This is the most optimal usage of biometric technology. In this regard, the major market applications of biometric technology can be detailed as follows.

Physical Access Control

Physical access entry refers to giving an individual (such as an employee) access to a secure building, or a secure room within an office building.

Traditionally, keys and badges have been used in order to gain access. But the main problem is that these tools can be very easily lost, stolen, replicated, or even given to other individuals who have no business in physically being at that particular location.

Once again, biometric technology has been used here to replace the entire lock/key and ID badge approach. In this type of market application, a biometric device can be wired to an electronic lock strike, and once the employee has been verified by the biometric system, the door will automatically open.

The advantage to this obvious: no more lost, stolen, or fraudulent use of keys and ID badges, only the legitimate individual whose identity has been one hundred percent confirmed by the biometric system will gain access.

Any type of biometric modality will work here, but the dominant technologies used in this type of scenario are hand geometry recognition and fingerprint recognition.

In a particular market application, the biometric systems can operate either in a stand-alone mode or in a networked mode. Typically, small businesses will pick the former approach and larger businesses will opt for the latter approach, in order to accommodate the greater number of employees.

Time and Attendance

Businesses and corporations, at all levels of industry, have to keep track of the hours their employees have worked so that they get paid fairly for the amount of work produced.

Keeping track of the time when employees have worked can be done by numerous methods, such as using a timecard, utilizing a sign-in/sign-out roster at the main place of entry of the business, entering the hours worked into a spreadsheet, or even using an online portal to record the clock-in and clock-out times.

But using these manual approaches has proved to be a massive headache in terms of administration on at least two fronts:

- Using these manual methods of processing the hours worked and calculating payroll can be very tedious, laborious, time-consuming and costly;

- Using these manual methods just described fraud and forgery can very easily take place, especially with regard to what is known as "buddy punching." This is where one employee fraudulently reports the time worked for another employee who did not even physically appear for work.

The various biometric modalities can play an integral role here in time and attendance applications and alleviate the above two headaches.

Again, any type of biometric modality can work here, but it has been hand geometry recognition and fingerprint recognition which have been traditionally utilized. But iris recognition and even vein pattern recognition are becoming more widely used now.

Biometrics-based time and attendance systems can operate in either a stand-alone or network mode, but it is the latter which offers the most advantages.

For example, a business can have central control and administrative functions from within a central server, and, best of all, all of the administrative tasks associated with processing payroll and distributing paychecks can now be completely automated, thus reducing paperwork and overhead costs.

Logical Access Control

Logical access control refers to gaining access to a computer network, either at the office, or via a remote connection from the employee's home, or wireless access if they are on the road. Computer network access is a broad term, but for the context here, it can be defined as anything which relates to a place of business or organization.

This can include accessing the corporate intranet all the way to accessing the most confidential files and resources on a corporate server.

The security tool which is most commonly used here is the traditional username and password. While this may have worked effectively for the last couple of decades or so, it is now definitely showing its signs of severe weaknesses.

For instance, people (especially employees) write down their passwords on a yellow Post-It note, and stick it to their monitor in plain sight (this is also known as the "Post-It syndrome"). Also, employees concoct passwords which anybody could hack into (for instance, even the word "password" is used as an actual password).

As a result, to combat these weaknesses, employers have greatly tightened their security policies, requiring employees to create passwords which are way too complex to remember (such as requiring a capital letter, a number, or a punctuation mark at different locations in the password). All of this has led to greatly increased administrative password-reset costs, which can amount to as much as $300 per year per employee for any business.

To fight these escalating costs, as well as employee/employer frustrations with passwords, biometrics has been called upon to replace the use of passwords totally.

The use of biometrics in this regard is referred to as "single-sign-on solutions," or SSOs for short, because with one swipe of your finger, or even just one scan of your iris, you can be logged into any computer network without having to type in a password.

Mobile and Wireless

This is probably one of the most recent and booming market segments for biometric technology. The most needed here is to provide the end-user with another way of securing and logging into his or her particular wireless device – instead again of having to enter in a password or a personal identification number.

The most common biometric modalities used here are fingerprint recognition, iris recognition, voice recognition, and even facial recognition. With a simple scan or an image taken, the end-user can quickly and easily log into his or her wireless device.

In fact, the major cellular operators have already implemented fingerprint recognition technology into the actual hardware of the smartphone. The best example of this is the iPhone. Starting with the 5S series, Apple has embedded an optical sensor in the casing of the iPhone.

The catalyst for this was when the Apple Corporation outright acquired another biometric vendor known as Authentec, one of the leading manufacturers at the time of fingerprint recognition sensors.

Mobile and E-Commerce

This specific market application has been around for some time, ever since the dawn of the Internet era. For instance, rather than having to visit a traditional brick-and-mortar store, an end-user or a customer can just visit the online store of a merchant, and with just a few clicks of the mouse can make his or her product selections, enter in his or her credit card information, and have them all shipped to their doorsteps in just a matter of a few days.

There have been security issues here as well, such as confirming the actual identification of an end-user. However, the use of biometric technology has almost eliminated the problem. However, this e-commerce model has now deployed itself into the wireless world.

For example, customers can now use their particular brand of smartphone to buy products online as they would from their desk computer or laptop. Now a variation of this has taken off in the other parts of the world, where biometric technology is being used to help secure what are known as "virtual payments."

Through the use of radio frequency identification (RFID) technology, a customer does not even have to take out his or her credit card or cash to make a payment – it can be all done by tapping the smartphone on the point-of-sale terminal. Once again, Apple Corporation has pioneered the use of this technology in the United States, with their method of payment known as Apple Pay.

With this, a customer can use his or her iPhone to pay for products and services. However, there have also been grave security issues, and once again the use of biometric technology has been called upon to solve them.

Surveillance

The last application of biometric technology is surveillance. This is probably what the public fears the most, and as a result has literally impeded its growth here in the United States.

What scares the public most about biometrics is the covert nature in which it can be used, without having any prior knowledge that they are being watched, recorded, and subsequently analyzed by various biometric devices.

For example, facial recognition systems can be embedded very easily now into CCTV cameras, and these can be placed in public places, without anybody's knowledge of the facial recognition system being used in conjunction with the CCTV cameras.

Given this covert nature of biometric technology, many citizens here in the United States fear that law enforcement and especially the Federal Government are watching our every move. Thus, this stokes up fears of George Orwell's "Big Brother is watching."

However, it is important to keep in mind that not all types of surveillance are associated with law enforcement.

For instance, any person or any business who knows how to set up a surveillance system can implement it in just a matter of a short period of time, and potentially spy on another business competitor, or even spy on customers as they shop, in order to determine their buying patterns.

In fact, under the umbrella of surveillance, another large market application for biometrics is conducting surveillance operations here and abroad on potential terrorist groups and terror suspects. With all of this in mind, it is important to discriminate what the types of surveillance activities actually are, and there are five major types:

(1) Overt surveillance;

(2) Covert surveillance;

(3) Tracking individuals on watch lists;

(4) Tracking individuals for suspicious behavior;

(5) Tracking individuals for suspicious types of activities.

With overt surveillance, the public, the individuals, and even the businesses in question know that they are being watched, whether it is directly disclosed, or it is perceived. The primary goal of overt surveillance is to prevent and discourage unlawful behavior.

In terms of covert surveillance, no individual or business entity has any knowledge that they are being watched and recorded. As mentioned, it is this segment of surveillance of which the public is the most afraid of in terms of biometric technology usage.

With regard to watchlist surveillance, the primary objective is to find an individual or group of individuals whose identity can be confirmed, but whose exact whereabouts are totally unknown. A good example of this are the so-called terror watch lists used at the major international airports here in the United States.

The security officials have the names of the suspects on that particular list, and if after checking a passenger's travel documents there is a match in names, then that person is obviously much further scrutinized.

In terms of the fourth type of surveillance, which is suspicious behavior surveillance, the goal here is to question individuals whose behavior tends to be very erratic, abnormal, or totally out of the norm.

This can considered to be a "macro" type of surveillance, because the exact identity of the individual is not known ahead of time; instead, one is trying to filter out undesirable behavior in a group of people in a public or even private setting.

Finally, with the last type of surveillance, which is looking out for suspicious activities, an individual is on the lookout for a potential suspect whose activities are illegal and can lead to great harm to the public and businesses in general.

Again, the goal here is to collect direct evidence which can be used in a court of law to convict a potential suspect before the actual activity is carried out. A good example of this is the current war on terrorism, where federal law enforcement agencies have kept tabs on potential terror suspects in order to ascertain whether their activities are illegal or not.

The form of biometric technology which has been widely used with these types of surveillance activities has been and continues to be facial recognition, being used in conjunction with CCTV technology. Obviously with surveillance, you want a contactless form of biometric technology to be used – which is why facial recognition is the popular choice.

Now that we have examined some of the major concepts behind Biometric technology, we turn our attention to reviewing some of the specific biometric modalities once again. By this, we will examine in somewhat more technical detail how they work, from the hardware perspective.

In order to truly get an understanding of what kind of software applications need to be created for a corporation's or a business's specific security needs, a good understanding of the biometric hardware is needed. With this in mind, the main emphasis of the next section will be upon the hardware which is associated with fingerprint recognition, iris recognition, and facial recognition.

A Technical Review of the Major Biometric Modalities

In this section, we give more technical insight into the major biometric modalities which exist today. As described throughout this book, these modalities fall into one of two major categories: (1) physical-based biometrics or (2) behavioral-based biometrics. With the former, it is snapshot of our physical selves which is captured at a certain point in time.

For instance, this includes capturing an image of the fingerprint, the eye, the face, the hand, the voice, and even the vein pattern structure which exists just underneath the fingertip or the palm. From here, the unique features are extracted, in order to provide a basis for confirming the identity of a particular individual.

The same is true of behavioral biometrics. In this, samples of the way we type on a computer keyboard or how we sign our name are captured. Although these specific biometric modalities are not used perhaps as commonly as the physical biometrics, they are now starting to gain some traction in terms of the major market applications.

The primary reason for this is that the behavioral-based biometrics are much easier to procure, deploy, and install. For instance, with keystroke recognition (this is the modality which measures our unique typing pattern on the keyboard), it is simply a software-based solution. There is no hardware to procure, and the end-user training is very simple.

In fact, even the software is very easy to install – it does not need a security administrator, even an end-user who is well versed in computer technology can do it. With regard to signature recognition (the modality which measures the mannerisms with which we sign our name), the main component is software, which too is very easy to deploy and install.

Although signature recognition does require some specialized hardware, such as the writing tablet and the stylus with which to sign the name, it is actually very cheap to acquire, when compared to the cost of some of the higher-end physical biometrics, such as iris recognition and facial recognition.

Signature recognition also has a very shallow learning curve, in that all the end-user has to know is how to sign his or her name comfortably on the writing tablet. In the beginning, there might be some unfamiliarity with it, but after a few practice runs the end-user will be able to feel comfortable with it.

One of the largest applications for signature recognition is actually the retail market segment. For example, when customers present their credit card for payment at the checkout lane, they not only have to sign their name to authorize the transaction, but they may also be required to present a form of identification in order to confirm who they are.

But with signature recognition, this particular modality can serve both purposes quite easily and effectively. For instance, not only can the writing tablet of the signature recognition device be used to authorize the sales transaction, it can also be used to confirm the identity of the cardholder in just a matter of seconds.

The remainder of this section now provides a more in-depth technical review, first with the physical biometric modalities, followed by the behavioral biometric modalities.

Physical Biometrics – Hand Geometry Recognition

To start the enrollment process with a hand geometry scanner, a combination of prisms and light emitting diodes (LEDs) from within the scanner are used, to help capture the raw images of the hand. The technology can capture images of the back of the hand as well as the palm. This creates a two-dimensional image of the hand.

In order to capture a three-dimensional image of the hand, five guiding pegs are located just underneath the camera, to help the end-user position their hand properly. Although this is advantageous, this method also possesses one serious disadvantage. For instance, the images of these pegs are also captured in the raw image. This results in greatly increased processing time because the images of the pegs have to be removed. Also, because of this, the extraction algorithm cannot take into account variances due to hand rotation and differences in the placement of the hand. To create the enrollment template, the average of the measurements described previously is calculated, and is then converted into a binary mathematical file. This is very small, only nine bytes.

A problem in the construction of the enrollment and verification templates is that the geometric features of the hand share quite a bit of resemblance or correlation with another, which can greatly hinder the process of unique feature extraction.

To help alleviate this problem, a method known as principal component analysis, or PCA, is used to produce a set of geometric features which are uncorrelated, and thus unique features can be extracted.

The small biometric template of hand geometry scanning gives it a rather distinct advantage. For example, hand geometry recognition works very effectively and is very interoperable as a multimodal security solution for both physical and logical access entry, as well as for time and attendance applications.

As a stand-alone device, a hand geometry recognition device can store upwards of 40,000 unique biometric templates.

Finally, in terms of the enrollment process, some 96+ measurements of the hand are taken, and this includes the following variables:

- The overall shape of the hand;
- The various dimensions of the palm;
- The length and width of all 10 fingers;
- The measurement between the joints of the hand;

- The various shapes of the knuckles;
- The geometrical circumference of the fingers;
- Any distinct landmark features which can be found on the hand.

Physical Biometrics – Vein Pattern Recognition

With a vein pattern recognition (VPR) system, the end-user can place either their palm or fingertip within the scanner, and in order to properly position them guides can be used.

The latter part is the only contact which is required, and there is no direct contact with either the palm or the fingertip on the actual sensor itself, thus giving VPR its contactless feature.

From this point onwards, after the palm or fingertip is properly positioned, the NIR light is then flashed towards the target, and in order to illuminate the unique pattern of blood vessels two techniques are used, and are described as follows:

(1) Diffused illumination: with this method, the NIR light source and the sensor are located on the same side of the VPR. As a result, the NIR light which is reflected back from either the palm or the fingertip is then used to capture the raw image of the vein pattern. The thickness of the skin is not a factor with this method.

(2) Direct illumination: with this technique, the NIR light is flashed directly at either the palm or the fingerprint, and through the target. This gives the impression of the ability to see the vein patterns right through the skin. This technique is directly affected by the thickness of the skin. The NIR light can be flashed from either the top, below, or on the sides of the VPR scanner.

From within the VPR system itself, specialized software is used to normalize the raw images of the vein pattern which has just been captured, and also remove any types of obstructions such as skin hair on the palms or on the fingertips.

The extraction algorithms then extract the unique features of the vein pattern, and the enrollment template remains encrypted in the database of the VPR system.

Physical Biometrics – Facial Recognition

Facial recognition technology relies upon the physical features of the face, which are determined by genetics. Also, this technology can be deployed either as a fully automated system or as a semi-automated system.

With the former, no human interaction is needed: all of the verification and identification decisions are made by the technology itself. With the latter, human intervention is required to a certain degree, and this is actually the preferred method for deploying a facial recognition system.

Given some of the serious obstacles it still does face, it is always better to err on the side of caution and have an actual human being involved as well in rendering a verification or identification decision.

Facial recognition systems of today focus on those parts of the face which are not as easily prone to the hurdles just described. These regions of the face include:

(1) The ridges between the eyebrows;

(2) The cheekbones;

(3) The mouth edges;

(4) The distance between the eyes;

(5) The width of the nose;

(6) The contour and the profile of the jawline;

(7) The chin.

The methodology to capture the raw images of the face is much different when compared to the other biometric technologies. Although facial recognition is a contactless technology, the image capture processes are much more complex, and more cooperation is required on part of the end-user.

To start the process of raw image collection, the individual must first either stand before a camera, or unknowingly have their face captured with covert surveillance methods, such as using a CCTV camera system (with the technology that is available today, facial recognition can literally be implanted in a CCTV).

Once the raw images are collected by the camera, the data are then either aligned or normalized to help refine the raw images at a much more granular level.

The refinement techniques involved include adjusting the face to be in the middle of the pictures which have been taken, and adjusting the size and the angle of the face so that the best unique features can be extracted and later converted to the appropriate verification and enrollment templates.

All of this is done via mathematical algorithms. As mentioned previously, facial recognition is complicated by a number of major obstacles, but even more so at the raw image acquisition phase.

These include a lack of subtle differentiation between the faces and other obstructive variables in the external environment, various different facial expressions and poses in subsequent raw image captures, and capturing a landmark orienting feature such as the eyes.

Physical Biometrics – Voice Recognition

The first step in voice recognition is for an individual to produce an actual voice sample. Voice production is a fact of life which we take for granted every day, and the actual process is complicated. The production of sound originates at the vocal cords.

In between the vocal cords is a gap. When we attempt to communicate, the muscles which control the vocal cords contract.

As a result, the gap narrows, and, as we exhale, the breath passes through the gap, which creates sound. The unique patterns of an individual's voice are then produced by the vocal tract.

The vocal tract consists of the laryngeal pharynx, oral pharynx, oral cavity, nasal pharynx, and the nasal cavity. It is these unique patterns created by the vocal tract which is used by voice recognition systems.

Even though people may sound alike to the human ear, everybody, to some degree, has different or unique pronunciation in their speech.

To ensure a good-quality voice sample, the individual usually recites some sort of text, which can either be a verbal phrase, a series of numbers, or even repeating a passage of text, which is usually prompted by the voice recognition system. The individual usually has to repeat this a number of times.

The most common devices used to capture an individual's voice samples are computer microphones, cell (mobile) phones, and land-line-based telephones. As a result, a key advantage of voice recognition is that it can use existing telephony technology, with minimal disruption to an entity's business processes.

In terms of noise disruption, computer microphones and cell phones create the most, and land-line-based telephones create the least.

Physical Biometrics – Iris Recognition

With NIR light shone into the iris, various grayscale images are captured, and then compiled into one primary composite photograph. Special software then removes any obstructions from the iris image, which can include portions of the pupil, eyelashes, eyelids, and any resulting glare from the iris camera.

From this composite image, the unique features of the iris (as described before) are then "zoned off" into hundreds of phasors (also known as vectors), whose measurements and amplitude level are then extracted (using Gabor wavelet mathematics), and then subsequently converted into a binary mathematical file, which is not greater than 500 bytes. Because of this very small template size, verification of an individual can occur in just less than one second.

In the traditional iris recognition methods, this mathematical file then becomes the actual iris biometric template, which is also known as the "IrisCode."

However, in order to positively verify or identify an individual from the database, these iris-based enrollment and verification templates (the IrisCode) must be first compared with one another. In order to accomplish this task, the IrisCodes are compared against one another byte by byte, looking for any dissimilarities amongst the string of binary digits.

In other words, to what extent do the zeros and ones in the iris-based enrollment and verification templates match and do not match? This answer is found by using a technique known as "Hamming distances," which is used in iris recognition algorithms today.

After these distances are measured, tests of statistical independence are then carried out, using high-level Boolean mathematics (such as exclusive OR operators [XOR] and masked operators).

Finally, if the test of statistical independence is passed, the individual is then positively verified or identified, but if the tests of statistical independence are failed, then the person is **not** positively verified or identified.

Physical Biometrics – Fingerprint Recognition

Fingerprint recognition is one those biometric technologies which not only works well for verification types of scenarios, but it also works very effectively for identity applications, which is best exemplified by the gargantuan databases administered by the FBI. But whether it is identification or verification which is being called for, fingerprint recognition follows a distinct methodology which can be broken down into the following steps:

(1) Raw data acquisition: the actual, raw images of the fingerprint are acquired through the sensor technology which is being utilized. At this point, a quality check is also included. This means that the raw images which are collected are eventually examined by the biometric system to see if there are too many extraneous data in the fingerprint image, which could interfere in the acquisition of unique data. If there is too much of an obstruction found, the fingerprint device will automatically discard that particular image, and prompt the end-user to place their finger into the platen for another raw image of

the fingerprint to be collected. If the raw images are accepted, they are subsequently sent over to the processing unit, which is located within the fingerprint recognition device.

(2) With the raw images which have now been accepted by the system, the unique features are then extracted and stored as the enrollment template. If fingerprint recognition is being used by a smartphone, a smart card is then utilized to store the actual enrollment template, and can even provide some processing features for the smartphone.

(3) Once the end-user wishes to gain physical or logical access, he or she then has to place their finger onto the sensor of the fingerprint recognition system, so that the raw images and unique features can be extracted as described above, and this becomes the enrollment template. The enrollment and verification templates are then compared to one another, to determine the degree of similarity/non-similarity with one another.

(4) If the enrollment and verification templates are deemed to be close in similarity, the end-user is then verified and/or identified, and is then granted either physical or logical access to what they are seeking.

The unique features of the fingerprint can be broken down into the following categories:

(1) Arches: these are the ridges which just flow in one direction, without doubling back, or going backwards. These only comprise about 5% of the features of the fingerprint.

(2) Loops: in this feature, the ridges go backwards, and go from either the left to the right or the right to the left. There are two distinct types of loop: (a) radial loops, which go downward and (b) the ulnar loop, which goes upwards on the fingerprint. These make up 65% of the features within the fingerprint.

(3) Whorls: the ridges in the fingerprint make a circle around a core, and these comprise 30% of the features in the fingerprint.

In addition to the above features which are collected by a fingerprint recognition system, the actual number of ridges and the way that these ridges are positioned (specifically their orientation) can also prove to be a very distinctive feature, and can help to contribute to the verification and/or identification of an individual. Other distinctive features which can be extracted, but are not as commonly used, include the following:

(1) Prints/islands: these are the very short ridges found on the fingerprint;

(2) Lakes: these are the special indentations/depressions located right in the middle of the ridge;

(3) Spurs: these are the actual crossovers from one ridge to another.

Behavioral Biometrics – Signature Recognition

Today's signature recognition devices can now collect and analyze such variables as speed, acceleration, pauses, and the changes in pressure with which the individual signs their name on the special writing tablet.

Neural network technology can also be incorporated with signature recognition, which can literally learn the slightest changes and variations in the way an individual signs their name over a pre-established period of time, and make the necessary changes to the database.

Signature recognition technology involves the use of a pen and a special writing tablet, which are connected to a local or central computer for processing and verification. To acquire the signature data during the enrollment process, an individual is required to sign his or her name several times on the writing tablet. It should be noted that the robustness of the signature recognition enrollment template is a direct function of the quality of the writing tablet. With signature recognition templates, different values or "weights" are assigned to each unique feature. These templates are therefore as small as 3 kB.

One of the biggest challenges in signature recognition is the constant variability in the signatures themselves. This is primarily due to the fact that an individual never signs their signature in the same fashion any given two successive times.

Behavioral Biometrics – Keystroke Recognition

To start the enrollment process, an individual is required to type a specific word or group of words (text or phrases). In most cases, the individual's username and password are used. It is very important that the same words or phrases are used during both the enrollment and verification processes.

If not, the behavioral typing characteristics will be significantly different, and, as a result, a mismatch will arise between the enrollment and verification templates.

The distinctive behavioral characteristics measured by keystroke recognition include:

(1) The cumulative typing speed;

(2) The time that elapses between consecutive keystrokes;

(3) The time that each key is held down (also known as the dwell time);

(4) The frequency with which other keys, such as the number pad or function keys, are used;

(5) The key release and timing in the sequence used to type a capital letter (whether the shift or letter key is released first);

(6) The length of time it takes an individual to move from one key to another (also known as the flight time);

(7) Any error rates, such as using the backspace key.

These behavioral characteristics are subsequently used to create statistical profiles, which essentially serve as enrollment and verification templates. The templates also store the actual username and password. The statistical profiles can either be "global" or "local."

Whereas a "global" profile combines all behavioral characteristics, a local profile measures the behavioral characteristics for each keystroke.

References

[1] https://en.wikipedia.org/wiki/Software_development_kit.

[2] Ravindra Das, *Biometric Technology: Authentication, Biocryptography, and Cloud-Based Architecture* (CRC Press, 2014).

3 | Iris Recognition

Physical and Behavioral Biometrics

Before we move onto our detailed discussion and analyses of iris recognition we examine what physical biometrics and behavioral biometrics are. Physical biometrics involves taking a biological or physiological snapshot of a part of our body, and behavioral biometrics involves taking a picture of our unique mannerisms, which make us different from everybody else.

But now, we need to provide much more precise, scientific definitions for these two terms. Physical biometrics can be defined as: "Acquiring physical biometric samples which involves taking a measurement from subjects. This does not require any specific action by the subject. A physical biometric is based primarily upon an anatomical or physiological characteristic rather than a learned behavior" [1].

Behavioral biometrics can be defined as: "Acquiring behavioral biometric samples which requires subjects to be active. They must perform a specific activity in the presence of a sensor. A behavioral trait is learned and acquired over time rather than based upon biology" [1].

The Differences Between Physical Biometrics and Behavioral Biometrics

As one can see, based upon these two definitions, some very subtle differences between physical biometrics and behavioral biometrics can be observed. Probably the biggest difference to be noted is the amount of activity required by the end-user.

With physical biometrics, no activity is needed on the part of the individual in order to collect that individual's physiological and biological unique features (whether it be the hand, the finger, the iris or retina, or even the vein patterns present under the palm or the fingertip). Of course, the end-user must be cooperative in order for an effective sample to be captured.

In other words, physical biometrics can be more or less considered as "garbage in, garbage out." The image is captured, unique features are extracted, and the individual is either verified or not verified. But with behavioral biometrics, a specific function, or an active part, must be carried out (such as typing on a keyboard or signing your name), which is learned over time.

As a result, because of this learned behavior, deviations or changes in the behavioral-based biometric templates which are collected can occur over time, at a higher level than with physical-based biometric templates.

Hence, research and development is already under way in which a behavioral-based biometric system can literally learn and take into account such changes in the behavior and mannerisms which can occur over the lifetime of an individual.

A perfect example of this would be the use of neural network technology. With this type of technology, computer-based learning and reasoning takes place in an attempt to closely follow the actions and patterns of the human brain.

Another difference between physical biometrics and behavioral biometrics which is evident from the above definitions is the number of measurements taken in order to extract the unique features, although in both types of technologies multiple images or multiple samples are collected.

But in physical biometrics, only one composite image is utilized to extract the unique features from. Thus, with physical biometrics, it is considered that only one measurement is taken.

With behavioral biometrics, multiple samples are collected, but a composite sample is not created from which to extract the unique features. Rather, statistical profiles are created from each individual sample in order to positively verify or identify an individual.

For example, with keystroke recognition, an end-user has to type multiple lines of text. Statistical profiles (using hidden Markov models primarily) are created on the basis of each line of text typed, and from there the unique patterns are noted, and then the individual is either fully verified or not verified at all.

The Eye: The Iris and the Retina

Out of all of the biometric technologies available today, it is the eye, and its subcomponents, especially the retina and the iris, which possesses the most unique information and data by which to identify and verify an individual. As of now, it is the retina which is deemed to be the most unique biometric of all. The iris is deemed to be the next most unique biometric, right after the retina.

Although the main focus of this chapter is about the iris and the major scientific studies which have taken place in this field, it is also equally important to review the retina in detail. The primary reason for this is that they both can be considered to be part of the same "organ," which is of course the eye.

And although in a technical sense they both are located in two very distinct parts of the eye, on a theoretical level they both also work together in order for us to see with almost one hundred percent clarity, and also to understand and interpret the visual information and data that we process almost every second, non-stop, in our daily lives.

The Retina

Very often, there is a lot of confusion between the retina and the iris. As previously discussed, the iris is located at the front of the eye, but the retina is located at the back of the eye. Unlike the iris, the retina is actually a grouping of blood vessels which lead into the optic disc, and from there visual information is transmitted to the brain for processing via the optic nerve, which lies in between the optic disc and the brain.

The scanning of the retina is also known as retinal recognition, and at the present time is deemed to be the most unique biometric of all because of the richness of the data it possesses, from which the unique features can be extracted.

Retinal recognition technology was first conceived of in the mid 1970s, but the first retinal recognition biometric device did not come onto the marketplace until the early 1980s. Although retinal recognition does possess some very distinct advantages over the other biometric technologies, this technology has extremely limited market applications.

The primary reasons for this are the high cost of retinal recognition devices (which can be as high as $5000 per device), their bulkiness, and the fact that it is very user-invasive. Although retinal recognition technology is a contactless technology, the end-user has to sit very close to the scanner, and place his or her eye near the scanning device, thus making it very cumbersome and not very comfortable for the end-user. An image of the retina can be seen in Figure 3.1.

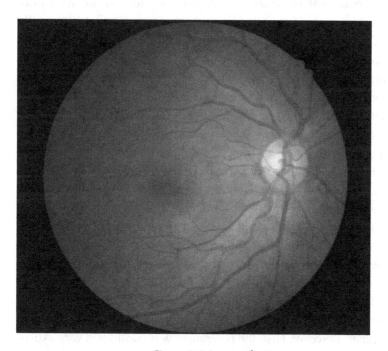

Figure 3.1 Image of retina
Source: memorisz/Shutterstock.com

The Physiology of the Retina

It is said that the retina "is to the eye as film is to a camera" [2].

The retina consists of multiple layers of sensory tissue and millions of photoreceptors whose function is to transform light rays into electrical impulses. These impulses subsequently travel to the brain via the optic nerve, where they are converted to images. Two distinct types of photoreceptors exist within the retina: the rods and the cones.

While the cones (of which each eye contains approximately 6 million) help us to see different colors, the rods (which number 125 million per eye) facilitate night and peripheral vision. It is the blood vessel pattern in the retina that forms the foundation for retinal recognition as a science and technology.

Because of its position within the eye, the retina is not exposed to the external environment. As a biometric, it is therefore very stable. It is from here that information is transmitted to and received from the brain. The circle in the diagram indicates the area that is typically captured by a retinal scanning device. It contains a unique pattern of blood vessels.

There are two famous studies that have confirmed the uniqueness of the blood vessel pattern found in the retina. The first was published by Dr Carleton Simon and Dr Isadore Goldstein in 1935, and describes how every retina contains a unique blood vessel pattern.

In a later paper, they even suggest using photographs of these patterns as a means of identification. The second study was conducted in the 1950s by Dr Paul Tower. He discovered that – even among identical twins – the blood vessel patterns of the retina are unique and different.

The first company to become involved in the research, development and manufacture of retinal scanning devices was EyeDentify Inc. The company was established in 1976 and its first retina capturing devices were known as "fundus cameras."

While intended for use by ophthalmologists, modified versions of the camera were used to obtain retina images. The device had several shortcomings, however. First, the equipment was considered very expensive and difficult to operate. Second, the light used to illuminate the retina was considered too bright and too discomforting for the user. Further research and development yielded the first true prototype scanning device, which was unveiled in 1981.

The device used infrared light to illuminate the blood vessel pattern of the retina. The advantage of infrared light is that the blood vessel pattern in the retina can "absorb" such light much faster than other parts of the eye tissue.

The reflected light is subsequently captured by the scanning device for processing. In addition to a scanner, several algorithms were developed for the extraction of unique features.

Further research and development gave birth to the first true retinal scanning device to reach the market: the EyeDentification System 7.5. The device utilized a complex system of scanning optics, mirrors, and targeting systems to capture the blood vessel pattern of the retina.

Ongoing development resulted in devices with much simpler designs. Later scanners consisted of integrated retinal scanning optics, which sharply reduced manufacturing costs (compared to the EyeDentification System 7.5.).

The last retinal scanner to be manufactured by EyeDentify was the ICAM 2001, a device capable of storing up to 3000 templates and 3300 transactions. The product was eventually withdrawn from the market on account of its price as well as user concerns.

The Process of Retinal Recognition

The overall retinal scanning process may be broken down into three sub-processes:

(1) Image/signal acquisition and processing: this sub-process involves capturing an image of the retina and converting it to a digital format;

(2) Matching: a computer system is used to verify and identify the user (as is the case with the other biometric technologies reviewed in previous articles);

(3) Representation: the unique features of the retina are presented as a template.

The process for enrolling and verifying/identifying a retinal scan is the same as the process applied to other biometric technologies (acquisition and processing of images; unique feature extraction; template creation).

The image acquisition and processing phase is the most complicated. The speed and ease with which this sub-process may be completed largely depend on user cooperation. To obtain a scan, the user must position his/her eye very close to the lens.

To safeguard the quality of the captured image, the user must also remain perfectly still at this point. Moreover, glasses must be removed to avoid signal interference (after all, lenses are designed to reflect). On looking into the scanner, the user sees a green light against a white background.

Once the scanner is activated, the green light moves in a complete circle (360 degrees). The blood vessel pattern of the retina is captured during this process.

Generally speaking, three to five images are captured at this stage. Depending on the level of user cooperation, the capturing phase can take as long as one minute.

This is a very long time compared to other biometric techniques. The next stage involves data extraction. One very considerable advantage of retinal recognition becomes evident at this stage.

As genetic factors do not dictate the pattern of the blood vessels, the retina contains a diversity of unique features. This allows up to 400 unique data points to be obtained from the retina. For other biometrics, such as fingerprints, only 30–40 data points (the minutiae) are available.

During the third and final stage of the process, the unique retina pattern is converted to an enrollment template. At only 96 bytes, the retina template is considered one of the smallest biometric templates.

As is the case with other biometric technologies, the performance of the retinal scanning device may be affected by a number of variables, which could prevent an accurate scan from being captured. Poor-quality scans may be attributable to:

(1) Lack of cooperation on the part of the user – as indicated, the user must remain very still throughout the entire process, especially when

the image is being acquired. Any movement can seriously affect lens alignment;

(2) The distance between the eye and the lens is incorrect and/or fluctuates – for a high quality scan to be captured, the user must place his or her eye in very close proximity to the lens. In this sense, iris scanning technology is much more user-friendly; a quality scan can be captured at a distance of up to three feet from the lens;

(3) A dirty lens on the retinal scanning device: this will obviously interfere with the scanning process;

(4) Other types of light interference from an external source;

(5) The size of the user's pupil: a small pupil reduces the amount of light that travels to (and from) the retina. This problem is exacerbated if the pupil constricts as a result of bright lighting conditions, which can result in a higher false reject rate.

The Advantages and Disadvantages of Retinal Recognition

All biometric technologies are rated against a set of performance standards. As far as retinal recognition is concerned, there are two performance standards: the false reject rate and the ability to verify rate.

As mentioned back in Chapter 1, the false rejection rate (FRR) describes the probability of a legitimate user being denied authorization by the retinal scanning system. Retinal recognition is most affected by the false reject rate.

This is because the factors described above have a tangible impact on the quality of the retinal scan, causing a legitimate user to be rejected. Also, the ability to verify rate describes the probability of an entire user group being verified on a given day. For retinal recognition, the relevant percentage has been as low as 85%.

This is primarily attributable to user-related concerns and the need to place one's eye in very close proximity to the scanner lens.

Just like all other biometric technologies, retinal recognition has its own unique strengths and weaknesses. The strengths may be summed up as follows:

(1) The blood vessel pattern of the retina rarely changes during a person's life (unless he or she is afflicted by an eye disease such as glaucoma, cataracts, etc.);

(2) The size of the actual template is only 96 bytes, which is very small by any standards. In turn, verification and identification processing times are much shorter than they are for larger files;

(3) The rich, unique structure of the blood vessel pattern of the retina allows up to 400 data points to be created;

(4) As the retina is located inside the eye, it is not exposed to (threats posed by) the external environment. For other biometrics, such as fingerprints, hand geometry, etc., the opposite holds true.

The most relevant weaknesses of retinal recognition are:

(1) The public perceives retinal scanning to be a health threat; some people believe that a retinal scan damages the eye;

(2) User unease about the need to position the eye in such close proximity of the scanner lens;

(3) User motivation: of all biometric technologies, successful retinal scanning demands the highest level of user motivation and patience;

(4) Retinal scanning technology cannot accommodate people wearing glasses (which must be removed prior to scanning);

(5) At this stage, retinal scanning devices are very expensive to procure and implement.

As retinal recognition systems are user-invasive as well as expensive to install and maintain, retinal recognition has not been as widely deployed as other biometric technologies (particularly fingerprint recognition). To date, retinal recognition has primarily been used in combination with access control systems at high security facilities.

This includes military installations, nuclear facilities, and laboratories. One of the best-documented applications involves the State of Illinois, which used retinal recognition to reduce welfare fraud by identifying welfare recipients (thus preventing multiple benefit payments). This project also made use of fingerprint recognition.

Retinal recognition was first introduced in Granite City and East Alton (southern Illinois) towards mid-1996. Once the fingerprint recognition program had been initiated, the authorities drew up a comparison between fingerprint and retinal recognition, concluding that "retinal scanning is not client or staff friendly and requires considerable time to secure biometric records. Based on these factors, retinal scanning technology is not yet ready for state-wide adaptation to the Illinois welfare department ..." [2]. As a result, the use of retinal recognition systems was stopped.

Retinal recognition can also be compared to the seven criteria the other technologies have been compared to. But while retinal recognition does possess some very significant advantages, overall, it does not fare as well (meaning the negatives far outweigh the positives), which seriously limits its adoption rate in the market place.

The Seven Criteria to Evaluate Retinal Recognition

(1) Universality: virtually everybody, unless they have some extreme form of blindness, possesses a retina, thus, at least on a theoretical level, people can have their retina scanned;

(2) Uniqueness: as described, the retina is very unique, even amongst identical twins. This is probably its greatest strength;

(3) Permanence: unlike the other physiological components of our bodies, the biological fundamentals of the retina hardly change in the lifetime of the individual. But it should be noted that if any thing affects the iris, then the retina can be subject to degradation as well. Also, it should be noted that the retina is prone to degradation via diabetes, glaucoma, high blood pressure, and even heart disease;

(4) Collectability: the scan area of the retina is very small, and the end-user must place their eye in a very user-invasive eye receptacle, and

he or she must remove contact lenses or eye glasses in order for a good-quality scan to be captured. Because of this very constrained environment, the end-user must remain cooperative, and the system's administrator must make sure that the retina is scanned in an appropriate time frame, if not, the FTE (failure to enroll rate) will be high;

(5) Performance: as a flip side to the user invasiveness which is involved, retinal recognition has extremely high levels of accuracy, in fact, it is claimed that the error rate is as low as one in one million;

(6) Acceptability: retinal recognition works best with those end-users who are absolutely required to use it in order to perform their required job functions;

(7) Resistance to circumvention: it is almost impossible to spoof a retinal recognition system, and a live retina is required for either verification or identification to take place.

Because of the high expense and user invasiveness involved, retinal recognition is only used for ultra-high-security applications, such as for the government and the military. As a result, there is a high level of preference given to iris recognition over retinal recognition.

The Iris

The popularity of iris recognition dates all the way back to the mid nineties, when the first mathematical algorithms were developed and created by Dr. John Daugman of the University of Cambridge. At the time, only one iris recognition vendor existed, known as Iridian Technologies, Inc.

For well over a decade, this company owned the intellectual property as well as the mathematical algorithms involved with iris recognition at the time. As a result, a very strong monopoly was held, and customers could only utilize just one type of iris recognition product or solution.

The system, although considered to be very advanced at the time, was quite expensive, and bulky to deploy and maintain. But eventually, just a couple of years ago, Iridian Technologies was bought out by a much larger biometrics vendor, and at the same time the patents surrounding the original algorithms and technology expired, thus breaking the monopoly which was held for such a long time.

As a result, there has been a huge explosion of iris recognition just in the past couple of years, offering many new types of products and solutions for the customer.

The advantage to this of course is that the customer now has a much greater depth and breadth of picking and even customizing their own iris recognition solution which will fit their exact needs and requirements, unlike before, where people were basically forced to buy just one product or solution.

In fact, iris recognition has developed so quickly that now images of the iris can be captured at much greater distances, as well as when people are in movement. Previously, an end-user had to stand directly in front of the iris recognition camera, in very close proximity. And now, even the unique pattern of the blood vessels can also be scanned, and this will be examined.

The Physiological Structure of the Iris

The iris lies between the pupil and the white of the eye, which is known as the sclera. The color of the iris varies from individual to individual, but there is a commonality to the colors, and these include green, blue, brown, and, in rare cases, even a hazel color can occur.

Even in the most extreme cases, a combination of these colors can be seen in the iris. The color of the iris is primarily determined by the DNA code inherited from our parents.

The unique patterns of the iris starts to form after the human embryo is conceived; usually this happens during the third month of fetal gestation.

The phenotype of the iris is shaped and formed in a process known as chaotic morphogenesis, and the unique structures of the iris are completely formed during the first two years of child development.

The primary purpose of the iris is to control the diameter and the size of the pupil. The pupil is that part of the eye which allows light to enter into the eye, which in turn reaches the retina, which is located in the back of the eye. Of course, the amount of light that can enter the pupil is a direct function of how much it can expand and contract, which is governed by the muscles of the iris.

The iris is primarily composed of two layers: (1) a fibrovascular tissue known as the stroma and (2) the stroma is in turn connected to a grouping of muscles known as the sphincter muscles.

It is these muscles which are responsible for the contraction of the pupil, and another group of muscles known as the dilator muscles govern the expansion of the pupil. When you look at your iris in the mirror, you will notice a radiating pattern.

This pattern is known as the trabecular meshwork. When near infrared light (NIR) is flashed onto the iris, many unique features can be observed.

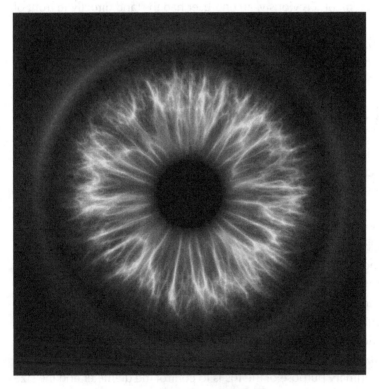

Figure 3.2 Image of iris
Source: Juergen Faelchle/Shutterstock.com

These features include ridges, folds, freckles, furrows, arches, crypts, coronas, as well as other patterns which appear in various, discernible fashions.

Finally, the collarette of the iris is the thickest region of it, which gives the iris its two distinct regions, known as the pupillary zone (this forms the boundary of the pupil) and the ciliary zone (which fills up the rest of the iris). Other unique features can also be seen in the collarette region.

The iris is deemed to be one of the most unique structures of human physiology, and in fact each individual has a different iris structure in each eye. In fact, scientific studies have shown that even identical twins have different iris structures. An image of an actual iris can be seen in Figure 3.2.

A view of the iris and the retina working in synchrony with each other can be seen in Figure 3.3.

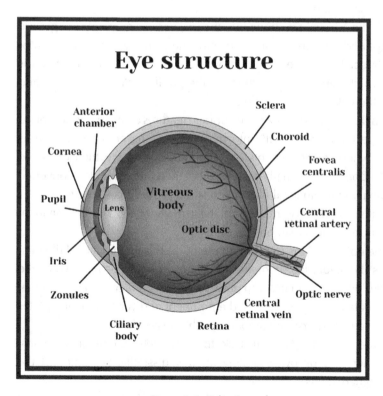

Figure 3.3 Side view of eye
Source: Mrs_Bazilio/Shutterstock.com

How Iris Recognition Works: The Mathematical Algorithms

The "Father" of Iris Recognition – Dr. John Daugman

The idea of using the iris to confirm the identity of an individual dates all the way back to 1936, when an ophthalmologist by the name of Frank Burch first proposed the idea. This idea was then patented in 1987, and by the mid-nineties Dr. John Daugman of the University of Cambridge had developed the first mathematical algorithms for it. Traditional iris recognition technology requires the end-user to stand no more than 10 inches away from the camera.

With the NIR light is shone into the iris, various grayscale images are then captured, and then compiled into one primary composite photograph. Special software then removes any obstructions from the iris image, which can include portions of the pupil, eyelashes, eyelids, and any resulting glare from the iris camera.

From this composite image, the unique features of the iris (as described before) are then "zoned off" into hundreds of phasors (also known as vectors), whose measurements and amplitude level are then extracted (using Gabor wavelet mathematics), and then subsequently converted into a binary mathematical file, which is not greater than 500 bytes.

Because of this very small template size, verification of an individual can occur in just less than one second.

In the traditional iris recognition methods, this mathematical file then becomes the actual iris biometric template, which is also known as the "IrisCode." However, in order to positively verify or identify an individual from the database, these iris-based enrollment and verification templates (the IrisCode) must first be compared with one another.

In order to accomplish this task, the IrisCodes are compared against one another byte by byte, looking for any dissimilarities amongst the string of binary digits.

In other words, to what extent do the zeros and ones in the iris-based enrollment and verification templates match and do not match? This answer is found by using a technique known as "Hamming distances," which is used in iris recognition algorithms today.

After these distances are measured, tests of statistical independence are then carried out, using high-level Boolean mathematics (such as exclusive OR operators [XOR] and masked operators). Finally, if the test of statistical independence is passed, the individual is then positively verified or identified, but if the tests of statistical independence are failed, then the person is **not** positively verified or identified.

The mathematical algorithms as developed by Dr. John Daugman have so far remained the most widely used in iris recognition devices today. The primary reasons for this are not only the robustness of the Gabor wavelet mathematical algorithms, but, with the expiration of the patents, they are now available for the biometrics industry to use at large.

With the expiration of these patents also came the explosion of many new iris recognition vendors. They have developed their own types of mathematical algorithms; however, some of them still use the Gabor wavelet algorithms as the theoretical underpinning in the creation and development of their own set of algorithms.

It is important to keep in mind as well that all of the iris recognition vendors have chosen to adopt the framework as developed by Dr. John Daugman. However, they have ventured forth and created/tested their own unique brands of both enrollment and verification mathematical algorithms. The goal of this section of the chapter is to review the theoretical constructs of these kinds of algorithm.

But, no matter what is being created and implemented, a common theme will persist in this section. That is, they all follow a common set of rules to take the actual image of the iris, and to extract the unique features in order to create not only the enrollment templates, but the verification templates as well. These steps can be described as follows:

(1) Image acquisition;

(2) Segmentation;

(3) Normalization;

(4) Feature encoding;

(5) Feature matching.

The Theoretical Framework of Iris Recognition – Tarawneh and Thunibat

A scientific study conducted by Rasha Tarawneh and Omamah Thunibat of Mutah University provides a good example of these above-mentioned processes. It is interesting to note that their research does not hinge upon the work of Dr. John Daugman; as described earlier, these scientists have developed their own set of mathematical algorithms which will be reviewed in greater detail as we go through each technique as described above.

Image Acquisition

As the scientists describe in this phase, image acquisition is primarily involved with capturing a sequence of iris images. In fact, this procedure is common across all of the biometric technologies, both physical-based and behavioral-based. For instance, take the example of fingerprint recognition. When an end-user first enrolls in the system, he or she will be prompted to have their fingertip scanned multiple times. The premise behind this is that a complete snapshot of the finger should be created. This can only be done when these multiple images are combined to create a master, composite image of the fingerprint. In fact, it is where the unique feature extraction process commences.

But in this regard, iris recognition is different from fingerprint recognition. The former can be referred to as a "contactless" type of technology, in that cameras are actually used to capture the sequence of iris images. The end-user has no direct contact with the iris system, as they are required just to stand in front of the camera(s) at a predetermined distance.

But, as also discussed in this chapter, iris recognition is also a dynamic type of technology, in that images of the iris can be captured of individuals as they are walking. A prime example of this is at international airports, where iris recognition is used to confirm or deny the identity of all of the passengers embarking and disembarking at their point of origin or point of destination, respectively.

As in the case of fingerprint recognition, a complete image of the iris is required in order to capture the unique features. It should be noted also that some kind of preprocessing techniques may be further required to further enhance the composite image of the iris.

Segmentation

This process involves actually further breaking down the composite image of the iris after it has been completely refined, as described in the last subsection. Tarawneh and Thunibat, in their research, identified two steps in this process:

(1) The actual segmentation:

This is where the image of the iris is broken down into various subcomponents. In other words, it is completely divided up in order to extract as many unique as features as possible from the composite image of the iris. The premise behind this is simple: the more unique data points that can be collected, the greater are the chances of positively confirming the identity of the individual in question.

(2) The act of approximation:

This is the part where the divided images of the iris as described previously can be mathematically represented by two distinct circles:

- A circle for the boundary between iris and the sclera (this part is also referred to as the "white of the eye."
- A circle to denote the boundary between the iris and the pupil.

Once these particular circles have been created and identified, a mathematical technique known as the "Hough transform" is first used to detect the horizontal position of the eyelids, as well as to detect the vertical position of the boundaries of the iris.

The eyelids have been deemed to be an interference when dividing up the image of the iris, so derivates are calculated in order to reduce the impact they have upon the composite of the iris. It should be noted at this point that the Hough transform will be examined in further detail in this section of the chapter.

Also, an "edge map" is created to help determine both the center radius coordinates of the region which lies in between the pupil and the iris. This is achieved by calculating the first derivatives of the composite image of the iris by using this formula created by Tarawneh and Thunibat:

$$x_c^2 + y_c^2 - r^2 = 0 \qquad \text{Equation 3.1 [3]}$$

where:

x_c and y_c = the center coordinates of the iris

r = the radius of the iris.

Just as much as the eyelids are a source of interference for the composite image of the iris, so are the eyelashes. In this case, there are two types of eyelash:

(1) The separable eyelash:

This is where the actual eyelashes can be further isolated from the composite of the iris.

(2) Multiple eyelashes:

These are layers of eyelashes which are literally "bunched" together and actually overlap and create cross interference with the composite image of the iris.

In summary, once the effects of the eyelashes and the eyelids have been removed from the segmented images of the composite image of the iris, they can be considered as "noise-free." In the end, it is important to remove the effects of the eyelashes and the eyelids, as they can greatly degrade the accuracy and performance of the iris recognition system.

Normalization

After the composite image of the iris has been divided, or segmented into smaller data points as described in the last section, by the various methodologies, the next step involved in creating robust and effective enrollment and verification templates of the iris is known as "normalization."

This step transforms the regions of the iris which were captured in the composite image into various fixed dimensions for quick comparisons.

Despite the fact that the effects of the eyelids and the eyelashes are greatly diminished in the segmentation process, there is still a great deal of variability which can be encountered from within the iris itself. One of the factors which leads to these great fluctuations is the actual dilation of the pupil itself.

The term "dilation" simply means that the pupils are further widened in order for more light to reach the retina. As discussed in detail in the section on the retina, the retina is located in the back of the eye, and from there forms the optic nerve. This nerve then enters into the brain and feeds it data so that the visual information, which essentially becomes our line of sight, is thus created. This process is completely natural and is also known in medical terms as "mydriasis." An image of a dilated pupil can be seen in Figure 3.4:

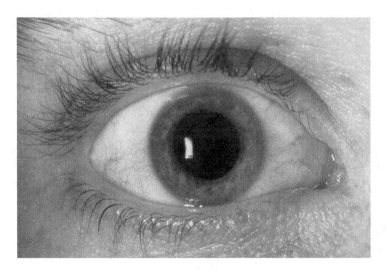

Figure 3.4 Image of dilated pupil
Source: Tim Mainiero/Shutterstock.com

In fact, the next series of mathematical algorithms to be reviewed deals with the issue of pupil dilation, and its effect upon the subsequent creation of the enrollment and verification templates.

The normalization process essentially involves further unwrapping the divided or segmented components of the composite image into what is known as its "polar" equivalent.

At the present time, there are three scientific methods by which the entire normalization process can be achieved, which are as follows:

(1)   The rubber sheet model by Dr. John Daugman;

(2)   The image registration model by Wildes et al.;

(3)   The virtual circles model by Boles et al.

However, it is the rubber sheet model which is the most widely used normalization technique. In mathematical terms, it can be represented as follows:

$$r' = \sqrt{\alpha\beta} \pm \sqrt{\alpha\beta^2 - \alpha - r_i^2}$$

with

$$\alpha = o_x^2 + o_y^2$$

$$\beta = \cos\left(\pi - \arctan\left(\frac{o_y}{o_x}\right) - \theta\right) \qquad \text{Equation 3.2 [3]}$$

where:

o_x and o_y = the displacement of the center of the pupil in comparison to the relative position of the center of the iris

r' = the distance between both the edges of the iris and the pupil at a predetermined angle

θ = the region around both the pupil and the iris

r_i^2 = the radius of the iris.

The process of normalization using the rubber sheet model involves the following steps:

(1) Radial vectors are first created, which pass through the entire region of the iris. This in turn creates various radial lines;

(2) After these vectors have been passed through, a select number of data points are then chosen amongst the set of these established radial lines. This becomes known as the "radial resolution." However, the total number of radial lines which **go around and do not intersect** the iris becomes known as the "angular resolution."

(3) At the end of this process, various two-dimensional (2D) arrays are then created from both the angular and radial resolution factors.

It should be noted that the rubber sheet model does not take into consideration the rotational inconsistencies which are found in the composite image of the iris. Thus, when compared to the other models described above, this is one of the greatest weaknesses of the rubber sheet model.

Feature Encoding

After the composite image has been segmented and normalized, the next step is known as "feature encoding." This is the process in which both the enrollment and verification templates contain only the most unique features of the iris.

At the present time, there are five main models which have been formulated in order to carry out the feature encoding process. They are as follows:

1) Gabor wavelets by Dr. John Daugman;

2) Log-Gabor filters by D. Field;

3) Haar wavelets by Lim et al.;

4) Zero crossing by Boles and Boashash;

5) Laplacian or Gaussian filters.

Once again, it is the Gabor wavelets model which is used the most for the feature encoding process. Mathematically it can be represented as follows:

$$H(r,\theta) = e^{-i\omega(\theta-\theta_0)}e^{-(r-r_0)^2/\alpha^2}e^{-i(\theta-\theta_0)^2/\beta^2}$$

Equation 3.3 [3]

where:

r_0 and θ_0 = the center frequency of the Gabor wavelet filters

α and β = the effective width and height of the respective Gabor wavelet filters.

It is important to note that a Gabor wavelet filter can be literally either a sine or a cosine functionality. These filters are further governed by a Gaussian continuous probability distribution, which is thus applied onto the entire composite image of the iris. From this point onwards, the unique features of the iris are then extracted and further examined as well as analyzed via a demodulation process where the specific outputs of the Gabor wavelet filters are compressed. Once this has been accomplished, the respective enrollment and verification templates are created.

This demodulation process can be mathematically represented as follows:

$$h_{\{Re,Im\}} = sgn_{\{Re,Im\}}\int_{\rho}\int_{\phi}I(\rho,\phi)e^{-i\omega(\theta_0-\phi)}e^{-(r_0-\rho)^2/\alpha^2}e^{-(\theta_0-\phi)^2/\beta^2}\rho d\rho d\phi$$

Equation 3.4 [3]

where:

$h_{\{Re,\,Im\}}$ = a bit which consists of both real and imaginary numerical values

$I(\rho,\theta)$ = the actual image of the iris in a complex polar coordinate system.

It should also be noted at this point that both the real and imaginary numbers create a preset number of bits represented by a binary pattern which are encoded into both the enrollment and verification templates. The total number of bits required can be calculated by this formula:

angular resolution * radial resolution * 2 * the total number of Gabor wavelet filters

Feature Matching

As the name implies, the primary objective of feature matching is to compare the relative closeness of the enrollment template versus the verification template. If there is enough statistically based closeness between the two, then the identity of the individual is confirmed, and he or she is then allowed to have access to whatever resources that they are seeking.

It is important to keep in mind that in this regard, the two major aspects of access are physical access entry and logical access entry. The enrollment template is actually created when the end-user enrolls in the biometric system (whether it be physical or behavioral-based). This is when multiple images of the iris are taken, and then the composite image is created, and the unique features are extracted.

In fact, it is the enrollment template which is stored permanently in the database, until it is deleted by the systems/network administrator. It should also be noted that the verification template is created in the same manner as the enrollment template, but it is **not stored** in the database of the biometric system.

Rather, it is used just one time. This means that if the individual in question wishes to gain either physical or logical access at a subsequent point in time, he or she will then have to go through this entire process as just described.

As also discussed in great detail in our first book, the enrollment and verification templates are not the actual images or recordings of either the physical or the behavioral which were collected. Rather, they are mathematical files. But the type of mathematical file which is created is dependent upon the biometric system which is being used. For example, in the case of both fingerprint and hand geometry recognition, it is a binary mathematical file which forms both the enrollment and verification templates. In other words, it is a simply a series of zeros and ones, as illustrated below:

0001000101011111010100001111101010101001010101010100011110101010

In the case of facial recognition and voice recognition as well as all of the behavioral-based biometrics (which includes the likes of both keystroke and signature recognition) statistical-based profiling is used to create both the enrollment and verification templates: primarily hidden Markov models (HMMs) are used.

Iris recognition uses a completely different approach when comparing the enrollment and the verification templates and the statistical closeness between the two. Three methods have been developed for this, and they are as follows:

(1) The Hamming distance model developed by Dr. John Daugman;

(2) The weighted Euclidean distance model developed by Zhu et al.;

(3) The normalized correlation model developed by Wildes.

The Hamming distance model is used the most by iris recognition vendors in the iris-based technologies that they create.

In order to fully compare the degree of similarity between the enrollment and verification templates in an iris recognition system, Dr. John Daugman created a metric known as the "Hamming distance." What is unique about this, on a technical level, is that it actually looks for **the degree of dissimilarity** between the enrollment and the verification templates.

This is determined by the difference between "bits" in the enrollment and the verification templates. The Hamming distance can be mathematically represented as follows:

$$1/N\sum_{j}(XOR)B_{j}$$

When calculating the Hamming distance, the various shifts of the bits are closely examined. For example, a bit is defined as one shift to the left, followed by one shift to the right. This process is carried out over several iterations, with the end result being that there are numerous Hamming distances calculated, which takes into account any type of inconsistency in the iris structure.

Boolean XOR operators are used to calculate the Hamming distance(s) as well, as described earlier in this chapter. The basic theoretical construct behind the Hamming distance model is that the iris patterns from

Table 3.1 Hamming distance calculations

Template 1	10 00 11 00 10 01	
Template 2	00 11 00 10 01 10	Hamming distance = 0.83
	← Shift 2 bits to the left	
Template 1	00 11 00 10 01 10	Hamming distance = 0.83
Template 2	00 11 00 10 01 10	
	→ Shift 2 bits to the right	
Template 1	01 10 00 11 00 10	Hamming distance = 0.33
Template 2	00 11 00 10 01 10	

the same iris are not different from each other when compared to patterns from different irises.

Explained in terms of the Hamming distance, if the Hamming distance between two bit patterns is calculated to be 0.5, it means that there is a strong level of difference between the two irises, but if the Hamming distance between two bit patterns is 0, it means they arise from the same iris.

Table 3.1 represents these kinds of calculations with a greater level of clarity.

Reducing the Effects of Pupil Dilation and Constriction – Proenca and Neves

As mentioned in the last section, In the segmentation phase of creating the iris-based enrollment and verification templates, a major constraint in breaking down the composite image into useful, smaller ones is the dilation and the constriction of the pupils. Normally, as it was discussed, our pupils dilate when there is not enough light in the external environment, and then they constrict once there is enough light.

But in many cases, this may not be the case. For example, an end-user may have impaired vision in which they require more light to enter their pupils. As a result, their pupils will be dilated for a longer period.

The scientific work of Proenca and Neves examined various methods in which this constraint of the dilation and the constriction of the pupils can be greatly reduced. As a result of their work, they came up with a newer set of mathematical algorithms, termed IRINA. This stands for **I**ris **R**ecognition that is robust against **INA**ccurately segmented iris samples.

They noted two major weaknesses that are present in the modern iris recognition technologies and systems. These can be described as follows:

(1) The inaccurate mathematical parameterization and segmentation to achieve an adequate level of normalization. They noted that many of the feature-matching techniques which are available today are vector-phase-based, which can result in a higher than expected false rejection rate (also known as the FRR).

(2) Pupils which are severely dilated or constricted can also lead to a higher false rejection in the iris recognition system. Other impacts include a non-linear deformation of the iris texture, and any extraneous movements of the pupil can actually put extra lateral pressure on the iris, with the result being that some muscle fibers can actually fold just beneath the structure of the iris itself.

The basic construct of IRINA is divided into three distinct steps (or three different "processing chains"), which are detailed as follows:

(1) The statistical estimation of the posterior probabilities:

Proenca and Neves make the assumption that the patches from two very distinct iris samples can actually correspond to one another, even in the situations where severe dilation and constriction of the pupils can lead to non-linear texture deformations. They have termed this phenomenon "corresponding patches," and it will be subsequently discussed in greater detail. The information and data which are collected are then analyzed by a "convolution neural network," or CNN. This system helps to discriminate the differences in both the corresponding and the non-corresponding patches of the iris structure.

(2) An assumption of a free-form 2D vector field:

This phase makes use of the hidden Markov models (HMMs) to represent these corresponding patches as a set of normal X and Y coordinates in a Cartesian plane.

(3) Observations in the deformation field:

This simply refers to the images, or the samples, of the iris which are collected from the irises of the same end-user. The mathematical assumption being made here is that the 2D vectors are much smaller than those of an "impostor." In order to ascertain this and collect the relevant information and data, first and second statistical manipulations are called upon to find any differences and relevant discriminations.

The concept of "corresponding patches" was previously discussed. In their work, Proenca and Neves specifically define this as the following: "The patches between pairs of iris based images ... this is the key to learn the typical non-linear deformations in the normalized representations of the iris due to the pupillary dilation / constriction and segmentation errors" [4].

To actually find the differences in these corresponding patches, normalized iris samples are collected from the end-user and analyzed. From here, the control points are the mathematically computed from the various regions by using this formulation:

$$f(x) = \lambda^T [\varphi, p(x)],$$

$$f_r(x) = \lambda^T [\varphi, p(x)], \tag{4}$$

where

$$\varphi = [\varphi(|x - x_{1|2}) \ldots \varphi = [(|x - x_{n|2}).$$

The information and data for the IRINA-based mathematical algorithms came from four distinct sources:

(1) The CASIA-Iris V3 Lamp;

(2) The CASIA-Iris V4 Lamp;

(3) The CASIA-Iris V4 Thousand;

(4) WVU.

It is important to define these terms:

(1) CASIA:

This stands for the Chinese Academy of Sciences – Institute of Automation iris image database. This consists of 756 grayscale iris-based images with 108 unique eye classes.

(2) WVU:

The West Virginia University iris dataset.

From these datasets, the following types of iris-based image were collected:

(1) Off-angle irises;

(2) Occluded irises;

(3) Dilated/constricted pupils;

(4) Iris shadows.

Overall, 500 datasets were used from the CASIA database, and 10 datasets were taken from the WVU database. All of these iris-based images went through a comprehensive segmentation process by using a different technique known as the "geodesic active contours algorithm."

This process helped to ensure that the iris images met the stringent requirements of maintaining 20 degrees of freedom for the pupil boundaries which intersected with the iris, and 2 degrees of freedom for the sclera boundaries which also intersected with the iris.

The performance of the IRINA-based mathematical algorithms was determined and evaluated in two types of scenarios:

(1) The **accurate** parameterizations of the boundaries of the iris with other components of the eye, namely the pupil and the sclera.

(2)   The **decrease** in the parameterizations of the boundaries of the iris with other components of the eye, namely the pupil and the sclera.

In terms of the first one, iris-based data which were deemed to be of high quality were used. Based upon the experimental results, it was deemed that the IRINA mathematical algorithms outperformed any other models. It was also discovered that the best data sets came from the CASIA-Iris V3 Lamp, in which sharp decreases in both the false acceptance rate (FAR) and the equal error rate (ERR) were of the order of one magnitude. The results of this can be seen in Table 3.2.

   With regard to the last setting, Proenca and Neves implemented two types of error, which were the translation and the scale to the various parameterizations which were set forth by the iris boundaries (these are the intersections of the iris with both the pupil and the sclera). These introduced error rates were as high as 21%. The metric used in this type of setting is the "magnitude," as previously described.

   In this regard, the order of magnitude can be defined as "the maximum Euclidean distance between the boundary points in the original and in the inaccurate segmentation parameterizations" [4]. Proenca and Neves discovered that it is in these conditions where the IRINA-based mathematical algorithms perform the best.

   Overall, they concluded that IRINA not only performs well with the good-quality datasets, but can also be very effective in greatly eradicating the segmentation errors and other types of issue with pupillary contraction and constriction.

Table 3.2 Results of datasets

Method	AUC	D'	EER
CASIA-Iris V3 Lamp	$0.999 \pm 1E^{-4}$	12.623 ± 0.176	0.006 ± 0.001
CASIA-Iris V4 Lamp	$0.995 \pm .0.002$	6.623 ± 0.454	0.026 ± 0.005
CASIA-Iris V4 Thousand	0.996 ± 0.001	6.179 ± 0.380	0.030 ± 0.005
WVU	0.991 ± 0.002	5.179 ± 0.361	0.042 ± 0.008

AUC = area under curve; EER = the equal error rate; D' = the decidability index.

Reducing the Effects of Eyelids and Eyelashes – Lin et al. and Zhou and Sun

It should be noted at this point that many of the theoretical constructs as well as the technological platforms for iris recognition follow the four steps in terms of unique feature extraction and template matching. But the key difference in all of this is that different mathematical algorithms are being used in most of these theories as well as the iris recognition systems.

In fact, many of these platforms use the theories created by Dr. John Daugman to form the basis of the iris recognition model.

Such is the case in the iris recognition models as developed by Lin et al. For example, they followed the basic constructs that were established by Dr. John Daugman, but modified to fit the model algorithm they were specifically using, which is known as the Morlet wave transformation.

It can be defined as a wavelet which is composed of a complex exponential carrier that is multiplied by a Gaussian window. In fact, this wavelet has been modeled after the theories which form the basis for human perception. Also, Lin et al. make use of the same four steps, which are as follows, but make further modifications and revisions:

(1) Iris localization:

In their research, they also note that the eyelashes can be a major impediment in the creation of a high-quality, robust composite image of the iris. Thus, they introduced the use of various grayscale projection techniques which in turn would create what is specifically known as a "pupil center detection center operator."

With this, the center of the pupil is identified and confirmed, and four inner boundaries and four outer boundaries (for a total of eight distinct boundaries) are located. This is accomplished by using the direction edge variable which is in the Morlet wave transformation, which is formulated as follows:

$$(x) = \pi^{-1/4}(e^{i\alpha x} - e^{-\alpha 2})e^{-x2}/2 \qquad [5,6]$$

(2)   Iris normalization:

This process is very similar to the one developed by Dr. John Daugman, but instead of using the final version of the composite image, Lin et al. use the initial or the first version of the composite image which was created. This is also known as the "primitive image." A polar coordinate transformation is used throughout this entire process, and thus the final image of the iris is fitted into a 512 column * 64 row grid.

(3)   Feature extraction:

In order to completely extract the unique features of the iris, the imaginary coefficients of the of the Morlet wavelet transformation are used. More specifically, one-dimensional (1D) transformations are utilized, and are applied to row by row in the final, composite image of the iris as described previously. The end result is that different scales and statistical distribution coefficients are developed. The primary goal of this is to reflect the unique information and data which can be found in the texture of the iris.

4)   Iris code matching:

In manner **not similar** to Dr. John Daugman's technique, two sets of iris codes are created and developed, which are as follows:

- Register code [m] [x] [y];

- Enroll code [m] [x] [y].

- In this case, an "AND" operator is created from the Morlet wave transformation and is utilized to compute the match between the registering iris (which is done at the enrollment phase) and the entering iris (this is done at the verification phase). For example, when two iris codes are being compared with one another, the code of the registering iris is shifted several pixels to the right or left and the code of the entering iris is shifted several pixels either down or up in a vertical fashion in a Cartesian geometric plane.

In the theoretical work conducted by Zhou and Sun, a mathematical algorithm known as the "canny edge operator" is utilized. This specific algorithm operates by making use of five different steps, which are described as follows:

(1) Smoothing:

Any extraneous filtering and blurring of the initial composite image of the iris are removed.

(2) Finding gradients:

Anywhere a color pattern is identified in the initial composite of the iris, all of the relevant pixels and points are grouped together.

(3) Non-maximum suppression:

The initial composite image of the iris is further processed into a non-linear and circular (or convexed) image, and the edges of the iris are identified and further refined.

(4) Double thresholding:

Any other edges or boundaries located amongst the pupil and sclera are identified and further refined.

(5) Edge tracking by hysteresis:

Finally, all identified and known iris images are suppressed in order to create the final composite image of the iris.

Once again, the scientific work of Zhou and Sun made use of the four procedures as described previously in order to extract the unique features of the iris, and to examine the statistical closeness of the iris-based enrollment template and verification template. But Zhou and Sun made further modifications to this, which are described as follows;

(1) Iris localization:

A statistical technique known specifically as "histogram analysis" was utilized to further locate any other unseen or undiscovered boundaries of the iris with both the pupil and the sclera. Also, canny edge detectors and parabolic curves were used to detect the presence of both the eyelashes and the eyelids.

(2) Iris normalization:

The rubber sheet model developed by Dr. John Daugman was utilized in order to transform the Cartesian geometric plane coordinates into polar-based coordinates. The end result is that the initial composite image of the iris is broken down into a rectangular shape, by rows and columns.

(3) Feature extraction:

In this process, 1D logarithmic-based Gabor wavelets were used to extract the unique features from the final composite of the iris (which is also the normalized image in step 2). This is mathematically represented as follows:

$$G(f) = \exp\left(\frac{-\left(\log(f / f_0)\right)^2}{2\left(\log(\sigma / f_0)\right)^2}\right) \qquad \text{Equation 3.5 [5,6]}$$

Iris codes were also created and developed by using this logarithmic-based approach, by creating feature vectors from the extracted information and data.

(4) Feature matching:

In order to compare the iris based enrollment template against the verification template, a "K-dimensional tree" was created and utilized. In this type of tree, there is a left child node, a right child node, and an iris-based object. Unlike other research studies, these nodes were developed in order to make the comparison process between enrollment and verification templates quick and efficient. The Hamming distance was used to determine the actual degree of closeness or dissimilarity. For example, if the Hamming distance between the input iris code and the iris code for the K-dimensional (K-D) tree is zero, an exact match is found between the enrollment and verification templates (in other words, the identity of the end-user is confirmed). But if the Hamming distance between the input iris code and the iris code for the K-D tree is between 0 and 1, then there is an inexact match (in other words, the identity of the end-user cannot be absolutely confirmed, there is a false match). It is also important to note that the Hamming distance is calculated from the input iris code and the iris code in the K-D tree.

Reducing the Signal Noise in the Eye Image – Shivani and Sharma

So far in this chapter, and especially in this section, we have examined a number of the key mathematical algorithms which are currently being used in iris recognition technology. To review, these include the following:

(1) Gabor wavelets;

(2) Morlet wavelets;

(3) The K-D tree method.

The research conducted by Shivani and Sharma introduced yet another sophisticated mathematical algorithm to iris recognition. This particular one is known as the "reverse biorthogonal wavelet." This particular kind of algorithm is used in the feature extraction process, in order to improve the accuracy rate of actually locating the iris and completely eradicating any type of noise signal that might be present in the entire process from raw image collection to creating both the iris-based enrollment and verification templates.

As discussed earlier in this chapter, but to elaborate upon further, it is the iris which surrounds the pupil, which is of course at the center of the eye. The primary function of the iris is to moderate and control the actual amount of light which enters the eye.

It should be noted that in terms of physiology, the average diameter of the iris is around 12–14 mm, and the absolute size of the pupil can actually vary greatly. According to Shivani and Sharma, there is a large range, with the variance being from 10% to 80% of the total diameter of the iris.

As can easily be seen in a mirror, the pupil of the eye remains a constant color – which is black. It is located at the center of the eye, and normal light (whether it is natural or from a lighting device) enters it. This light then gets transmitted to the retina, which processes the information and data into meaningful visual cues.

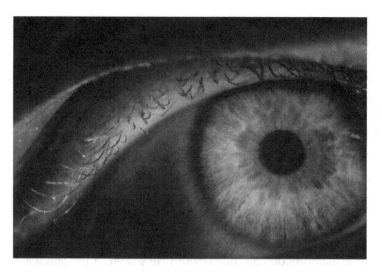

Figure 3.5 Image of normal pupil
Source: Jevgenij Avin/Shutterstock.com

So, when more light is required by the brain, the pupil of course expands to a certain degree in order to accommodate this extra light. If lesser amounts of light are required, the pupil actually shrinks in size. This expansion and contraction of the pupil is governed by a set of muscles. A dilated pupil can be seen in Figure 3.4. A normal pupil can be seen below in Figure 3.5.

The reverse biorthogonal wavelet algorithm can be broken down into the following four processes, the same as discussed previously with the other mathematical algorithms. However, the primary difference is that further modifications have been made to it, especially in the feature extraction process:

(1) Image acquisition:

This is where multiple images of the iris are captured in order to create the initial composite image.

(2) Segmentation:

This process converts the initial composite image of the iris into various grayscale images. In this particular research by Shivani and

Sharma, each pixel of the grayscale image is composed of a single numerical value which indicates the intensity of the grayscale. It should be noted that this value can range anywhere from 0 to 255. As discussed earlier in this sub-section, the canny edge operator is primarily used to determine and locate both the inner and the outer edges of the iris. In fact, it has three of its own processes as well in order to carry out this task. These can be described as follows:

- Determining the gradient level of the iris;
- Ascertaining the correct level for non-maximum suppression of the iris;
- Confirming the level of the hysteresis thresholding.
- The primary advantage of using the canny edge detector is to actually reduce the number of pixels used in the grayscale images. This will in turn make the subsequent processes much more efficient.
- In order to determine the boundaries that which intersect between the iris and the pupil further use is made of yet another mathematical algorithm, known as the "integro-differential operator." With this particular method, a gradient image in a conjunction boundary between the iris and the pupil literally searches for any type of increasing radii in both the pupil and the iris. From here, a maximum sum of all of these circles is determined to find the center of the pupil as well as its corresponding radius. All of this is done in order to prepare for the next process, which is normalization.

(3) Normalization:

In this process, the pupil image is removed from the iris image. As reviewed previously, the rubber sheet model is used to "unwrap" or separate the image of the iris from the pupil. In terms of mathematics, this is done by converting the iris image into Cartesian geometric plane coordinates. In other words, the value of (x,y) is transformed into a polar coordinate value of (r,θ). This technique is used primarily because the outer circles of the pupil are **not** concentric in nature. From here, the various images of the iris are broken down into rows and columns, thus giving its rectangular shape.

(4) Feature extraction:

In this process, the reverse biorthogonal wavelet is used to trans-form the input data from the raw images of the iris into a set of cer-tain, distinct areas from which the unique features of the iris can be extracted. Once these unique features have been extracted, they are converted into a binary format. It is important to note at this point that the wavelet component of the reverse biorthogonal ranges in value from −1 to +1. In fact, it incorporates a time and frequency domain as well, which thus creates very simple "wave forms." In fact, both of these variables are the characteristics of a proper wavelet transformation.

(5) Feature matching:

This is the last process to be accomplished, in which the iris-based enrollment template is compared against the iris-based verification template. For the purposes of the research conducted by Shivani and Sharma, a set of 765 grayscale images with up to 108 unique features were collected from a database known as the "UBIIRIS.v1." In order to make these particular comparisons, the Hamming distance was once again used. The mathematical formula used to calculate the Hamming distance is as follows:

$$HD = 1/n \sum nj = 1 Xj \oplus Yj \qquad [7]$$

where:

X and Y = the two bitwise templates to be compared

n = the total number of bits represented by each template.

It is important to note that this mathematical formula is quite different from the other formula, which just represented the Hamming distance. As an example of the above formula, the calculated Hamming distance is 0.445. If there is a value which falls below this threshold (<0.445), then it means that the images of the iris are from the same eye. However, if the value is above this threshold (>0.445), then this means that the images of the iris come from different eyes.

Table 3.3 Comparison of Hamming distance values

Time	12 seconds
Separation point	0.445
Inner mean	0.40
Inter mean	0.54

It is very important to note at this point that the primary objective of the Hamming distance is to separate the intra-class and inter-class images of the iris that have been collected. With the former, this is the Hamming distance between the iris images from the same individual, whereas with the latter this is the Hamming distance between the iris images from different individuals.

An optimal iris recognition system will try to close the gap between the intra-class and the inter-class to a value that is as small as possible. This value then becomes what is known as the "equal error rate," or the ERR for short.

This is where the false acceptance rate (the FAR) and the false rejection rate (the FRR) equal one another. This is the point, in theory at least, that every kind of biometric system, both physical and behavioral-based, should be at.

Overall, the research conducted by Shivani and Sharma demonstrates that the average time to compare the iris-based enrollment and verification templates for a particular individual is 12 seconds at a Hamming distance value of 0.445. The overall results can be seen in Table 3.3.

The Applications of Iris Recognition

As we have reviewed at the beginning of this book as well as in our previous two books detailed in Chapter 1, iris recognition in today's times holds its place as a leading biometric technology in terms of market applications.

It should be noted that although iris recognition does have a long history (not quite as long as either fingerprint recognition or hand geometry recognition), it did not make its entry into the market until after the tragic incidents of "9/11."

Just like facial recognition, there was also a strong interest in iris recognition in terms of securing our borders and major international airports.

But at this time, there was only one iris recognition company, which held the monopoly on the intellectual property and the mathematical algorithms, and this business entity was known specifically as Iridian Technologies, Inc.

Their primary markets at the time were the Federal Government sector, as well as some physical access entry applications on a large scale. It wasn't until after the patents expired on these mathematical algorithms that the explosion in the use of iris recognition actually occurred, late in the last decade.

Today, as reviewed at the beginning of this chapter, there is a plethora of iris recognition vendors, using all different kinds of mathematical algorithms. But it is interesting to see that the work conducted by Dr. John Daugman still serves as the basis for these algorithms.

When iris recognition first came out, there was a lot of hesitancy towards its use, especially by the public. The primary reason for this is that there were strong levels of apprehension about having one's eyes scanned in close proximity. They compared the level of intrusiveness in this regard to that of retinal recognition.

At the time, iris recognition did require end-user to stay very close to the camera in order to have their irises scanned. But the technology has evolved to the point now that iris recognition can now scan the irises of people at a distance, even when they are in motion, without their knowledge of what is actually happening to them.

In this regard, a prime example is international airports. Just like facial recognition, iris recognition can be used to scan the eyes of foreign travelers as they walk to their next airline connection or embark in their country of destination. Of course, there are other social issues related to this, especially that of the violation of privacy rights. This topic was explored in great detail in our second book.

Overview of the Major Applications

Today, we see iris recognition being used at the same level as the other biometric technologies are being used. In summary, these applications include the following:

(1) Physical access entry:

   Traditionally, it has been either hand geometry recognition or finger-print recognition (or even a combination of them) which has been used in this particular market segment. But now, iris recognition is making its entrance here as well, and one of the primary reasons for this is the contactless nature of iris recognition. This can save time when trying to gain access through a secure door.

(2) Time and attendance:

   Once again, it has been fingerprint recognition and/or hand geom-etry recognition which has been used to keep track of both the clock-in and clock-out times of employees. But again, iris recognition is making its entrance here as well, primarily because of its contactless nature. In fact, in this regard, by using iris recognition, an employee of a business or a corporation can clock in and out faster, which in turn means a greater level of productivity.

(3) Logical access entry – single-sign-on solutions:

   This is where iris recognition can be used to gain access to shared network resources from a server(s) which is located at a business or a corporation. In this regard, the most common traditional method of authentication has been the use of a password. We are now seeing just how vulnerable this is, especially when it comes to its covert hijacking and use by a malicious third party. Because of this, security policies now mandate the use of much longer and much more com-plex passwords, thus making it hard for employees to remember them. As a result, they write them down, which in the end defeats the entire purpose of creating a long and complex password in the first place. Also, the resetting of a password can carry a huge financial burden as well to a business or a corporation: up to $300 per employee. As a result of all of this, organizations are starting to realize the benefits of using iris recognition as a means of replacing the traditional pass-word. For example, with just one scan of your iris, you can not only be logged into your computer, but you can also gain access to the shared resources at the very same time, in just a matter of seconds. Because of this, iris recognition is also regarded as what is known as a "single-sign-on solution," or SSO for short.

(4) Secure documents:

The traditional paper passport has been primarily used as a means of confirming the identity of a foreign traveler as they disembark/ embark, in the county of destination or country of origin, respectively. But as also reviewed extensively in our second book, this too has its own set of major security vulnerabilities. To help combat this, the nations around the world have come up with a replacement to the traditional paper passport, and this is known as the "biometric passport," or the "e-passport." Essentially, this is an electronic version of the traditional paper passport, with a major addition to it. It also contains a memory chip (such as those used on smart cards), in which the biometric templates of the foreign traveler can be stored. In this regard, it is fingerprint recognition, facial recognition, and iris recognition which are being used for the e-passport. The primary benefits of this are the 100% confirmation of the identity of the foreign traveler, as well as greatly expedited immigration processing times.

In this part of the chapter, we can continue to look at the scientific studies which have explored the use of iris recognition in other applications as well, which include the following:

(1) Spoofing – print attacks;

(2) Wireless networks;

(3) Fuzzy neural networks;

(4) Biocryptography.

Spoofing – Print Attacks – Gupta et al.

As reviewed extensively in the last section in terms of the mathematical algorithms, the Iris recognition template is not the actual image of the iris itself. Rather, it is just a mathematical representation of it. But very often the question gets asked by the end-user: "What if this template is hacked into? Can in it be used for launching identity theft attacks in a manner similar to credit card theft?" On a theoretical level, the answer to this is no. On a technical level, the answer is still no, but keep in mind that an Iris recognition system is still just a technological tool, and thus it can be prone to very sophisticated as well as very covert cyber-based attacks.

One such potential attack on an iris recognition system could be what is known as a "spoofing attack." The work of Gupta et al., in their research, further examines the implications and reality of it actually occurring. The cyber threat here is known specifically as "iris spoofing": this refers to a cyber attacker using the iris image of a legitimate user in order to literally "spoof" the iris recognition system.

There are a number of reasons why this can occur, and they are as follows:

(1) Pupil dilation:

Any extreme in the expansion of the pupil can result in the patterns being indiscernible by the iris recognition device.

(2) Textured contact lenses:

A contact lens which has varying levels of texture and coloring to it can cause the iris recognition to be "confused."

(3) Print attack:

This involves literally printing an image of the actual iris, and from there scanning it in in an attempt to spoof the iris recognition system. On a theoretical level, if the right printer and paper combination is used, this could actually happen.

To further elaborate upon the latter, a print-based attack can be defined specifically as follows: "the image of the iris patterns is first printed on a paper and then scanned via a regular scanner ... or when a photo is captured via an iris scanner" [8]. Based on this definition, the former can be referred to as a "print + scan attack," and the latter can be referred to as a "print + capture attack." This can then be broken down into the following types of attack:

(1) Type 1:

A fake image of the iris is presented to the sensor.

(2) Type 2:

A stolen iris recognition template is hijacked from a database, and is used to spoof the iris recognition system.

There have been several methodologies which have been developed to eradicate these two types of attack, as follows:

(1) Frequency spectrum analysis (Daugman et al.);

(2) Use of the Purkinje image (Lee et al.);

(3) The use of neural network technology to differentiate between fake and live iris images (Takano and Nakamura).

But, as Gupta et al. have pointed out, there have been no existing scientific studies on iris recognition spoofing which have taken the following permutations into account:

(1) The use of a large-scale iris-based database;

(2) Analysis of the impacts a print attack can have on an iris recognition system;

(3) Finding other methods to detect any covert variations in Iris recognition spoofing.

In order to address these permutations, Gupta et al. first utilized an iris database known as the "IIITD Contact Lens Iris (CLI)" database. As they discovered, this particular database consists of images of the iris with the following characteristics:

(1) No contact lens (described as "normal CLI");

(2) Transparent lenses present (described as "transparent CLI");

(3) Colored lenses present (described as "color CLI").

Images of transparent lenses and colored lenses can be seen in Figures 3.6 and 3.7, respectively.

Figure 3.6 Image of transparent lens
Source: buradaki/Shutterstock.com

Figure 3.7 Image of colored lens
Source: Kichigan/Shutterstock.com

Table 3.4 The IIITD iris spoofing database

Number of subjects	101
Number of textured lens images per subject	6
Number of without-lens images per subject	3
Number of transparent lens images per subject	3
Number of iris-based sensors	2
Number of spoofing scenarios	2
Total number of images in the iris database	$101 \times 12 \times 2 \times 2 = 4848$ iris images

It should be noted that this particular database consists of at least 6,750 iris-based images, collected from 101 end-users. It is important to note that these iris images were collected by making use of two types of optical sensor:

(1) The Cogent CIS 202 dual iris scanner;
(2) The Vista FA2E single iris sensor.

Table 3.4 further elaborates upon the details of the IIITD iris spoofing database:

As Gupta et al. noted, the first issue to be addressed is the affects that a print attack will have upon an iris recognition system, in terms of performance. In order to conduct this task, a software development kit (SDK) was used, known as the "VeriEye." From this, the following metrics were established:

(1) A score of "0" is given for any matches between the iris-based enrollment and verification templates which are deemed to be "impostor like."

(2) Any score which is greater than "0" (>0) is deemed to be "genuine like." It should be noted that the more this score is above 0, the stronger the statistical closeness will be between the iris-based enrollment and verification templates.

In order to launch the cyber-based print attacks, the data sets from the IIITD contact lens iris were utilized, and two "galleries" were created by

Table 3.5 Results of cyber-based print attacks

Probe	Cogent	Vista
CLI normal	97.77	100
CLI transparent lens	94.30	95.54
CLI textured lens	26.49	46.29
Print + scan normal	47.94	62.37
Print + scan transparent lens	41.02	46.61
Print + scan textured lens	5.33	6.54
Print + capture normal	24.76	4.57
Print + capture transparent lens	23.77	6.37
Print + capture textured lens	3.67	0.63

Gupta et al. Each gallery consisted of 202 normalized iris images, which were collected by the Vista- and Cogent-based optical sensors. In the end, a total of 2424 iris images were used.

The results of this are as follows:

(1) When normal iris images of the same individual are compared, there is a very high "genuine" score developed. It should be noted that there are no contact lenses utilized in this part of the study.

(2) When the original iris images are compared with those of a spoofed image(s), instead of having a value of 0, a high "genuine" score is obtained.

These results are further quantified in Table 3.5.

Gupta et al. concluded that, based on this table, the Cogent-based optical sensor is much more susceptible to cyber-based print attacks, whereas the Vista-based optical sensor is not prone to this security vulnerability. Also, if colored contact lenses are used, then the iris recognition system is not prone to these kinds of attack. On the contrary, it is difficult for an end-user to actually conceal their identity if they are required to be scanned by an iris recognition system.

These findings are further substantiated by Tables 3.6 to 3.9, which display the minimum, maximum, and mean Genuine and Impostor scores which were collected and analyzed by the VeriEye SDK.

Table 3.6 The Cogent-based optical sensor – genuine scores

Probe type	[Min, max]	Statistical mean
CLI normal	[0, 3235]	1132
CLI transparent	[0, 1146]	375.69
CLI textured	[0, 182]	**29**
Print + scan normal	[0, 256]	**27.21**
Print + scan transparent	[0, 345]	25.11
Print + scan textured	[0, 64]	4.85
Print + capture normal	[0, 574]	45.55
Print + capture transparent	[0, 386]	36.44
Print + capture textured	[0, 106]	10.13

Table 3.7 The Cogent-based optical sensor – impostor scores

Probe type	[Min, max]	Statistical mean
CLI normal	[0, 67]	3.86
CLI transparent	[0, 211]	3.87
CLI textured	[0, 68]	3.57
Print + scan normal	[0, 45]	0.37
Print + scan transparent	[0, 57]	0.38
Print + scan textured	[0, 44]	0.80
Print + capture normal	[0, 79]	4.16
Print + capture transparent	[0, 70]	3.80
Print + capture textured	[0, 76]	4.89

In order to combat the threats posed by the cyber-based print attacks, Gupta et al. first examined the use of spoof-detection algorithms. They discovered that creating such mathematical algorithms would simply tax the memory and the processing power of the iris recognition system to its limits. Thus, they examined the use of image descriptors, which can be described as follows:

(1) The local binary pattern (LBP) descriptor:

This encodes the texture feature of the iris image(s).

Table 3.8 The Vista-based optical sensor – genuine scores

Probe type	[Min, max]	Statistical mean
CLI normal	[0, 3235]	1944
CLI transparent	[0, 3235]	496.98
CLI textured	[0, 165]	39.72
Print + scan normal	[0, 278]	43.63
Print + scan transparent	[0, 345]	27.61
Print + scan textured	[0, 89]	5.47
Print + capture normal	[0, 212]	8.43
Print + capture transparent	[0, 216]	10.55
Print + capture textured	[0, 80]	3.97

Table 3.9 The Vista-based optical sensor – impostor scores

Probe type	[Min, max]	Statistical mean
CLI normal	[0, 55]	3.08
CLI transparent	[0, 181]	3.09
CLI textured	[0, 67]	3.02
Print + scan normal	[0, 45]	0.36
Print + scan transparent	[0, 50]	0.38
Print + scan textured	[0, 44]	0.78
Print + capture normal	[0, 421]	3.16
Print + capture transparent	[0, 514]	2.89
Print + capture textured	[0, 105]	3.39

(2)   The GIST descriptor (GIST):

This provides low-dimensional images of the iris which include the color, spatial frequency, the texture, and the size and position of the unique features which can be found in the iris.

(3)   The histogram of oriented gradients descriptor (HOGS):

This actually locates the iris appearance and shape, by making use of the local intensity gradients. A support vector machine is then used to match the statistical histograms which are then created.

In order to ascertain whether these descriptors will mitigate the effects of a cyber-based print attack, the images of the iris are further segmented and cropped to a much smaller size. Then a binary mask is used to assign a 0 value to each pixel value which falls off the image of the iris. The actual image of the iris then becomes a region of interest, and then the above-mentioned descriptors are then applied

It was discovered by Gupta et al. that both the LBP and HOG descriptors could be used to combat the threats posed by a cyber-based print attack.

Wireless Networks – Ibrahim et al.

As we know today, wireless communications is fast becoming the de facto standard by which, as a society, we communicate with others not just on a personal level, but on a professional level as well. This includes not only the transmission of pictures, messages, and videos, but it also the sending of very confidential and sensitive corporate information and data.

The device which we use today that makes the most use of wireless-based network protocols is the smartphone, and other mobile devices as well.

Because of this, there is also a strong level of interest of in the process of confirming the identity of an individual via a wireless channel. Of course, this brings some key advantages. For example, if a business or a corporation has remote offices worldwide, there is no need to conduct the actual authentication processes at these remote locations.

Instead, the end-user can have his or her iris scanned, and have the verification template which was created compared with the enrollment template stored in the databases at the main corporate office. Of course, this verification template would have to be transmitted via a wireless communications channel.

This is the research work conducted by Ibrahim et al. [9]. They discussed one key issue which is prevalent when confirming the identity of an individual via a wireless communications channel:

The confirmation of the identity of an individual has to occur within a matter of seconds, in fact, in a time shorter than if this were to happen locally (this simply refers to the fact that the enrollment templates are stored into the database of the iris recognition device, and the comparison of the iris-based enrollment template and the iris-based verification template occurs at the device level).

Ibrahim et al. refer to this specifically as "automatic authentication." The basic premise here is to totally eradicate the use of PIN codes and passwords, given the grave security vulnerabilities that they possess. They point out that in this regard, iris recognition is deemed to be the most reliable automatic authentication system available, when compared to the other physical and behavioral-based biometric modalities.

In fact the statistical probability of two individuals possessing the same type of iris pattern is almost zero percent, and the chances of the same individual having the same type of iris pattern in both eyes is even statistically lower.

But, in order for the wireless-based iris recognition system to be effective, the actual iris image and its related information/data must be compressed to a level (or degree) that it can cause a reduction in the storage space amongst the data packets which house them as they traverse a wide variety of network connections.

In most if not all instances, in this kind of wireless environment, the images of the iris and its related information/data have to transferred across a wireless network (also known as a "Wi-Fi") to a certain geographic location. In this regard, this must be transmitted across a network medium which could quite possibly have a very low bandwidth and latency capability.

As stated earlier, the image of the iris has to be compressed in such a way that a minimal amount of information and data is actually transmitted across a wireless network medium.

Ibrahim et al. proposed a brand new technological model for the creation and the implementation of an iris-based wireless system. It consists of three parts, which are as follows:

(1) Two methods for the comparison of the iris-based verification and enrollment templates;

(2) A single method for both the compression and the decompression of the iris-based images and their related information/data;

(3) The design and implementation of the constructs of an actual wireless system.

Two Methods for the Comparison of the Iris-Based Verification and Enrollment Templates: The Libor Masek Algorithm

In this part of the process, iris images were collected and utilized from the Chinese Academy of Sciences Institute of Automation, also known as "CASIA" for short. The processing of the actual iris image involves two sub-steps, as follows:

- Iris segmentation:

  In this regard, it is the Hough transformation technique is utilized, which locates and ascertains the actual iris itself, along with the pupil which it surrounds. Also, the occluding eyelids as well as the eyelashes and any reflections which they may create are located by making use of further linear Hough transformation methods.

- Iris normalization:

  As reviewed extensively before, the rubber sheet model (as developed by Dr. Joh Daugman) was used to further segment the actual iris image into a geometric rectangle so that any imaging inconsistencies can be taken into consideration. The end result of all of this is the creation of various 2D mathematical vectors. One vector consists of the normalized iris region, whereas the other vector consists of the extraneous noises which are contributed by the eyelids, eyelashes, and other kind or type of light-based reflections.

In order to extract the unique features from the iris, 1D log Gabor wavelets were utilized (this was also reviewed in detail earlier in this chapter). At this point, these unique features are then further encoded in order to create a 2D iris-based enrollment template.

In order to fully ascertain the statistical closeness of both the iris-based enrollment and verification templates, the respective Hamming distances were calculated as well (also examined in detail earlier in this chapter).

A Single Method for Both the Compression and the Decompression of the Iris-Based Images: The Genetic Algorithm Optimization

Overall, the use of genetic algorithms is meant to lead to optimization. In other words, they are called upon in order to ascertain and determine the most optimal solution to a given problem, in this case how to decrease the transmission time of the iris-based templates as they traverse the network medium and various connections.

This is further accomplished by either maximizing or minimizing the usage of specific mathematical functions. For the purposes of the work conducted by Ibrahim et al., the maximizing function is used to locate and determine the best-fit statistical score between the iris-based enrollment and verification templates.

The technique known as principal component analysis or PCA is utilized to reduce the data-based dimensions of both the templates. When this particular technique is utilized, there is hardly any loss of information or data. When PCA is used as an image compression algorithm, it takes the various grayscale images and computes the arithmetic mean of them.

From there, the respective covariance matrix can be calculated, as well as the respective eigenvectors and the eigenvalues. Finally, a compressed image matrix is created and further decompressed by making use of the technique known as the inverse principal component analysis or IPCA for short. Illustrations of both PCA and IPCA can be seen in Figure 3 A and B.

The Design and Implementation of the Constructs of an Actual Wireless System

In terms of the network design of the wireless-based Iris recognition System, an infrastructure topology is assumed. For example, the central server(s) which house the database(s) of the enrollment and verification templates is connected to a main router. Also, the iris recognition device which is assumed to be located at a remote office (away from the main corporate office) is also connected to the same router.

In this type of setup, two network connectivity lines are also established, and these are as follows:

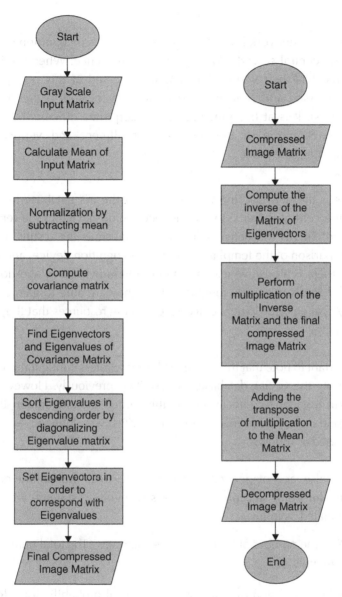

Figure 3.A The principal component
analysis algorithm

Figure 3.B The inverse principal
component analysis algorithm

(1) Line 1:

This is the network line which connects the iris recognition device to the central server(s) located at the main office. When the individual has their verification template created at this point, it is compressed and sent to the iris database located in the central server(s). It is at this juncture (at the corporate office) where the comparison the of the iris-based enrollment and verification templates take place.

(2) Line 2:

This is the network line which connects the iris database located in the central server(s) to the iris recognition device at the remote office. This is the network line which transmits the results of the comparison of the templates to the iris recognition device, and tells it if there is a positive match or not of the individual in question. If he or she is positively identified, then they are able to gain either physical entry or logical entry access to the resources that they are seeking.

It is important to note that this entire iris-based wireless configuration was tested using the CASIA database, as described previously. However, in order to truly gauge the effectiveness of this particular configuration, three very important key performance indicators (KPIs) were utilized, and can be described as follows:

(1) The false acceptance rate (this the statistical probability of an **impostor** being **accepted** by the iris recognition system), which is calculated as follows:

FAR = The number of falsely accepted samples / The total number of all attempts

(2) The false rejection rate (this is the statistical probability of a **legitimate individual** being **denied** by the iris recognition system), which is calculated as follows:

FRR = The number of falsely rejected samples / The total number of all attempts

(3)   The correct recognition rate is calculated as follows:

CRR = The total number of correctly accepted samples / The total number of all presented samples.

The results of the experiments which followed can be seen in Tables 3.10 to 3.15.

In terms of performance results, for the first 150 samples using the Libor Masek algorithm, the FAR value is zero and the FRR value is at 1.33%. But when the population size increases to 324, the FRR increases to 4.33%, but the FAR still remains at zero. With regard to the CRR, for 150 iris samples, it is at 98.66%, and then further decreases to 95.06% when 324 iris samples are presented.

Table 3.10 The Libor Masek algorithm – performance results

Total number of samples	FAR %	FRR %	CCR %
75	0.00	1.33	98.66
150	0.00	1.33	98.66
324	0.00	4.93	95.06

Table 3.11 The genetic algorithm – performance results

Total number of samples	FAR %	FRR %	CRR %
75	0.00	0.00	100.00
150	0.66	0.66	99.33
324	1.54	2.77	97.22

Table 3.12 The Libor Masek algorithm – timing results (average transmission time/second)

Line 1	Line 2
24.66	25.55

Table 3.13 The genetic algorithm – timing results (average transmission time/second)

Line 1	Line 2
23.3	25.55

Table 3.14 The Libor Masek algorithm – timing results (average recognition time/second)

Line 1	Line 2
135.7	11.5

Table 3.15 The genetic algorithm – timing results (average recognition time/second)

Line 1	Line 2
9.3	6.5

With regard to the genetic algorithm, for a population size of 75 iris samples, a 100% CRR % and a 100% recognition rate have been established. But when 324 iris samples are presented, the FAR % increases from 0.66% (with 150 samples) to 1.54%, and the CRR % decreases from 99.33% (with 150 samples) to 97.22%. It should be noted that the FRR % is increased from 0.66% to 2.77%.

In terms of the timing results, Line 1 represents the decompressed iris image using the PCA/IPCA techniques previously discussed. Line 2 represents a non-compressed iris image which is being transferred. When the Libor Masek algorithm is used, the recognition time is 137.5 seconds for a decompressed iris image, but when the genetic algorithm is used in this regard, the recognition time falls dramatically down to 9.3 seconds.

In terms of transmission time results, Line 1 is at 24.6 seconds, and Line 2 is at 25.5 seconds.

Overall, Ibrahim et al. concluded that the genetic algorithm is far more accurate than the Libor Masek algorithm, and also that compressed iris images have a much shorter transmission time than decompressed iris images.

Fuzzy Neural Networks – Karthikeyan

The research work of Karthikeyan [10] focused also upon using the same four processes for capturing an image all the way down to the comparison of the iris-based enrollment and verification templates. In fact, this has been the theme behind iris recognition. Most if not all iris recognition vendors incorporate these four processes when developing their respective iris recognition technologies; but there are often changes made in order to fit the particular mathematical algorithms which are being used.

Such is the work by Karthikeyan:

(1) Image acquisition:

They identified that this probably not only the most important, but probably the hardest process in iris recognition. The primary reason for this is that it is the composite image of the iris which lays down the foundation for the other three processes, which will be subsequently reviewed as well. They make the correlation that a good, composite image of the iris is a direct function of the type and quality of the camera used to capture the raw images of the iris. For example, in this particular research, a charged couple device (CCD) camera was utilized, and the image resolution was set to a constant 640 × 480.

(2) Iris pre-processing:

As described previously throughout this chapter, this process heavily involves ascertaining and locating those parts of the iris which are relevant, and the removal of those components which are irrelevant, such as the eyelid, pupil, eyelashes, etc. In order to accomplish this task, the composite image of the iris is converted mathematically into a binary format. This simply means that this format only consists of black and white pixels. Karthikeyan further elaborated on the point that both the inner and outer boundaries of the iris can be deemed as circular in nature, but they are also not concentric in nature. Next, the pupil is located, and the canny operator (also reviewed in detail in this chapter) is used in order to determine the particular gradient image of the iris.

(3) Iris mapping:

Once the mathematical limits of the iris boundaries have been determined, the next step is to actually separate the iris data from the pupil data, as well as any other types of extraneous noise. The dilation and constriction of the pupils need to be taken into account as well. In this process the mathematical coordinate system is changed in order to accommodate the "unwrapping" of the lower part of the iris, and find all of the unique features within the boundaries of this particular region of the iris. These unique features are then converted into their polar equivalents. A size of 100×402 pixels was eventually used, which simply means that equal amounts of iris-based unique features are captured from every angle possible. In order to unwrap the lower segment of the iris, bilinear transformations are used. As a result, the values of these pixels are mathematically correlated with the previous iris-based grayscale images.

(4) Feature extraction:

It is important to note at this point that the unique features of the iris can be considered to be an "arrangement." These particular arrangements are actually determined by the order of the elements of which it is actually composed, not its intrinsic nature. In order to extract the unique features of the iris, a mathematical algorithm known as the "Haar wavelet" is used. Although Gabor wavelets have been used to extract the unique features of the iris, their main disadvantage is that they can take up a lot of the iris recognition system's processing power. Thus one of the primary goals which has been laid out is to keep the computational time as low as possible (in these instances, any computations which have to be done have to accomplished in just a matter of a few seconds). When the Haar wavelet algorithm is used to further break down (or decompose) the 100×402 composite images of the iris, there are once again five separate values which are computed in both a horizontal and a vertical plane in a Cartesian coordinate system. These computed values can be represented as a system of variables. So with the former, the computed values can be represented as cD1 h to cD5h and cD1 v to cD5 v, respectively. Any diagonal values can be represented as cD1 d to cD5 d. Any redundant computed value across any direction should be eliminated. In other words, a combination of six different linear matrices can be represented as follows:

cD4 h and cD5 h

cD4 v and cD5 v

cD4 d and cD5 d

All of these computed matrices are then formulated into one matrix, which is known as the "feature vector." Because of the fixed pixel size, which was established previously at 100 × 402, then all of the feature vectors which have been created will also have a fixed length as well. In other words, for the purposes of this particular research, the feature vectors which have been established have a size of 702 elements, as opposed to the 1024 feature vectors which were established by Dr. John Daugman using Gabor wavelet algorithms. The primary reason for this is actually quite simple: Dr. John Daugman captured a composite image of the entire iris, as opposed to Karthikeyan, who mapped only the lower part of the iris.

As discussed in the last sub-section, it is very important for the iris recognition to possess the ability to compress the image of an iris in order to fully realize faster transmission times, especially if it is being used across a wireless network. This is where a mathematical process known as "EZW coding" can be quite useful.

The EZW encoder which was developed is derived by using the quantization method, based upon the principles of progressive encoding. The basic premise here is to have the ability to compress the composite image of the iris into a bit stream, so once decoded in the iris recognition process, more unique features can be discovered and revealed. In fact, this entire process can be referred to as "embedded encoding." The end result of all this is that an effective composite image of the iris is thus created, which can be compressed and decompressed quickly and efficiently.

The Concepts of the Fuzzy Neural Network

In the world of research and development of today, there is much focus being given to using neural technology. Essentially what this is is the ability of a computer (or for that matter, any other kind of technological device) to think like the human brain and, in an appropriate way, to have the ability to act on thoughts and emotions.

Specifically, a neural network can be defined as follows:

> A neural network is a system of hardware and/or software patterned after the operation of neurons in the human brain. Neural networks – also called artificial neural networks – are a variety of deep learning technologies.
>
> (http://searchnetworking.techtarget.com/definition/neural-network)

An illustration of a fuzzy neural network can be seen in Figure 3.8.

Thus, as one can see from the definition, the goal is also not just for the computer or related device to interpret and act on thoughts and

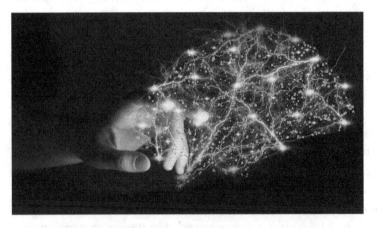

Figure 3.8 Image of fuzzy neural network
Source: sdecoret.com/Shutterstock.com

emotions. The other objective for it is to have the ability to learn from a set of parameters and permutations it has been given and apply it to future patterns and/or problems that it is given.

A prime of example of the use of neural networks is once again in biometrics, especially when it comes to the statistical comparison of the iris-based enrollment and verification templates, and whether it is a positive match or not (in other words, whether the person's identity has been positively confirmed or not). An objective here is that if the neural network can do these types of comparison, then this will be a catalyst in speeding up these kinds of processing transaction.

The use of neural network technology was introduced in the last subsection, and we see it here being used once in the work of Karthikeyan. But an approach is used in that what is known as a "fuzzy neural network" is created and deployed. They too make the hypothesis that the use of neural networks can yield much higher accuracy rates, especially when it comes to comparing the iris-based enrollment and verification templates.

The fuzzy neural network is composed of steps, which are described as follows:

(1) The input parameters are ascertained and established:

In this process, an "n" continuous valued input can be categorized as at least two or more numerically populated sets. In turn, these sets are then converted into a specific binary format. For instance, if the populated set is small enough, this can be mathematically represented as {li is small}, and in terms of a binary format it can be represented as [0,1]. Likewise, if the dataset is large enough, it can be mathematically represented as {li is large}, and in terms of a binary format it can be represented as [0.1]. The end result of this is that there can be an infinite number of valued parameters, and these in turn can be converted to a $2n$ set of inputs, which can be represented as binary digits.

(2) The implementation of a two-layer feed-forward back-propagation technique:

In this process, the fuzzy neural network algorithm is created and deployed, where the same concept of $2n$ inputs are used, with the only caveat being that there can be only as many output nodes as there are classes in the various datasets which are being used. As described previously from the definition which was provided, once this fuzzy neural network has been trained on the datasets which it has been designed to learn from, the "dominant neuron" is then extracted and used in the iris recognition process. This can be accomplished by determining the specific value for each data input of li (whether it is large or small) and which one carries the "highest" or the most statistically significant value associated with it. However, it is important that these permutations are not absolute, and that they can be relaxed by using what is known as the "pruning process." This procedure sorts the specific input parameters into either a descending or ascending order based upon the statistical value of their maximum weights. The pruning process then commences, whereby each single input parameter with the smallest statistical value is examined and analyzed first. But as Karthikeyan also noted, there is a disadvantage with the pruning process: it assumes that the effect of the input parameter depends upon its maximum weight, and thus can affect the sequencing of the neuron activation for the iris recognition system. As they surmised, those specific input values that need to be pruned can escape the pruning process, thus diminishing the effectiveness of the fuzzy neural network algorithm. This is turn will affect the accuracy of the statistical comparison of the iris-based enrollment and verification templates.

(3) The establishment of the creation and deployment of a binary coding scheme:

In this last process of the development of the fuzzy neural network algorithm, the feature vector which was created earlier is then encoded by using the following set of established parameters:

If $Coef(i) < 0$, then $Coef(i) = 0$

If $Coef(i) \geq 0$, then $Coef(i) = 1$

It should be mentioned at this point that Karthikeyan noted that the feature vectors used either had a maximum numerical value which was greater than zero or had a minimum value which was less than zero.

The fuzzy neural network algorithm was then tested on the iris pairs of 20 subjects, with the results displayed in Table 3.16.

Table 3.16 Results of the fuzzy neural network algorithm

Edge detection efficiency	Mapping efficiency	Feature extraction efficiency	Binary code generation efficiency
96%	100%	96%	100%

Table 3.17 Results of the accuracy rate of the fuzzy neural network algorithm

Methodology	Accuracy rate
Wavelet	92.64%
Wavelet with a zero tree	94.9%
Fuzzy neural network	99.25%

This system achieved a recognition rate (when the iris-based enrollment and verification templates were compared) of 93%, with an average processing time of 31 nanoseconds. After this step was accomplished, the next step was to have the fuzzy neural network learn from a dataset of both iris-based enrollment and verification templates.

In this regard, two iris-based images are used for both training and testing. The end result of this was that once the fuzzy neural network had learned from these datasets, the recognition rate remarkably increased to 99.25%.

The results of the accuracy rate of the fuzzy neural network when compared to other techniques can be seen in Table 3.17.

Overall, Karthikeyan concluded that the use of the fuzzy neural network algorithm is quite competitive in terms of fast processing times and accuracy (when in both instances the two templates are compared), and thus its use should be given serious consideration in the development and improvement of future iris-based recognition systems.

Biocryptography

As reviewed in our last two books and in this chapter, the actual composite images or recordings of either the physical or behavioral modalities are not what is actually stored in the database of the biometric system for subsequent comparison.

Rather, these images and recordings get converted into mathematical files, such as either binary mathematical files (such as is the case with fingerprint recognition, hand geometry recognition and vein pattern recognition), or some sort of statistical profile (widely used with the behavioral-based biometric modalities such as keystroke recognition and signature recognition).

Very often, the question is asked whether, if these biometric templates were actually stolen or hijacked, anything malicious can be done with them. On a theoretical basis, no, nothing can be done by the cyber attacker. This is so for a number for reasons. First, each biometric vendor has its own set of proprietary mathematical algorithms to create both the enrollment and the verification templates.

So, if they were to be hacked into or stolen, these biometric templates could not be used in another biometric modality. For instance, if the enrollment and verification templates from a fingerprint recognition system were hijacked, it could not be used in an iris recognition system.

Second, most biometric systems require an image or recording to be taken from a live, actual person – not somebody who is deceased, which is very much contrary to popular belief. Third, the actual composite image or recording cannot be reconstructed by reverse engineering either the enrollment or the verification template.

But on a technical level it is very important to keep in mind that a biometric system and its corresponding enrollment and verification templates are just pieces of technology – thus they do have their limitations in terms of what they can and cannot do, as well as their susceptibility to cyber-based attacks.

Because of this, the actual biometric template does need an extra layer of protection – this is where the principles of cryptography come into play. Thus, this becomes known specifically as "biocryptography," because it is the concepts of cryptography which are being used to fortify the biometric templates. But before this topic is reviewed, it is very important at this stage to review the basic principles of Cryptography first. **Also, one of the research works examined in this chapter demonstrated, at least on a theoretical level, that a composite image can be spoofed. Thus, the role of biocryptography in iris recognition becomes very important.**

Introduction to Cryptography

Cryptography is a science which dates all the way to the back to the times of Julius Caesar. In its simplest terms, the science of cryptography is merely the scrambling and the descrambling of text, or written messages between two individual parties.

These individual parties can also be referred to as the sender and the receiver. It is the former that creates the text or the written message which needs to be sent, and in turn it is the latter that receives the text or the written message, and then reads it and appropriately responds.

In normal, everyday communications, we always trust that the individual party who is receiving the text or written message will receive it accordingly, without any type of problem. While this does mostly happen in our daily lives, given especially the high-tech world we live in today, this sometimes does not occur.

And, when this does actually happen, we always assume that the worst has occurred. But, what is the worst that could happen? Well, the text or the written message could be intercepted by a third party, and maliciously used.

Now once again, in normal everyday conversations, while we would normally trust the other party (the receiving party) to keep the details of the conversation privileged, there is always a chance that a third party could be covertly listening in, and use that very privileged information for purposes of personal gain or exploitation, such as identity theft.

We can also extend this example to electronic communications of all types. For example, when we hit the "send" button, what assurances do we have that the receiving party will get our message, or that it will not be intercepted by a third party? Obviously, we cannot really ensure any type of safety, especially when it comes to electronic communications, like email, which is transmitted all over the worldwide networks and the Internet.

But the only thing that can be guaranteed is that if any type of message were to be captured by a third party, it would be rendered useless. But, how is this task actually accomplished? It is done by the scrambling and the descrambling of the text or the written message.

Much more specifically, the text or the written message is scrambled by the sending party, and it remains scrambled while it is in transit, until the receiving party gets the text or the written message.

Message Scrambling and Descrambling

Then at this point the text or the written message must be unscrambled in order for it to make comprehensible sense for the receiving party. For example, a very simple example of this is "I LOVE YOU." The sending party would scramble this message by rearranging the letters as "UYO I VEOL." This message would then stay in this scrambled format while it is in transit, until it is received by the receiving party.

They would then descramble it, so it would read once again "I LOVE YOU." So, if this message were to have been captured by a third party, the content would be rendered useless and totally undecipherable to the third party. This, in very simple terms, is the science of cryptography.

It is basically the art of scrambling, and in turn, the descrambling of the text or the written message into a readable and comprehensible format, once again.

Specifically, cryptography can be defined as "the practice and study of techniques for secure communication in the presence of third parties (called adversaries). More generally, it is about constructing and analyzing that overcome the influence of adversaries and which are related to the various aspects of data confidentiality, data integrity, authentication, and repudiation" [11].

Encryption and Decryption

In terms of cryptography, the terms scrambling and descrambling have much more specific terms associated with them. Respectively, scrambling and descrambling are also known as "encryption" and "decryption."

So for instance, the written message "I LOVE YOU" when it is scrambled by the sending party becomes what is known as the "encrypted message," meaning that the written message has been disguised in such a manner that it would be totally meaningless or, in the terms of cryptography, it would be what is known as "undecipherable."

Encryption can also be further defined and described as "conversion of information from a readable state to apparent nonsense" [11]. Now, when the receiving party receives this encrypted written message, it must be descrambled into a comprehensible state. This process of descrambling is also known as "decryption."

So, rather than saying that cryptography is the science of scrambling and descrambling, it can now be referred to as the science of encryption and decryption. There are also specific terms which are used for the encrypted message as well as the decrypted message.

For example, the decrypted message, when it is returned to its plain or original state which is comprehensible and decipherable, is also known as the "cleartext" or the "plaintext."

Ciphertexts

When the decrypted message is once again encrypted into a state which is totally incomprehensible and undecipherable, this is known as the "ciphertext." So, to illustrate all of this, with the previous example, when the sending party creates the written message "I LOVE YOU," this is the plaintext or the cleartext.

Once this message is encrypted into the format "UYO I VEOL," and while it is in transit, it becomes known as the ciphertext. Then, once the receiving party gets this ciphertext and then decrypts it into the comprehensible form "I LOVE YOU," this message then becomes the plaintext or the cleartext, once again.

At this point, the question that often gets asked is how the sending party actually encrypts the text or the written message, and how the receiving party then actually decrypts the ciphertext (which is, again, the text or written message which is encrypted).

Well, in its simplest form, the text or the written message is encrypted via a special mathematical formula. This formula is known as the "encryption algorithm." Because the ciphertext is now encrypted by this special mathematical algorithm, it would be rendered useless to a third party with malicious intent, because of its totally garbled nature.

When the receiving party receives this ciphertext, it remains in its garbled format until is it is descrambled. To do this, a "key" is used, which is only known by the sending party and the receiving party. In terms of cryptography, this key is also known as the "cipher," and it is usually a short string of characters, which is needed to break the ciphertext.

As will be examined later in this chapter, interestingly enough, the encryption algorithm may actually be publicly known, and be available for everyone to use. Therefore, the key or the ciphertext must remain a secret between the sending party and the receiving party.

In order to send the ciphertext between the sending party and the receiving party, and to share the key that is needed to encrypt and decrypt the ciphertext, specific cryptographic systems are needed. Today, there are two such types of cryptographic system which exist. They are known as symmetric key systems and asymmetric key systems.

Symmetric Key Systems and Asymmetric Key Systems

The primary difference between these two types of cryptographic system is that the former uses only one key for encryption and decryption, which is known as the private key of the ciphertext. With the latter, two types of key are utilized for encryption and decryption of the ciphertext, and these are known as the public key and the private key.

We look at both of these cryptographic systems, starting with symmetric key systems. One of the simplest methodologies in symmetric key systems is the Caesar cipher, which can be traced as far back as Julius Caesar (thus its name).

The Mathematical Algorithms with Symmetric Cryptography

There are a number of key mathematical algorithms which are associated with symmetric cryptography, and they can be described as follows:

(1) The Needham-Schroder algorithm: this algorithm was specifically designed for KDC systems, in order to deal with sending and receiving parties from within the place of business or organization, who appear to be offline. For example, if the sending party sends a ciphertext message to the receiving party, and after sending the message they go offline, the KDC system could just "hang," and maintain an open session indefinitely, until the sending party comes back online again. With this particular algorithm, this problem is averted by immediately terminating the communication session once either party goes offline.

(2) The digital encryption standard algorithm (DES): this mathematical algorithm was developed in 1975, and by 1981 it had become the de facto algorithm for symmetric cryptography systems. This is a powerful algorithm, as it puts the ciphertext through 16 iterations in order to ensure full encryption.

(3) The triple-digit encryption standard algorithm (3DES): this mathematical algorithm was developed as an upgrade to the previous DES algorithm just described. The primary difference between the two is that 3DES puts the ciphertext through three times as many iterations as the DES algorithm.

(4) The international data encryption algorithm (IDEA): this is a newer mathematical algorithm than 3DES, and constantly shifts the letters of the ciphertext message around, until is decrypted by the receiving party. It is three times faster than any of the other DES algorithms just reviewed, and as a result it does not consume as much processor power as the DES algorithms do.

(5) The advanced encryption standard algorithm (AES): this is the latest symmetric cryptography algorithm, and was developed in 2000, primarily designed for use by the Federal Government.

Asymmetric Key Cryptography

These keys are called the public and the private key, and are also used to encrypt and decrypt the ciphertext which is sent between the sending and the receiving parties as they communicate with another. In the most simplistic terms, asymmetric cryptography can be likened to a safety box at a local bank. In this example, normally, there are two set of keys which are used.

One key is the one that the bank gives you. This can be referred to as the public key, because it is used over and over again by past renters of this particular safety deposit box, and by other, future renters as well. The second key is the private key, which the bank keeps in its possession at all times, and only the bank personnel know where it is kept.

The world of asymmetric cryptography is just like this example, but of course it is much more complex than this in practice. To start with, typically, in asymmetric cryptography, it is the receiving party that is primarily responsible for generating both the public and the private key. In this situation, let us refer to the public key as "pk," and the private key as "sk."

So, to represent both of these keys together, it would be mathematically represented as (pk,sk). It is then the sending party which uses the public key (pk) to encrypt the message they wish to send to the receiving party, which then uses the private key (sk), which they have privately and personally formulated to decrypt the encrypted ciphertext from the sending party.

Remember, one of the primary goals of asymmetric cryptography is to avoid the need for both the sending and the receiving parties to meet literally face to face in order to decide how to protect (or encrypt) their communications with another. So, at this point, the question arises: how does the sending party know about the public key (pk) generated by the receiving party so that the two can communicate with each other?

Keys and Public Private Keys

There are two distinct scenarios in which this can be accomplished: (1) the receiving party can deliberately notify the sending party of the public key (pk) in a public channel, so that communications can be initiated and then further established; and (2) the sending party and the receiving party do not know anything about each other in advance.

In this case, the receiving party makes their public key known on a global basis, so that whoever wishes to communicate with the receiving party can do so.

Now, this brings up a very important point: the public key is literally "public," meaning that anybody can use it, even all of the hackers in the world. If this is the case, how does asymmetric cryptography remain secure?

It relies solely on the privacy of the private key (sk) that is being utilized. In these cases, it is up to the receiving party to share the private key (sk) with any other party, no matter how much they are trusted.

If the privacy of the secret key (sk) is compromised in any way, then the security scheme of asymmetric cryptography is totally compromised. In order to help ensure that the private keys remain private, asymmetric cryptography uses the power of prime numbers. The basic idea here is to create a very large number as a product of multiplying two very large prime numbers together.

Mathematically put, the basic premise is that it will take a hacker a very long time to figure out the two prime number factors of a very large product which is several hundred integers long, and thus give up in frustration.

As a result, only one portion of the (pk,sk) is figured out, and the asymmetric cryptography technique utilized by the sending and the receiving parties still remains intact and secure. In other words, the hacker cannot reverse engineer one key to get to the other key to break the ciphertext. It should also be noted than in asymmetric key cryptography, the same public key can be used by multiple, different sending parties to communicate with the single receiving party, thus forming a one to many, or $1:N$, mathematical relationship.

The Differences Between Asymmetric and Symmetric Cryptography

Now that we have provided a starting point in asymmetric cryptography, it is important at this juncture to review some of the important distinctions and the differences between this and symmetric cryptography. First, with symmetric cryptography, the complete 100% secrecy of the key must be ensured, whereas, as has just been described, asymmetric cryptography requires only half of the secrecy, namely that of the private key (sk).

Although this might seem like just a minor difference, the implications of this are great. For example, with symmetric cryptography, both the sender and the receiver need to be able to communicate the secret key generated to each other first, and the only way that this can happen is if both parties meet face to face, before the encrypted communication can take place between both parties.

And, to complicate matters even more, it is absolutely imperative that this private or secret key is not shared with anybody else, or intercepted by a third party, whereas once again in asymmetric cryptography the public key can be shared virtually indiscriminately with others, without the fear of compromising security.

Second, symmetric cryptography utilizes the same secret key for the encryption and decryption of the ciphertext, but with asymmetric cryptography two different keys (namely the public and the private keys) are used for the encryption and the decryption of the ciphertext.

In other words, in asymmetric cryptography, the roles of the sender and the receiver are not interchangeable as in symmetric cryptography. This means that with asymmetric cryptography, the communication is only one way.

As discussed, because of this, multiple senders can send their ciphertexts to just one receiver, but in symmetric cryptography only one sending party can communicate with just one receiving party.

Also, asymmetric cryptography possesses two essential advantages: (1) it allows for the sending party(s) and the receiving party to communicate with another, even if their lines of communication are being observed by a third party; and (2) because of the multiple key nature, the receiving party needs to keep only one private key to communicate with the multiple sending parties.

The Mathematical Algorithms of Asymmetric Cryptography

There are number of mathematical algorithms which serve as the basis for asymmetric cryptography and, of course, widely differ from the ones used with symmetric cryptography. The algorithms used in asymmetric cryptography are as follows:

(1) The RSA algorithm;

(2) The Diffie-Hellman algorithm;

(3)   The elliptical wave theory algorithm.

In terms of the RSA algorithm, this is probably the most famous and widely used asymmetric cryptography algorithm. In fact, this very algorithm will serve as the foundation for biocryptography later in this chapter. The RSA algorithm originates from the RSA Data Security Corporation, and is named after the inventors who created it, who are Ron Rivest, Adi Shamir, and Leonard Adelman.

The RSA algorithm uses the power of prime numbers, as reviewed previously, to create both the public key and the private key. But using such large keys to encrypt large amounts of data is totally infeasible, from the standpoint of the processing power and central server resources.

Instead, ironically, the encryption is done by symmetric algorithms (such as those reviewed previously), then the private key is further encrypted by the receiving party's public key.

Once the receiving party obtains the ciphertext from the sending party, then the private key generated by the symmetric cryptography algorithm is decrypted, and the public key which was generated by asymmetric cryptography can then be used to decrypt the rest of the ciphertext.

With regard to the Diffie Hellman asymmetric algorithm, it is named after its inventors as well, who are Whit Diffie and Martin Hellman. It is also known as the DH algorithm for short. But interestingly enough, this algorithm is not used for the encryption of the ciphertext, rather its main concern is to solve the problem of sending a key over a secure channel.

Here is a summary of how it works, on a very simple level:

(1)   The receiving party as usual has the public key and the private key that they have generated, but this time they are both created by the DH algorithm;

(2)   The sending party receives the public key generated by the receiving party and uses the DH algorithm to generate another set of public keys and private keys, but on a temporary basis;

(3)   The sending party now takes this newly created temporary private key and the public key sent by the receiving party to generate a random, secret number – this becomes known as the "session key";

(4) The sending party uses this newly established session key to encrypt the ciphertext message, and sends this forward to the receiving party, with the public key that they have temporarily generated;

(5) When the receiving party finally receives the ciphertext from the sending party, the session key can be derived mathematically;

(6) Once the above step has been completed, the receiving party can decrypt the rest of the ciphertext.

Finally, elliptical wave theory is a much newer type of asymmetric mathematical algorithm. It can be used to encrypt very large amounts of data, and its main advantage is that it is very quick, and does not require a lot of server overhead or processing time. As its name implies, elliptical wave theory first starts with a parabolic curve drawn on a normal X,Y coordinate Cartesian plane.

After the first series of X and Y coordinates are plotted, various lines are then drawn through the image of the curve, and this process continues until many more curves are created and their corresponding, intersecting lines are also created.

Once this process has been completed, the plotted X and Y coordinates of each of the intersected lines and parabolic curves are extracted. Once this extraction has been completed, then all of the hundreds and hundreds of X and Y coordinates are added together in order to create the public and the private key.

However, the trick to decrypting a ciphertext message encrypted by elliptical wave theory is that the receiving party has to know the shape of the original elliptical curve, and all of the X and Y coordinates of the lines where they intersect with the various curves, and the actual point at which the addition of the X and Y coordinates first started.

An Introduction to Biocryptography

Biocryptography provides the means to further secure biometric templates at these critical junctures. As reviewed at the beginning of this chapter, cryptography is the science of scrambling information and data in transit across a network medium, and then descrambling them at the receiving end into a comprehensible format.

That way, if the scrambled information and data were to be intercepted by a third party, there is not much that can be done unless they possess the keys for descrambling the information. These concepts of scrambling and descrambling can be very easily applied to biometrics. This is formally known as "biocryptography."

In other words, the biometric templates are protected by scrambling and descrambling keys while they are stored in the database, or in movement across a network.

To review, whenever we send a message to our intended recipient, whether it is by email, instant message, or even just a text message on our smartphone, this message is often sent as a "plaintext," or "cleartext."

This means that the actual message is transmitted to the intended recipient in the way it was originally constructed by the originator of the message. Thus, the only true way to protect the information being sent is to scramble it, in other words, "encrypt the message." This encrypted (or scrambled) message is now known as the "ciphertext."

The reverse of this process is known as "decryption," with the end result being a readable message for the intended recipient. As all of this relates to biometrics, the data packet which houses the biometric template (such as the iris recognition template) can be viewed as the plaintext, or as the "plaintext biometric template."

The Cipher Biometric Template

When the iris template is encrypted, it can be viewed as the "cipher biometric template," and when it is decrypted, it can be viewed once again as the decrypted "plaintext biometric template." But other than just doing the above, biocryptography also has to provide the following three functions in order for it to be truly effective:

(1) Authentication: the receiver of the message (or the plaintext biometric template) should be able to, 100%, verify the origin of it;

(2) Integrity: the message in transit (or the plaintext biometric template) should not be modified in any way or form while it is in transit;

(3) Non-repudiation: the sender of the plaintext biometric template should not falsely deny that they have sent that particular template originally.

Biocryptography Keys

A component which is central to biocryptography is what is known as "keys." It is the key itself which is used to lock up the plaintext biometric template (or encrypt it) at the point of origination, and it is also used to unlock that same template at the receiving end.

The key itself is a series of mathematical values – obviously, the larger the value, the harder it is to break it while it is in transit. The range of possible mathematical values is referred to as the "keyspace."

There are many types of such keys used in biocryptography, such as signing keys, authentication keys, data encryption keys, session keys, etc. The number of keys which are generated depends primarily upon the mathematical algorithms which are used, which are primarily symmetric and asymmetric mathematical algorithms.

To further fortify the strengths of a biocryptography-based public key infrastructure, mathematical hashing functions are used to protect the integrity of the plaintext biometric template. For example, when the destination party receives the plaintext biometric template, the hashing function is included with it.

If the values within the hashing function have not changed after it is has been computed by the receiving end, then one can be assured that the plaintext biometric template has not been changed or altered in any way.

To prove the validity of the hashing functions, it should be noted that they can be calculated only in one direction (e.g. going from the sending point to the receiving point, where it is computed), but not in the other direction (e.g. going from the destination point to the origination point).

A Review of How Biocryptography Can Be Used to Further Protect Iris Templates

It is important to note that a biometric systems can take quite an array of system designs, deployments, and network architectures. To illustrate that the concepts of cryptography can be used with biometrics, three primary examples will be reviewed:

(1) From the standpoint of a single biometric system;

(2) A client-server setting, where the biometric devices are connected to a central sever;

(3) A hosted environment, where the biometric templates and the processing functions are placed in the hands of a third party.

Biocryptography in a Single Biometric System

With the biometric technology available today, most iris recognition scanners consist of the database and the processing functions in just one unit, meaning that enrollment and verification occur at a single point.

Obviously, there are many advantages to having this type of "stand-alone" system, with the two biggest ones being low overhead in terms of costs and very quick times in terms of processing the enrollment and verification templates.

This is how biocryptography would be used to protect the iris recognition templates in this type of environment:

(1) Assuming that the end-user wishes to gain physical access or logical access with their iris scan, a verification template must first be created. This template could be an IrisCode (for an iris template);

(2) Using the principles of symmetric cryptography, the verification templates would then be encrypted with the key that is generated by the system. This would occur right after the unique features from the print or the iris are extracted, and the template is created.

167

(3) Once the verification template reaches the level of the database, it would then be decrypted by the same key, and the statistical correlations would then be computed between the verification and the enrollment templates. If this correlation is within the bounds of the security threshold established, then either physical access or logical access would be granted by the biometric system.

In this illustration of the stand-alone iris recognition system, a number of key assumptions are made:

(1) Only verification, or a 1:1 match, is being used. And since it is being done at the local level, the configuration needs are low, thus symmetric algorithms are the key choice for cryptography. As a result, only one key is generated.

(2) Only the verification templates receive the added protection from encryption. This is because the iris recognition templates are created only once, and later discarded from the biometric system. In fact, in any biometric system, no matter what the magnitude of the application is, verification templates are used only once, and no more.

(3) The enrollment templates in the iris biometric system receive no added protection from encryption. There is no doubt that this is an inherent security risk, but one has to keep in mind also that the database is stored in the biometric device, and not located in multiple places, where the need for protection is much greater.

(4) In a biometric verification application at the local level, the processing power required is much less compared to the client-server or even the hosted approach. Thus, this further supports the need only for symmetric algorithms.

Biocryptography in a Client-Server Biometric System

In a client-server network topology in the traditional sense, there are a series of computers connected to a central server, via a network medium (for example, it could be a hard-wired network or wireless).

Within this central sever reside all of the resources and applications the end-user needs access to. Not only this, but databases are very often stored here, which contain all types of data, and this is also the point where database querying and processing takes place.

This type of infrastructure can be very small (also known as a local area network, or LAN), or it can be very large, covering great distances and international boundaries (this is known as a wide area network, or WAN).

This type of setup can also be extrapolated to biometrics. Multiple biometric devices can be networked to a central server, in a very similar fashion to that described above. But the key difference in a biometrics client-server system is that the primary application is for verification and identification, template processing/querying, and nothing more.

Today, biometric client server applications do exist in business. Typically, they are medium to larger businesses which have this type of configuration, because many more resources are required, which can be a much greater expense compared to a single biometric system, discussed previously.

In this type of configuration, the most commonly used biometric devices are hand geometry scanners, fingerprint scanners, iris scanners, and facial recognition scanners. Different biometric devices can be used (such as fingerprint scanners being used in conjunction with iris scanners), or the same biometric devices (for example, all fingerprint scanners).

In the end, it really does not matter what hardware is used, because they are all accessing the same resource – namely, the central server. But with all of this comes an even greater risk – specifically the security threats which confront the system.

Again, biocryptography can play a huge part to ensure the protection of the biometric templates. For this configuration, asymmetric cryptography will be used, meaning a public key will be generated as well as a private key.

This is how biocryptography will be used in this type of environment:

(1) The end-user has an iris scan, and the usual verification templates are created by the biometric system;

(2) These iris verification templates will then be protected by a key, specifically, the public key;

(3) After the above two processes have been completed, the newly encrypted verification templates will then make their way across the appropriate network media, and finally make their way to the central server;

(4) It is here where the biometrics database is stored, which contains the relevant iris enrollment templates, and it is here where the private keys are stored and also encrypt these templates;

(5) Once the public and private keys have been decrypted, the appropriate statistical measures will be applied to determine the closeness or the dissimilarity between the verification and the enrollment templates;

(6) Based upon the results, the end-user will be granted or denied access to whatever application they are trying to gain access to (either physical access entry or logical access).

An important point needs to be made about this biometric client-server system:

> As is the case in the single biometric system, the verification templates, after they have been compared and evaluated, will be discarded along with their public keys. The enrollment templates will have to be decrypted as well, so that the comparison between the verification and the enrollment templates can be made. But, because the enrollment templates are stored outside the actual biometric device, they will have to be encrypted again to ensure maximum security while they are stored in the database in the central server. Thus, this type of configuration will need far more network resources and much more processing power. Also, there is no doubt that there will be extra overhead and quite possibly verification times will increase by a few more seconds (under normal conditions, this happens in less than one second).

Biocryptography in a Hosted Biometrics Environment

The world of information technology is now moving very quickly towards a new type of application which is known as "cloud computing," or "software as a service" (SaaS). This means that a business's entire IT infrastructure can be outsourced and managed by an independent third party, also known as a "hosting provider."

At this venue, all of the IT infrastructure hardware and software is set up and managed, maintained, and upgraded by them. All a business owner has to do is open an account with this hosting provider, and with a few clicks of the mouse set up the IT services they need or desire to have.

The primary advantages of this are: (1) total elimination of IT administrative headaches and hassles, because the hosting party is held entirely responsible for all of this; and (2) a business only pays for the software/hardware services they have subscribed to, at a fixed monthly cost.

This model of cloud computing can now be expanded to the world of biometrics, which can be termed as "biometrics as a service" (BaaS). This is also known as a "hosted biometrics environment." It would be established as follows:

(1) All that a business would have to do is purchase and acquire the requisite biometrics hardware; in this scenario, it would be the iris scanners;

(2) All of the servers, the databases which house the iris enrollment templates, the processing of the verification templates between the enrollment templates, and formulating the match/non-match result rests entirely with the hosting provider. Meaning, after the biometrics hardware is installed, all the business has to do is simply set up the services needed with their account, and all is set to go.

But because the iris and templates are placed in the hands of the hosting provider, security of these templates obviously becomes the prime concern.

Biocryptography and Virtual Private Networks

There is yet another tool of cryptography which would fit perfectly here – this is known as a "virtual private network," or VPN for short, as just previously reviewed in extensive detail. This is how it works with a BaaS type of application:

(1) The end-user in the previous examples has their iris scanned to create the verification template. This template then gets broken down into a separate data packet. This data packet (which contains the iris verification template) is then further encapsulated (or encrypted) into another data packet, so it eventually becomes invisible as it traverses the various network media, as it makes its way to the servers of the hosting provider.

(2) To ensure the integrity of the this double-layered data packet, it would also consist of headers which contain information about the size and type of the verification template. This would be a confirmation to the hosting provider, as they receive this data packet, that none of the iris or template data has been altered or changed en route.

(3) To create another layer of protection, a dedicated VPN channel can be created. This would be a direct line from the point of origin of the iris scanner all the way to the servers of the hosting party. This is known as "IP tunneling," and this channel cannot be seen by other people accessing the Internet across the same network media the data packets (which contain the verification templates) are also traveling across.

(4) Once this data packet arrives at the servers of the hosting provider, it is then decrypted, and the same processes of verification/enrollment template comparing, as detailed in the biometric client-server network system, will be followed.

(5) After a match or non-match has been determined, the result is then sent from the hosting provider back to the place of origin of the iris scanner, and the end-user is then allowed or not allowed access to the resources or applications they have requested.

Some special points need to be made about BaaS:

(1) Although this type of application is still very new (only voice biometrics thus far has been used as a BaaS), it could very well be the wave of the future. This is so because biometrics as a security technology is still perceived to be very expensive. But with a hosted approach, these high costs will be largely eliminated, because all that the business owner needs to purchase is the required biometric hardware, and also, like SaaS, BaaS would be a fixed monthly cost.

(2) With BaaS, the verification times and presenting the match/non-match result could take time, because all of the template processing and matching will take place at the hosting provider. The speed will be a direct function of the hardware and the software that is used, as well as the amount of network bandwidth that is consumed.

(3) Although BaaS holds great promise, one of the biggest obstacles which it will face is one which has constantly plagued the entire biometric industry, which is the issue of privacy rights. This issue will only proliferate more if the biometric templates are in the hands of an outside third party, which is the hosting provider.

In summary, the principles of cryptography and biometrics can be used together to provide maximum security for the most important component – namely the biometric templates which are created and stored. As of this writing, biocryptography is still very much an emerging field, and some observations have to be noted:

(1) The three examples described and discussed in this article are theoretical in nature – they have not yet been proven in the real world, and it is assumed that much research will have to be conducted before these applications are put to the test on a commercial basis.

(2) These examples, if proven to be viable in the real world, could become very complex, very quickly. This is so because there are two types of security technology becoming fused as one and, from that, many variations of all kinds could be created. Thus, great attention has to be paid to the actual biometric systems analysis and design right from the outset, in order to help ensure a smooth streamlined process, from the standpoint of troubleshooting and support.

(3) Another area which has haunted and plagued the Biometrics Industry is the lack or sheer absence of standards and best practices for the technology both in its current state and as it is being developed. As biocryptography emerges into the forefront of security, this is an absolute must, in order to avoid duplication of efforts, resulting in unneeded and bloated overheads. Also, as businesses and entities start to adopt biocryptography, a standards and best practices list will

help to provide the groundwork which is needed to create security applications, rather than having to reinvent the wheel every time.

(4) Finally, it is the author's point of view that biocryptography should be developed in an open model type of forum, where all parties involved, ranging from the private sector to academia to the level of the government, can collaborate and discuss new ideas with the goal of open communication and open dialogue. An open model would help to minimize any potential security threats and risks to biocryptography, because answers and solutions can be very quickly created. This is best exemplified by the use of the open-source model for software development versus the closed-source model.

Case Study: "The Afghan Girl – Sharbat Gula"

Probably the best example of using these traditional iris recognition techniques was in trying to confirm the identity of Sharbat Gula, also known as the "Afghan girl." The famous picture of the striking, green eyes of Sharbat Gula goes back over 30 years, to 1985.

She was originally from Afghanistan. During the time of the Soviet Union invasion of Afghanistan, she and her family fled into the Nasir Bagh refugee camp, located in Peshawar, Pakistan.

During this time, a world-famous photographer from *National Geographic* magazine, Steve McCurry, came to this region to capture the plight of the Afghanistan refugees in pictures. One of the refugees he met and took pictures of was Sharbat Gula, when she was only 13 years old.

Steve McCurry did not know her name, or anything else about her family. Of the many pictures he took of her, one stood out in particular – her piercing, green eyes.

During the course of the next 17 years, this picture became world-famous, appearing in books, magazines, newspapers, posters, and other forms of media.

Sharbat Gula knew nothing of her fame until she met Steve McCurry for the second time in January 2002. In January 2002, Steve McCurry returned to the same region in a final attempt to locate Sharbat Gula.

Steve McCurry and his team searched through numerous villages and came across various leads which proved to be false. Finally, the break came when an individual came forward and claimed that Sharbat Gula had been a next-door neighbor many years ago.

After several days of making this claim, this same individual brought back the brother of Sharbat Gula, who had the same color eyes. From that moment onwards, McCurry and his team felt that they had located the family of Sharbat Gula.

Because of her culture, Sharbat Gula was not allowed to meet other men. However, a female producer of *National Geographic* was allowed to initially meet her and take photographs of her. Finally, after a series of "negotiations" with her family, Steve McCurry was able to see Sharbat Gula.

After asking some questions and comparing the world-famous photograph to photographs just taken of her, Steve McCurry felt he had finally found the "Afghan girl" – 17 years later.

However, various tests had to be conducted in order to make sure that Sharbat Gula was truly the "Afghan girl." Numerous tests were conducted to confirm the identity of Sharbat Gula. Two sophisticated tests were utilized: facial recognition techniques developed by forensic examiners at the FBI, and iris recognition techniques developed by Dr. John Daugman and Iridian Technologies, Inc.

The pictures taken in 1985 were compared to the pictures taken in 2002, in both tests. The facial recognition techniques confirmed her identity; however, the ultimate test came down to iris recognition because of its reliability, as stated before in this book. However, the scientists at Iridian Technologies, Inc. had to overcome a number of obstacles.

First, the pictures taken by *National Geographic* of Sharbat Gula were not taken by iris recognition cameras, rather they were taken with other types of camera. As a result, the scientists had to eliminate the effects of the light reflections produced by these cameras, and also make various modifications to the image quality of these photographs.

The pictures of Sharbat Gula were then eventually scanned into a digital format. Second, iris recognition works by examining scans from live subjects, not static photographs – another major obstacle. After

Figure 3.9 Before image of a girl resembling Sharbat Gula
Source: Iapina/Shutterstock.com

Figure 3.10 After image of a woman resembling Sharbat Gula
Source: RZ Images/Shutterstock.com

making a series of adjustments to the iris recognition software, the scientists concluded that Sharbat Gula was positively the "Afghan girl":

> The match of Sharbat Gula's eyes to the eyes on the 1985 cover photo was irrefutable, as we achieved a 1 in 100 million probability of a false match. There is no doubt in my mind that National Geographic has found the girl in the cover photo. [12]

Before and after images of an Afghan girl resembling Sharbat Gula can be seen in Figures 3.9 and 3.10, respectively.

References

[1]   IEEE, *Certified Biometrics Learning System*, Module 2, Biometrics Standards. 2010, 2-1.

[2]   Robert "Buzz" Hill, Retina Identification. In Anil Jain, Ruud Bolle and Sharath Pankati, eds., *Biometrics: Personal Identification in Networked Society* (New York: Springer, 2006), p. 124.

[3]   Rasha Tarawneh and Omamah Thunibat, *Iris Recognition System* (PowerPoint presentation).

[4]   Hugo Proenca and Joao C. Neves, IRINA: Iris Recognition (Even) in Inaccurately Segmented Data. *Computer Vision and Pattern Recognition (CVPR), 2017 IEEE Conference*, pp. 538–547.

[5]   Steve Zhou and Junping Sun, A Novel Approach for Code Match in Iris Recognition. *12th International Conference on Computer and Information Science (ICIS), IEEE/ACIS* (2013), pp. 123–128.

[6]   Lin Ma, David Zhang, Namini Li, Yan Cai, Wangmeng Zuo and Kuanquan Wang, Iris-Based Medical Analysis by Geometric Deformation Features. *IEEE Journal of Biomedical And Health Informatics* 17:1 (2013).

[7]   Pooja Kaushik Shivani and Yuvraj Sharma, Design of Iris Recognition System Using Reverse Biorthogonal Wavelet for UBIRIS Database. *The International Journal of Scientific Research Engineering & Technology* 3:2 (2014), 232–236.

[8]   Gupta Priyanshu, Behera Shipra, Vatsa Mayank and Richa Singh, On Iris Spoofing Using Print Attack. *Pattern Recognition (ICPR), 2014 22nd International Conference*.

[9]   Ali Abdulhafidh Ibrahim, Thura Ali Khalaf and Bashar Mudhafar Ahmed, Design and Implementation of Iris Pattern Recognition Using Wireless

Network System. *Journal of Computer and Communications* 4:7 (2016), 15–21.

[10] T. Karthikeyan, Efficient Biometric Iris Recognition System Using Fuzzy Neural Network. *International Journal of Advanced Networking and Applications* 1:6 (2010), 371–376.

[11] J.F. Kurose and K.W. Ross, *Computer Networking: A Top-Down Approach* (Harlow: Pearson Education, 2008), p. 683.

[12] Quote from Ulf Cahn von Seelen, Director of Algorithms, Iridian Technologies, Inc. *Biometric Digest*, April 2002.

Bibliography

W.W. Boles and B. Boashash, A Human Identification Technique Using Images of the Iris and Wavelet Transform. *IEEE Transactions on Signal Processing* 46:4 (1998), 1185–1188.

J. Daugman, How Iris Recognition Works. *IEEE Transactions on Circuits and Systems for Video Technology* 14:1 (2004), 21–30.

D. Field, Relations Between the Statistics of Natural Images and the Response Properties of Cortical Cells. *Journal of the Optical Society of America* 4:12 (1987), 2379–2394.

Neha Kak and Rishi Gupta, Iris Recognition System. *The International Journal of Advanced Computer Science and Applications* 1:1 (2010), 34–38.

S. Lim, K. Lee, O. Byeon and T. Kim, Efficient Iris Recognition through Improvement of Feature Vector and Classifier. *ETRI Journal* 23:2 (2001).

Lakesh Sharma and Gautam Thakar, An Overview and Examination of Iris Recognition Algorithms. *The International Journal of Advanced Research and Management Studies* 2:8 (2014).

Amel Saeed Tuama, Iris Image Segmentation and Recognition. *International Journal of Computer Science and Emerging Technologies* 3:2 (2012).

R. Wildes, J. Asmuth, G. Green, S. Hsu, R. Kolczynski, J. Matey and S.E. McBride, A System for Automated Iris Recognition. Proceedings IEEE Workshop on Applications of Computer Vision, Sarasota, FL, 1994. pp. 121–128.

T. Zhu, T. Tan and Y. Wang, Biometric Personal Identification Based on Iris Patterns. *Proceedings of the 15th International Conference on Pattern Recognition*, Spain, Vol. 2 (2000).

4 | **Facial Recognition**

Which One to Use? Iris Recognition or Facial Recognition?

Now that we have reviewed iris recognition in detail, a question which often gets asked at this point is what type of biometric system should be used. In other words, should an iris or facial biometric system be utilized.

A big factor in which biometric system to choose will largely be the system analysis and design study which should have been conducted prior to the procurement and acquisition of a biometric system.

And of course, another big factor is the type of security application in which you are planning to use biometrics. For instance, are you looking at a verification or an identification type of scenario? Are you going to confirm the identity of an individual on a one to one level, or on a one to many basis?

When it comes to verification scenarios, either iris recognition or facial recognition will work. Probably the more robust biometric technologies to be used in this fashion would be fingerprint recognition, iris recognition, hand geometry recognition, and vein pattern recognition.

But, when it comes to identification scenarios, the only choice to use would be the physical-based biometrics. Behavioral-based biometrics are simply not robust enough to capture the identity of an individual in a large database.

Also, as will be discussed, at this point in time, facial recognition simply does not possess the capability to capture the dynamic changes of an individual's face which occur over the course of time.

In this regard, once again, iris recognition becomes the prime choice to be used for identification types of applications. For example, it has been used the most, and tested across very large databases.

Also, another critical factor in the choice of iris recognition or facial recognition is the ease of acquisition of the respective biometric templates in the specific environment they operate in. In other words, it is very important to choose a biometric system which will fit into the environment you want it to operate in.

For instance, facial recognition will work in small office-based environments, and iris recognition is more suited for usage in harsher environments, such as factories and warehouses.

Facial recognition is well suited for covert types of applications, such as tracking individuals in airport settings or at large sporting venues. In contrast, none of the behavioral-based biometrics are suited for large-scale environments.

Apart from all of these factors just described, there are other hurdles included as well, when choosing either an iris or a facial biometric system. These other factors include:

(1) The environment in which the biometric system will operate;
(2) The network bandwidth and data transmission needs in the transfer of the biometric templates as they traverse across the network medium;
(3) The size of the population and demographic specifics on which the biometric system will be used;
(4) The environmental comfort of the biometric system for the end-user (also known as ergonomics);
(5) The ability of the biometric system to operate in conjunction with legacy security systems;
(6) The end-user acceptance level of the biometric system which will be deployed.

Remember, in the end, there is no such thing as the perfect biometric system. They all have their strengths and weaknesses, as well as their technological flaws. Therefore, great thought needs to be given ahead of time to the biometric system which will best fit the needs of your business.

Although facial recognition does possess its suite of very strong advantages, it also possesses a list of disadvantages which can out-weigh them as well. The rest of this chapter is now dedicated to facial recognition.

An Introduction to Facial Recognition

Facial recognition is one of those biometric technologies which most people can associate with. For example, we all have a face, and, just like the fingerprint, the face has been used to verify and identify criminals and wanted suspects, as well as terrorists.

Probably one of the best examples of facial identification are the photos at the post office, as well as those facial images which are on the wanted portion of the major law enforcement websites.

But, unlike the other biometric technologies being used today, facial recognition is very prone to privacy rights issues and claims of civil liber-ties violations. The primary reason for this is that facial recognition can be used very covertly, without the knowledge or the consent of the individ-uals whom the system is trying to track down.

Facial recognition does have its fair share of technological flaws as well. For example, if a facial recognition system were to capture the image of an individual who is grossly overweight, and then capture another image of the same person who has gone through massive weight loss, the facial recognition system would not be able to make a positive match. In other words, the system can be very easily spoofed in these aspects.

But it is not just weight loss which can trick a facial recognition system, but such other things as the presence and the subsequent removal of facial hair, aging, as well as the presence and absence of other objects on the face, such as hats, sunglasses, as well as the switching from contact lenses to eyeglasses and vice versa.

But, one of the key advantages to facial recognition is that it can be used for both verification and identification scenarios, and for heavy-duty usage as well.

For instance, facial recognition is used quite frequently in the e-passport infrastructures of many nations around the world, and is also used for large-scale identification applications at the major international airports, especially in hunting down those suspects on the terrorist watch lists.

Facial Recognition: How it Works

Facial recognition technology relies upon the physical features of the face (see Figure 4.1), which are determined by genetics. This technology can be deployed either as a fully automated system or as a semi-automated system.

With the latter, no human interaction is needed: all of the verification and identification decisions are made by the technology itself. With the latter, human intervention to a certain degree is required, and this is actually the preferred method for deploying a facial recognition system.

Given some of the serious obstacles it still does face, it is always better to err on the side of caution and have an actual human being have involvement as well in rendering a verification or identification decision.

Facial recognition systems of today focus on those parts of the face which are not as easily prone to the hurdles just described. These regions of the face include:

(1) The ridges between the eyebrows;
(2) The cheekbones;
(3) The mouth edges;
(4) The distances between the eyes;
(5) The width of the nose;
(6) The contour and the profile of the jawline;
(7) The chin.

The methodology to capture the raw images of the face is much different when compared to the other biometric technologies. Although facial recognition is a contactless technology, the image capture processes are much more complex, and more cooperation is required on the part of the end-user.

To start the process of raw image collection, the individual must first either stand before a camera or, unknowingly, have their face captured with covert surveillance methods, such as using a CCTV camera system (with the technology that is available today, facial recognition can be implanted in a CCTV).

Once the raw images are collected by the camera, the data are then either aligned or normalized to help refine the raw images at a much more granular level.

The refinement techniques involved include adjusting the face to be in the middle of the pictures which have been taken, and adjusting the size and the angle of the face so that the best unique features can be extracted and later converted to the appropriate verification and enrollment templates.

All of this is done via mathematical algorithms. As mentioned previously, facial recognition is hampered by a number of major obstacles, but even more so at the raw image acquisition phase.

These include a lack of subtle differentiation between faces and other obstructive variables in the external environment, various different facial expressions and poses in subsequent raw image captures, and capturing a landmark orienting feature such as the eyes.

To help compensate for these obstacles, much research and development has been done in the area known as three-dimensional imaging. In this technique, a shape is formed and created, and using an existing 2D image, various features are created, and the result is a model which can be applied to any three-dimensional (3D) surface, and can also be used to help compensate for the above-mentioned differences.

However, it should be noted that these types of 3D facial recognition systems are not widely deployed in commercial applications yet, because this technique is still considered to be in the research and development phases.

Right now, it is primarily 2D facial recognition systems which are used on the commercial market. Three-dimensional facial recognition systems are only used as a complement to the 2D ones, in which higher imaging requirements are dictated, and the capture environment is much

Figure 4.1 Two-dimensional facial recognition image
Source: Franck Boston/Shutterstock.com

more challenging. An example of a 2D facial recognition image can be seen in Figure 4.1.

Defining the Effectiveness of a Facial Recognition System

According to the International Committee for Information Technology Standards, also known as INCITS, the raw image of a face must meet certain stringent requirements in order to guarantee its effectiveness and reliability in a facial recognition system. These requirements are as follows:

(1) The facial raw image must include an entire composite of the head, the individual must possess a full head of hair, and the raw image should capture the neck and shoulders as well;

(2) The roll, pitch, and yaw of the facial raw images collected must possess a variance of at least ± 5 degrees of rotation;

(3) Only plain and diffused lighting should be used to capture the facial raw images;

(4) In order for verification and/or identification to take place, no shadows whatsoever should be present in the raw images collected.

If a 3D facial recognition system is used, the following factors must be observed:

(1) Stereo imaging must utilize at least two cameras, which are mounted at a fixed distance;

(2) If structured lighting is used, the facial recognition system flashes a defined, structured pattern at the face, which is used to capture and compute depth;

(3) Laser scanners are the most robust form of sensing, but are very costly to implement as well as very slow; it take as long as 30 seconds or even more to capture and process the raw image of a face;

(4) Hybrid sensors do exist, and can use both the stereo imaging and structured lighting techniques.

The entire process of facial recognition starts with the location of the actual image of a face within a set frame. The presence of the actual face can be sensed or detected from various cues or triggers, such as skin color, any type of head rotation, the presence of the facial or head shape, as well as the detection and presence of both eyes in the face.

Some of the challenges involved in locating the face in the frame include identifying the differentiation between the tonality of the skin color and the background, the various shapes of the face (depending of course on the angle at which the raw image is actually presented to a facial recognition system), and even multiple images of faces may be captured in a single frame, especially if the facial recognition system has been used in a covert fashion, in a very large crowd.

The Techniques of Facial Recognition

To help alleviate these obstacles and to provide a solution in which a single facial image can be detected in just one frame, various techniques have been developed and applied to facial recognition. These techniques fall into two categories:

(1) Appearance based;
(2) Model based.

With appearance-based facial recognition techniques, a face can be represented in several object views, and it is based on one image only, and no 3D models are utilized. The specific methodologies here include principal component analysis and linear discriminant analysis.

Model-based facial recognition techniques construct a 3D model of the human face, and after that point the facial variations can be captured and computed. The specific methodology here includes elastic bunch graph mapping. All of these techniques will now be discussed in greater detail.

With principal component analysis (this is linear based, also known as PCA), this technique dates all the way back to 1988, when it was first used for facial recognition. This technique primarily uses what are known as "eigenfaces." Simply put, eigenfaces are just 2D spectral facial images, which are composed of grayscale features.

There are literally hundreds of eigenfaces which can be stored in the database of a facial recognition system. When facial images are collected by the system, this library of eigenfaces is placed over the raw images, and the eigenfaces are superimposed over one another.

At this point, the levels of variance between the eigenfaces and the raw images are then subsequently computed, averaged together, and then different weights are assigned.

The end result is a two-dimensional image of the face, which is then processed by the facial recognition system. In terms of mathematics,

PCA is merely a linear transformation in which the facial raw images get converted into a geometrical coordinate system.

Imagine, if you will, a quadrant-based system. With the PCA technique, the data set with the greatest variance lies upon the first coordinate of the quadrant system (this is also termed the first principal component analysis), the next data set with the second largest variance falls onto the second coordinate, and so on, until the two-dimensional face is created.

The biggest disadvantages with this technique are that it requires a full frontal image, and as a result a full image of the face is required. Thus, any changes in any facial feature requires a full recalculation of the entire eigenface process. However, a refined approach has been developed, thus greatly reducing the calculating and processing time required.

With linear discriminant analysis (this is linear based, also known as LDA), the is to project the face onto a vector space, with the primary objective being to speed up the verification and identification processes by cutting down drastically on the total number of features which need to be matched.

The mathematics behind LDA is to calculate the variations which occur between a single raw data point from a single raw data record. Based from these calculations, the linear relationships are then extrapolated and formulated.

One of the advantages of the LDA technique is that it can actually take into account the lighting differences and the various types of facial expressions which can occur, but still, a full face image is required.

After the linear relationship is drawn from the variance calculations, the pixel values are captured, and statistically plotted. The result is a computed raw image, which is simply a linear relationship of the various pixel values. This raw image is called a fisherface. Despite the advantages a major drawback of the LDA technique is that it does require a large database.

With the elastic bunch graph matching (this is model based, also known as EBGM) technique, this looks at the non-linear mathematical relationships of the face, which include such factors as lighting differences, and the differences in the facial poses and expressions. This technique uses a technique similar to that used in iris recognition, known as Gabor wavelet mathematics.

With the EBGM technique, a facial map is created. The facial image on the map is just a sequencing of graphs, with various nodes located at the landmark features of the face, which include the eyes, edges of the lips, tips of the nose, etc.

These edge features become 2D distance vectors, and during the identification and verification processes various Gabor mathematical filters are used to measure and calculate the variances of each node on the facial image.

Then, Gabor mathematical wavelets are used to capture up to five spatial frequencies, and up to eight different facial orientations. Although the EBGM technique does not require a full facial image, the main drawback with this technique is that the landmarks of the facial map must be marked extremely accurately, with great precision.

It is important to note that the above-mentioned techniques will be further reviewed in much greater detail in the next section of this chapter.

Facial Recognition: The Advantages and the Disadvantages

Facial recognition systems can also be evaluated against the same set of criteria. In this regard, there is a primary difference between this and the other biometric technologies, which is that while the face may not offer the most unique information and data like the iris and the retina, facial recognition can be very scalable, and like fingerprint recognition and hand geometry recognition, facial recognition can fit into a wide variety of application environments.

The evaluation of facial recognition can be broken down as follows:

(1) Universality: unlike all of the other biometric technologies, every individual possesses a face (no matter what the condition of the face is actually in), so, at least theoretically, it is possible for all end-users to be enrolled into a facial recognition system;

(2) Uniqueness: as mentioned, facial features are not distinctly unique at all, and members of the same family can genetically share the same types of facial features, as well identical twins (when it comes to the

DNA code, it is in the facial features that we inherit the most resembling characteristics);

(3) Permanence: given the strong effect of weight gain and weight loss (including voluntary changes in appearance), as well as the aging process we all experience, permanence of the face is a huge problem. In other words, the face is not at all stable over time, and can possess a large amount of variance. As a result, end-users may have to be re-enrolled in a facial recognition system time after time, thus wasting resources and processing power;

(4) Collectability: the collection of unique features can be very difficult, because of the vast differences in the environment which can occur during the image acquisition phase. This includes the differences in lighting, lighting angles, and the distances at which the raw images are captured, and also includes the extraneous variables such as sunglasses, contact lenses, eye glasses, and other types of facial clothing;

(5) Performance: in this regard, facial recognition has both positive and negative aspects, which are as follows:

- Accuracy: facial recognition, according to recent research, has a false acceptance rate (FAR) of .001, and a false rejection rate (FRR) of .001;

- Backward compatibility: any type of 2D photograph can be added quite easily to the database of the facial recognition system, and subsequently utilized for identification and verification;

- Lack of standardization: many facial recognition systems are in existence, but there is a severe lack of standards for the interoperability of these systems;

- Template size: the facial recognition biometric template can be very large, up to 3000 Mbytes, and as a result this can greatly increase the storage requirements as well as choke off the processing system of the facial recognition system;

- Degradation: the constant compression and decompression and recycling of the images can cause serious degradation to the facial images which are stored in the database over a period of time;

(6) Acceptability: in a broad sense, facial recognition can be widely accepted. However, when it is used for surveillance purposes, it is not at all accepted, because people believe that it is a sheer violation of privacy rights and civil liberties.

Also, some cultures prohibit the use of facial recognition systems, such as the Islamic culture, where women are required to wear head scarves, and hide their faces.

(6) Resistance to circumvention: facial recognition systems can be very easily spoofed and tricked by 2D facial images.

An Overview of the Facial Recognition Methodologies

Our last chapter reviewed in detail some of the major mathematical algorithms which are being used today to create both the enrollment and verification templates, as well comparing the two to determine the statistical degree of closeness. As discussed, if there is enough statistical correlation, then an individual in question can have their identity positively confirmed. But if for some reason the biometric system cannot render a statistical closeness between the enrollment and the verification templates, then the identity of the individual in question cannot be confirmed. As a result, he or she will have to go through the process over one or two more iterations, and if that does not work, then they must have their identity confirmed by a much less robust and secure traditional means.

In this regard, although the technology behind iris recognition is still advancing, the actual mathematical algorithms which drive the technology are actually maturing. A trend that is noticeable is that it is the work of Dr. John Daugman which still serves as the underlying construct behind the iris recognition algorithms of today.

But, it is important to note that facial recognition has not evolved nearly to the point where iris recognition has. As a result of this, there are more categories of mathematical algorithms which are still being developed and tested as well.

But what is most unique about facial recognition technology is that it does not just rely upon the principles of pure mathematics for the formulation of these specific algorithms. It uses the theories and principles of statistics as well.

As a result, as opposed to iris recognition, there are many more approaches which are being used in the development and improvement of facial recognition. In this section, we will first examine these various approaches which are being utilized, and from there the various mathematical and statistical algorithms will be examined. Also, we will review some scientific studies which have made specific use of these algorithms.

The Various Approaches to Facial Recognition

It is important to note that the scientific approaches used in facial recognition generally fall into five categories, which are as follows:

(1)   The geometry-based approach;

(2)   The template-based approach;

(3)   The bit by bit approach;

(4)   The appearance/model-based approach;

(5)   The neural network approach.

The Geometry-Based Approach

As discussed earlier in this chapter, when compared to the iris, there are many more features to the face which are examined. This includes the most prominent features such as the eyes, the eyebrows, the ears (to a certain degree), the lips, the chin, etc. and any distances which are computed relating to these major features.

Therefore, the primary goal of the geometry-based approach in facial recognition is to collect all of these prominent features of the face and compile them into one composite image, in a manner similar to iris recognition. But the primary difference here is that after the images of these prominent features are collected, the geometric relationships between them are calculated on a plane, primarily the Cartesian geometric plane.

As its name implies, the approaches used in this specific category are also known as "feature-based approaches." One of the most widely used mathematical algorithms here is elastic bunch graph matching.

But there are other approaches as well, and these include the use of 3D morphable models, which examines in detail the geometric points and coordinates of the prominent features of the face, as well as the texture of the face.

Using a geometry-based approach has been deemed to be very time-consuming (especially when the facial-based enrollment and verification templates have to be compared in less than a few seconds), and requires too much processing power on the part of the facial recognition system. As a result, this category is not used as much when confirming the identity of an individual when using facial recognition.

The Template-Based Approach

In this category, numerous mathematical and statistical-based algorithms have been created (and in fact are still being further developed) and are used to compare and determine the statistical closeness of the facial-based enrollment and verification templates.

A specific input image is used (which is really the composite image of the face) from which to extract the unique characteristics of the prominent features of the of face. In fact, this is the category in which we will be subsequently examining both the mathematical and statistical algorithms. In this regard, there are a numerous examples, some of them being:

(1)   Support vector machines (also known as "SVMs");

(2)   Principal component analysis (also known as "PCA");

(3)   Linear discriminant analysis (also known as "LDA");

(4)   Independent component analysis (also known as "ICA");

(5)   The kernel methods;

(6)   Trace transforms.

The Bit by Bit Approach

In this category, just small bits of the prominent features are utilized in order to confirm the identity of the individual in question. Put in a different way, it is the small bits of the various prominent features which can be compared, or just one prominent feature can be compared in a position which is relevant to the entire face.

In fact, the methods utilized in this category were the first to be used to examine the unique features of the face as a whole. One of the most widely used statistical methodologies which falls into this category is the hidden Markov model (HMM).

It should be noted that the examination of the various bits of the prominent features of the face and their geometric relationship to one another is far more important than examining just one prominent feature in comparison with the entire face.

The Appearance/Model-Based Approach

The goal of both the mathematical and the statistical algorithms which are used predominantly in this category is to create an **actual representation of the face, not use the prominent features of the face directly**. With this particular methodology, the actual image of the face is represented as a series of raw, very intense composite images. These are then converted over into one-dimensional (1D) based mathematical vectors.

From this point, various statistical methods (primarily the hidden Markov models) are used to capture the orientation of the prominent features of the face. This is then compared to a statistically derived training set. This can be referred to as the appearance-based approach to facial recognition. The model-based approach, tries to create a representative model of the face (as its name implies).

In other words, the composite image of the face of the individual in question is mapped against a model of a face, such models being scientifically known as "eigenfaces." From this point, the permutations and parameters established into the eigenface are then compared to the composite image of the individual in order to confirm his or her identity.

It is important to note at this point that a model-based approach can be classified as either 2D or 3D. As just reviewed, a model of the face is constructed in order to create an eigenface.

These types of models can be further classified as "morphable." This simply means that both the biological and physiological changes which occur to the face during a certain period of time can, at least on a theoretical level, be taken into account when confirming the identity of an individual.

It should also be noted that the 3D models are both structurally and mathematically much more complex, for the primary reason that a 3D model of the face is reconstructed from the composite image of the face. Some approaches used here are elastic bunch group matching as well as the 3D morphable models.

The appearance-based approach can be classified as either linear or non-linear in nature. For example, with the former, a specific technique known as linear dimension reduction is used. With this methodology, the various mathematical vectors of the face are constructed and then are further transformed into various projection coefficients in order to represent the prominent features of the face. In stark comparison, the non-linear approach tends to be much more complex, and various non-linear manifolds are created using the kernel PCA methodology.

The Neural Network Approach

The specific use of neural network technology was discussed in the last chapter, and how it can be used with an iris recognition system. The same kind of technology can be used with a facial recognition system, and in fact this is one of the quickly evolving areas in terms of research and development in facial recognition. There are two approaches used in this category:

(1) Template matching:

Neural networks are used to represent the prominent features of the face as a series of samples, models, curves, and textures. It is the distance between features that is used to help confirm the identity of a specific individual.

(2) The statistical approach:

Various discriminant functions are used to isolate and represent the prominent features of the face.

The Statistical Algorithms of Facial Recognition

An Overview of Facial Recognition Template Matching

As described in the last section, mathematical and the statistical algorithms are used most widely in the facial recognition technologies of today.

Although they have their own constructs, they basically comprise the use of the various pixels, textures, and samples from each composite image of the face that is created.

The end result is that any of these mathematical or statistical-based algorithms figure out or compute the differences between the prominent features of the face which have been captured in the verification template and compare them to what is contained in the information and data stored in the enrollment templates.

Put in another way, this is the general method that any facial recognition system uses to examine the degree of closeness between the facial-based enrollment and verification templates.

At the present time, facial recognition systems use primarily the mathematical and statistical algorithms which make use of a 33D approach. Although 2D approaches have been utilized, their primary disadvantage is that they are vulnerable to any changes to the orientation or illumination of the face. 3D approaches were developed in order to overcome these two primary disadvantages.

The use of 3D techniques does have its own disadvantages as well: as mentioned earlier in this chapter, the end-user (or the subject) must completely cooperate with the facial recognition system in order for a reliable composite image to be created.

But when facial recognition technology is applied to those situations where covert surveillance is required, it is obvious that the cooperation of the end-user is not a viable option to be had.

Therefore, in a manner similar to that of eigenfaces, training sets must be created for these 3D-based mathematical and statistical algorithms. One of the more efficient methods to conduct this task is to construct the 3D models from the 2D datasets.

According to a research study conducted by Blanz and Vetter [1], there are numerous ways in which the latter task can be completed, which can be described as follows:

(1) Match the geometric-based vertices of the face in the raw composite images of the face which are taken;

(2) Calculate any changes or deformations in the face which may have transpired over a specific period of time;

(3) Define via any textured and any non-textured areas which can also be found in the face. This can be determined by using illumination models which take into account both the direction and the intensity of the light which permeates from the external environment;

(4) From this point, various 3D models of the composite of the face are then created, and the unique features of the prominent features of the face are then captured to create the enrollment template. These templates are then stored permanently in a 3D database. It is important to note that this same process is also utilized to create the verification templates so that the identity of the individual in question can indeed be confirmed.

(5) Based upon the mathematical algorithm which was created by Blanz and Vetter, recognition rates were as high as 96% (this is when the facia-based enrollment and verification templates were compared).

Overall, this proves that when a 3D approach is utilized in the construction of both the mathematical and the statistical algorithms for facial recognition systems, the various issues found in the lighting from the external environment can be taken into consideration and be overcome.

One such statistical-based algorithm which makes use of this 3D approach is principal component analysis, which is examined next in further detail, as well as the other statistical-based algorithms which are used in facial recognition today.

Principal Component Analysis

It is important to note that in statistical-based approaches, each image of the face can be represented by a certain value known as "d." In other words, this can be thought of a vector in a Cartesian geometric plane in a "d" dimensional-based space. But on a theoretical level, there can be too many "d"-based coordinates for the facial recognition system to choose from.

As a result of this, the right techniques must be incorporated in order to ensure that the proper number of unique features are extracted from the prominent features of the face. Also, these techniques need to determine the appropriate Cartesian geometric plane coordinates so that the composite image of the face can be appropriately displayed.

When all of this is taken into consideration, not just linear-based unique features can be extracted, but curved, planed and hyperplaned unique features can be extracted as well. From here, the faces of different subjects can be grouped into different classes as well, thus offering the potential to create more eigenfaces which can be used in subsequent verification and identification-based scenarios. With regard to principal component analysis, it is a statistical-based algorithm which makes use of a dimensionality reduction technique to extract the unique features from the prominent places of the face, as described earlier in this chapter.

In other words, it is the "principal components" of the facial composite image which are extracted, thus the name of the statistical algorithm. The first step is to combine, in a linear-based manner, the original dimensions of the prominent features of the face which display the largest degree of statistical variability. Principal component analysis can be statistically represented as follows:

$$C_x = \Phi \Lambda \Phi^T \qquad [2]$$

It is important to note that the greatest statistical variance lies in the first coordinate in the Cartesian geometric plane which demonstrates the greatest statistical variability will decrease to the nth maximum variance in this particular plane. Also:

C_x = the covariance matrix of the statistical data compiled from the prominent features from the face

Λ = the diagonal matrix.

The eigenvalues $\lambda_1, \ldots, \lambda_n$ of C_x are located in the Cartesian geometric plane.

The covariance matrix can be mathematically represented as follows:

$$C_x = 1/m \sum X_i X_i^T \qquad [2]$$

The research work conducted by Javed [3] demonstrates how principal component analysis is applied to a facial recognition system. This is described below:

(1) Image acquisition:

Static digital cameras are used to capture and create the composite images of the individual in question.

(2) Image preprocessing:

The composite images which have been captured are aligned for the next step, and, in a manner similar to iris recognition, any extraneous features of the face are cropped out.

(3) Face detection:

The facial models can include the various appearances, shapes, as well as the different motions of the face of the individual in question. Other variables can also be taken into account, including the following:

• The blinking of the eyes;

• Any raised eyebrows;

• Flared nostrils;

• Any types of wrinkles on the forehead;

• An open mouth.

• It is important to note that in this particular phase, facial expressions on part of the individual in question cannot be accounted for. Once all of the above has been taken into account, then the composite image of the face is laid over an eigenface in a Cartesian geometric plane.

(4) Database creation:

A database is then created in order to store the composite images of the subject in question. It is assumed that the database will be a controlled environment, and the lighting from the external environment will be controlled and in a uniform fashion.

(5) The reshaping of the facial composite images:

Each composite image in the facial database has been converted from an $M \times N$ matrix (Table 4.1) into an M *ble $3 - N \times 1$ matrix (Table 4.2).

(6) Creation of the new data matrix:

The composite images of the face are reshaped from the $M \times N$ matrix (as illustrated above) into a new data matrix (Table 4.3).

Table 4.1 The M × N matrix

1	2	3
4	5	6
7	8	9

Table 4.2 The M * N × 1 matrix

1
2
3
4
5
6
7
8
9

Table 4.3 The new data matrix

2	2
3	3
8	4
9	5
7	6
6	7
5	8
4	1
1	0

(7) Creation of the new mean matrix:

An overall mean matrix (a composite-based one) is now created from all of the different matrices which were previously created. This is accomplished by the summation of the columns of the various matrices divided by the total number of columns of the various matrices. This is mathematically represented as follows:

$$\text{Mean} = 1/n \sum k = 1 \, l_k \qquad\qquad [3]$$

(8) The mean is subtracted from each column of the mean matrix:

in this step, the mean image is subtracted from all of the image matrices in order to calculate the mean subtracted data matrix. This is mathematically represented as follows:

$$A = [(l_1 - \text{mean}), (l_2 - \text{mean}), (l_8 - \text{mean})] \, .$$

(9) The creation of the covariance matrix:

The covariance matrix is now created by multiplying the mean of the subtracted matrix by its transposition in order to make into a square-based matrix. This is mathematically represented as follows:

$$C = A \, A^T \, .$$

(10) The determination of the eigenvalues and the eigenvectors:

These are then located in the facial composite images. It should be noted that for every "N" dimensional-based vector, there will be a corresponding number of "N"-based eigenvalues and eigenvectors.

(11) The creation of the eigenimages:

The respective eigenimages are then calculated by the multiplication of the mean subtracted from the data matrix by the eigenvectors computed in the previous step. This is mathematically represented as follows:

$$\text{EigImage} = (A)\,(\text{EigVec})\,.$$

(12) The determination of the highest-value eigenvectors:

At this point, the facial recognition system will choose those eigenvectors that possess the highest values. These then become the principal components of the data set which possess the highest number of unique features in order to create the respective facial enrollment and verification templates.

(13) The creation of the weight matrix:

This matrix is now created to be used in the verification and/or identification of the individual in question. This is computed by multiplying the eigenvectors with the largest values along with the mean from the subtracted data matrix. This can be mathematically represented as follows:

$$\text{WeightMat} = (\text{EigImage}^{T})(A) \tag{3}$$

It should be noted that at this point the facial recognition system can compare any facial image by comparing it with the main weighted matrix.

(14) Test imaging:

In this step, a test image is taken for comparison purposes. The same preprocessing step which occurred before will now occur on this test image.

(15) Matching:

> In this step, the facial composite which is in the Cartesian geometric plane is matched and compared with the test image.

(16) Output:

> The differences will then be compared from these two images, and the facial enrollment and verification templates will then be created.

Discrete Cosine Transform

This statistical algorithm which is also used in facial recognition can be referred to also as the "DCT-II" algorithm. When compared to some of the other statistical algorithms reviewed in this chapter, this has been deemed to be a more powerful one.

The primary reason for this is that the unique features of the prominent points on the face can be expressed as a linear series of data points as a sum of cosine functionality.

In other words, by using the DCT-II statistical algorithm, the unique features of the face which obviously change during the lifetime of an individual can be accounted for quite easily and effectively. It also possesses what are known as "strong energy compaction" properties, and the end result of this is that composite images of the face can be transformed according to the security requirements where the facial recognition system is going to be implemented, and in fact it can even compact the composite image to the required size.

It should be noted that the DC-II statistical algorithm has been used quite widely in this regard. The theoretical constructs of this algorithm are based upon the Fourier discrete transformation methodology.

The DCT-II statistical algorithm can be represented as follows:

$$\alpha_p = \begin{cases} 1/\sqrt{M}, p = 0 \\ \sqrt{2/M}, 1 \le p \le M-1 \end{cases} \qquad \alpha_q = \begin{cases} 1/\sqrt{N}, q = 0 \\ \sqrt{2/M}, 1 \le q \le N-1 \end{cases}$$

Equation 4.1 [3]

where:

M = the row size of the matrix

N = the column size of the matrix.

Linear Discriminant Analysis

This statistical algorithm, in a manner similar to the DCT-II algorithm, attempts to discover any hidden linear combinations of the prominent features on the face which have not been detected earlier when the initial raw images were collected and compiled. However, unlike the Principal component analysis algorithm, linear discriminant analysis can only take into account two separate eigenface classes.

Another factor differentiating this statistical algorithm from linear discriminant analysis is that data points for the unique features which have been captured have to be at a distance from one another. A prime example of this is the distance from the left earlobe to the bottom of the chin and the distance from the nose to the right eye.

Because of this, whenever linear discriminant analysis is used, different spatial vectors of the face are computed in order to create the enrollment and the verification templates. If more than two classes of eigenfaces are required in order to confirm the identity of a particular individual, then more than one linear discriminant analysis algorithm has to be used. This particular statistical algorithm can be represented as follows:

$$Aopt = argmax(a^\wedge TSba)/(a^\wedge TSta) \qquad [2]$$

Locality-Preserving Projections

This type of statistical algorithm was created and developed by He and Niyogi [4]. This has been considered by many facial recognition experts as an alternative to the principal component analysis algorithm.

For example, it has been primarily designed to actually preserve the properties of the composite image of the face which has been captured, and it also attempts to find the closest relationships between the prominent features of the face. The end result of this is that comparison between the facial-based enrollment and verification templates is much quicker.

It is important to note that the locality-preserving projection statistical algorithm is accomplished in three distinct steps, which are as follows:

(1) The development of the adjacency map:

A graph for these purposes is called "X" with a "y" number of nodes attached to it.

(2) Establishing the correct statistical weights:

The above-mentioned map is then converted into a weighted matrix, which can be represented as follows:

$$W_{ij} = e - (||X_i - X_j||)^{2/t} \qquad [2]$$

(3) The creation of the eigenface:

In this last step, a diagonal matrix is created where the prominent features of the face can be represented as follows:

$$D_{ii} = \Sigma_j W_{ij} \qquad [2]$$

The eigenface can then be computed as follows:

$$Y_a = XDX^T (XLX^T)^{-1} \qquad [2]$$

Gabor Wavelets

In a manner similar to iris recognition, Gabor wavelets can also be used in facial recognition. But apart from the statistical approach which can be taken, a physiological angle can be captured from this theory as well. For example, it has been shown on a theoretical level that the cell structure in the visual cortex of the brain can be viewed as a series of 2D Gabor wavelets.

However, in the instances of facial recognition, each face that is in a database can be represented as a Gabor wavelet as well, but in four distinct dimensions, which are as follows:

(1) Two can be considered as spatial dimensions;

(2) Two can be considered to represent the structures and the linear relationships of the prominent features of the face.

So, once process transformations have been completed, the various unique features of the prominent points of the face based on the composite image(s) can then be extracted in order to create the respective enrollment and verification templates.

Independent Component Analysis

With independent component analysis, the ultimate objective is to convert the unique features from the prominent features of the face into various linear combinations that are statistically independent of one another. In other words, the goal here is to make the data points in the facial-based composite image into points that are statistically uncorrelated.

Many experts view the independent component statistical algorithm as an alternative to the principal component analysis statistical algorithm in that it can actually provide a much more robust and sophisticated means of representing the unique features which are taken from the prominent features of the face.

This particular statistical algorithm can be represented as follows:

$$X = O^{1/2} U \qquad [2]$$

where

X = the facial image sample.

From this point, the computed facial image is then transformed into various eigenvectors, using the following equation:

$$C_x = O A O^T \qquad [2]$$

where

C_x = the covariance matrix.

205

The Kernel PCA

This type of statistical algorithm was created and developed by Scholkopf and Müller [5]. This algorithm primarily transforms the non-linear statistical relationships which exist in the prominent features of the face into linear inputs.

The linear inputs are computed by the following algorithm:

$$\text{input } (\Psi(x): R^N \rightarrow R^L) \tag{2}$$

where

N = the input space.

Once the linear inputs have been computed, they are then transformed into various eigenvectors to be represented on a Cartesian geometric plane, which is accomplished via the following algorithm:

$$M \, \lambda w = Kw \tag{2}$$

where

K = the diagonalized PCA value.

The Mathematical Algorithms

As described earlier in this chapter, when compared to iris recognition, facial recognition is still more or less an evolving biometric technology. Therefore, one will find more statistical and mathematical-based algorithms versus iris recognition in the scientific literature.

Our last section examined in detail the statistical algorithms that are associated with facial recognition, and in this section we now focus primarily on the mathematical algorithms of facial recognition.

The mathematical algorithms of facial recognition can be broken down as follows:

(1) Eigenfaces;

(2) Fisherfaces;

(3) Local binary pattern histograms;

(4) Neural networks.

Eigenfaces

The specific concept of eigenfaces was actually covered at the beginning of this chapter. Essentially, eigenfaces are merely a method of confirming the identity of a particular individual based upon the mathematical representations of the unique features of their face.

One of the primary objectives behind the use of eigenfaces is to locate and ascertain those parts of the composite image of the face which produce the most fluctuations or variations.

This kind of mathematical approach to facial recognition can be viewed as a "holistic" approach in that the **unique features of the entire** composite image(s) are taken into consideration, **not just the prominent features** of the face, which have been reviewed previously in this chapter.

In the world of eigenface mathematical algorithms, faces are broken down into different classes. In this regard, one specific class represents the face of one individual.

Thus, an entire database of eigenface mathematical algorithms will consist of many classes. It is also important to note that in the composite image of the face, one pixel represents one mathematical vector in the Cartesian geometric plane.

So, this simply means that a 100 × 100 pixel composite of the face is literally 10,000 different mathematical vectors.

It is important to note that the use of principal component analysis is also used as a theoretical foundation for eigenface mathematical algorithms. Also, as demonstrated before, covariance matrices are also heavily used in eigenface mathematical algorithms.

Here is a step by step process of how the eigenface mathematical algorithms are actually computed:

(1) The transformation of the facial composite images into the covariance matrix:

As just described, one pixel in the composite image(s) of the face represents a mathematical vector. Therefore, the numerous pixels can be transformed into an $N \times N$ covariance matrix where each component of the matrix represents one pixel. In mathematical terms, this can be represented as follows:

$$| f(x) \; I_1, \, I_2, \, I_3, \, I_4, \, \ldots \, I_m \qquad [6]$$

Also, the covariance matrix can be depicted as in Table 4.4.

(2) The adaptation of the covariance matrix I_1 into the mathematical vector of I_i:

In mathematical terms, the covariance matrices which are used in facial recognition utilize a higher-dimension space in the Cartesian geometric plane than the mathematical vectors. As a result, each row of the covariance matrix will have to be concatenated and then transposed into the mathematical vector. In other words:

$$I_1 \rightarrow I_i \qquad [6]$$

This can also be represented graphically as in Table 4.4. This is transformed into a series of mathematical vectors as represented in Table 4.5.

(3) The calculation of the average of the mathematical vectors li:

This is part is calculated by the following formula:

$$U = 1/m \sum I_i \qquad [6]$$

In specific terms, once each mathematical vector is calculated (represented as I_i), then the sum is actually divided by the total number of the facial-based composite image(s) which have been created. The result of this is the mathematical vector U, which in turn represents the average of all of the mathematical vectors based on the pixels from the composite image(s) of the face.

Table 4.4 The covariance matrix

I1	I2	I3
I4	I5	I6
I7	I8	I9

Table 4.5 The mathematical vectors of the covariance matrix

Ii
Ii
Ii
Ii
Ii

(4) The average of the covariance matrices is then subtracted from the mathematical vector of I_i:

This sub-process can be mathematically represented as

$$O_1 = I_i - U \qquad [6]$$

where

I_i = the mathematical vector

O_1 = the resultant of the subtractions.

(5) The computation of the special covariant matrix "C":

This matrix can be calculated by the following mathematical formula:

$$C = 1/M \sum O_n O_n^T = AA^T \qquad [6]$$

Depicted in terms of matrices, matrix A (Table 4.6) is multiplied by matrix A^T (Table 4.7), which results in the special covariant matrix "C" (Table 4.8).

After the special covariant matrix "C" has been computed, then the eigenvalues and eigenvectors which reside need to be computed (the

Table 4.6 Matrix A

O1	O2	O3
O4	O5	O6
O7	O8	O9

Table 4.7 Matrix A^{T}

O1	O2	O3	O4	O5
O6	O7	O8	O9	O10
O11	O12	O13	O14	O15
O16	O17	O18	O19	O20

Table 4.8 Covariant matrix C

N1	N2	N3	N4	N5
N6	N7	N8	N9	N10
N11	N12	N13	N14	N15
N16	N17	N18	N19	N20
N21	N22	N23	N24	N25

result of this will be used in the next step). This can be computed according to the following mathematical formula:

$$Av = \lambda v \text{ or } A - \lambda I4 \, v = 0 \qquad [6]$$

where

$v = $ is the eigenvector

$\lambda = $ is the eigenvalue

$I_n = $ the identity of matrix A.

6) Calculation of the eigenvectors and related eigenvalues:

As discussed, the values which were computed in the last step will now be used to compute the respective eigenvectors and eigenvalues which will be used to help confirm the identity of a particular individual. In this step, there are two known processes which can be used to compute the eigenvectors and the eigenvalues. These are defined mathematically as follows:

It can be calculated as:

$$U_i = f(x) \text{ of } AA^T \qquad [6]$$

or as:

$$V_i = (fx) \text{ of } A^TA \qquad [6]$$

Regardless of which of the above methods is utilized, the computed value of AA^T or A^TA will still yield the same covariance matrix of:

$$N^2 \times N^2 \qquad [6]$$

But overall, the preferred the method is the second mathematical algorithm. The primary reason for this is that the total number of facial-based composite images is actually smaller than the number of pixels which are actually in them. This in turn results in less processing power being utilized by the facial recognition system, and a quicker comparison time between the facial-based enrollment and verification templates.

Also, it is important to note that the "norms" of the eigenvectors are also calculated. The norm is simply the length of the particular eigenvector which has been computed. In order to figure out the norm of the eigenvector, the Pythagorean theorem is used, which is described as follows:

$$X^2 + Y^2 = V^2 \qquad [6]$$

Thus, the norm of an eigenvector can be computed with the following mathematical algorithm:

$$|| v || = \text{square root of } X^2 + Y^2 \qquad [6]$$

(7) Calculation of the "K" eigenvectors:

It is important to note that the above mathematical algorithm computes both what are known as "M" and "K" eigenvectors. But because "K" eigenvectors are smaller than the "M" eigenvectors, only the former is kept in the facial-based composite images. The mathematical formula which is used to decide the actual size of the "K" and "M" eigenvectors is as follows:

$$O_i = \sum W_j U_{j}, (W_j = U_j^T O_i) \tag{6}$$

where

U_j = the total number of eigenvectors at the index of j

O_i = the mage I – the average.

It is important to note that at this point in the process the eigenface is now finally created by combining certain segments of the facial-based composite image(s) with the associated eigenvectors which have thus far been calculated. This can be represented by the matrix in Table 4.9, where

W_1^i = the total projection of the eigenface i associated with the eigenvector at the index of 1.

(8) The comparison of the facial-based composite image(s) with the eigenface:

In this last step of this entire process, the facial-based composite image is compared with he eigenface. In order to do this, the eigenface is first projected onto what is known as an "eigenspace" in the Cartesian geometric plane. This is accomplished with the following mathematical algorithm:

$$O = \sum W_i U_{i}, (W_i = U_i^T O) \tag{6}$$

Table 4.9 Eigenvector matrix

W1^i
W2^i
W3^i
W4^i

The next step is to find the facial-based composite image which has the smallest distance to the eigenface. This distance is actually a Euclidean-based one, and is computed with the following algorithm:

$$E_r = \min \| U - U_i \| \qquad [6]$$

However, the "Mahalanobis distance" has been deemed to be more accurate than the Euclidean distance when it comes its use in a facial recognition system. For example, with the former, the E_r value can be compared to a preset threshold value. If the E_r value is smaller in this regard, then one can conclude that face of the particular individual does not actually exist in the database, and thus the associated facial-based composite image(s) are added.

But if the E_r value is greater than the preset threshold value, it is assumed that the facial-based composite image(s) of the individual in question actually exists in the database, and thus the comparison of the eigenface to the facial-based composite images can be initiated and processed.

As one can see, the Mahalanobis distance is actually a machine learning algorithm, and thus becomes much more reliable and efficient as new comparisons are made between the eigenfaces and the facial-based composite image(s).

Fisherfaces

Unlike the usage of eigenfaces, the approach used by fisherfaces tends to be a much more "holistic" or a macro-based one. The theory behind fisherfaces is actually a modification of eigenfaces, and it also makes heavy use of principal component analysis, which was described in detail in the last section of this chapter.

It is important to note that the primary difference between fisherfaces and eigenfaces is that the latter takes into account the different classes of faces which are used, whereas the former does not take this into account.

In other words, eigenfaces cannot discern the differences between the various classes of faces, but Fisherfaces can. In order to accomplish this task, fisherfaces makes use of what is known as linear discriminant analysis, also reviewed in detail in this chapter.

The ultimate goal here is to minimize variations within a face class compared to the variations found between the classes.

This particular task is accomplished by the following mathematical algorithm:

$$U_{ci} = 1/Q_i \sum R_k \qquad [6]$$

where

ci = the individual class i

Q_i = the total number of facial-based composite images in the class c.

Next, the various "scatter" facial-based covariant matrices are computed as follows:

$$S_w = \sum (R_k - U_{ci}) (R_k - U_{ci})^T \qquad [6])$$

where

S_w = the scatter facial-based covariant matrix.

After the above covariant matrices have been computed, the next step is to calculate the total number of the scatter-based covariant matrices. This is accomplished via the following mathematical formula:

$$S_t = \sum (R_i - U) (R_i - U)^T \qquad [6]$$

where:

S_t = the total number of scatter-based covariant matrices.

Finally, once all of the above calculations have been accomplished, the projection distance of the fisherface which will be overlaid over the facial-based composite image(s) is calculated as follows:

$$W_{opt} = \arg \max_w = |W^T S_b W| / |W^T S_w W| \qquad [6]$$

where

> W = the total projection range of the fisherface onto the facial-based composite image(s).

Local Binary Pattern Histograms (LBPH)

This mathematical algorithm is used in facial recognition to compare and contrast only the grayscale images of the facial-based composite image(s). As opposed to the fisherfaces approach, the use of the local binary pattern histogram is not considered to be a holistic approach when it comes to confirming the identity of a particular individual.

Rather, the goal is to examine just the 3 × 3 pixels of the facial-based composite images. In this type of methodology, the pixel which is deemed to be at the center of the facial-based composite image(s) is compared and contrasted against the neighboring pixels (these are also referred to as the "neighbors").

It should be noted that for any neighbor which possesses a value which is smaller than the pixel to which it is compared, a 0 will be subsequently assigned to a threshold square. However, if the value is greater, then a 1 will be added. When all of these comparisons have been made, then all of the results will be multiplied by a numerical weight, which is to the power of 2.

Each weight can range from 2^0 to 2^7. It is important to note that each pixel is deemed to have at least eight different neighbors associated with it, and in turn these represent one byte of the facial-based enrollment and verification templates. This can be demonstrated in the matrices shown in Tables 4.10–4.12.

To further explain this particular process, the example matrix displays a 3 × 3 pixel square. The threshold matrix then stores the results of the comparisons which have been calculated in the example matrix. The weights square determines the particular weight of each 3 × 3 pixel in the example matrix.

Thus, the resultant is the summation of 3 × 3 pixels in the threshold matrix based upon their assigned numerical weight, and from that point, a new value for the 3 × 3 pixels is then displayed in the example matrix. This can be mathematically represented as follows:

Table 4.10 The example matrix

5	2	9
7	4	4
3	2	3

Table 4.11 The thresholded matrix

1	0	1
1		1
0	0	0

Table 4.12 The weights matrix

128	64	32
1		16
2	4	8

The local binary patterns = 1 + 16 + 32 + 128 = 177

It should be noted that when this specific process has been completed for each of the 3 × 3 pixels of the facial-based composite image(s), it is then further divided up into a determinate number of regions.

At this point a statistical-based histogram is created for each of these specific regions and then subsequently extracted and concatenated in order to create the respective facial enrollment and verification templates.

In this regard, in order to fully compare the facial-based enrollment and verification templates, the various histograms are also compared with one another. The histogram that possesses the shortest numerical distance is then used for the final comparison of the templates.

Over the course of its development and usage, the local binary pattern mathematical algorithms have been modified, in order for them to fit the unique environments in which a particular facial recognition system will be used. One such modification is known as the "extended local binary pattern."

Rather than using a square like a covariant matrix, this enhanced methodology utilizes a circular neighborhood which is of course composed of a radius as well as a determinate number of pixel points. In this regard, the pixel can possess more than eight distinct neighbors, and if there are any pixels in the middle, they in turn can be compared to other pixels that are not close to it.

Another version of this enhanced extended local binary pattern mathematical algorithms is known as a "uniform pattern." This particular modification takes into account the number of transition points in a certain byte. These transition are represented in a binary fashion, for example, from a series of zeros to ones and vice versa. To further illustrate this, a pattern 12 bits long is considered to be one transition point, and a pattern 16 bits long is considered two transition points.

In fact, those bytes in a facial-based composite image that possess two transition points are the most commonly produced. In this regard, a regrouping process then takes place, and thus makes the computed histogram even smaller. This of course results in a much quicker comparison between the facial-based enrollment and verification templates.

Neural Networks

The use of neural network technology in the world of biometrics has just started to occur within the past decade. What neural networks are, and a specific definition of them, was delineated in the last chapter about iris recognition. In this regard, neural networks add a much more "intelligent" approach when biometric technology is utilized as a primary means of security.

For example, as reviewed in the last chapter, iris recognition has now evolved to the point where it can confirm the identity of individuals at a some distance, and even single out individuals as they are walking amongst a group of other individuals. This, of course, could not happen without the specific use of neural networks.

Figure 4.2 Group of people at an international airport
Source: urhan/Shutterstock.com

The algorithms which are used here work in conjunction, or in tandem, with the iris recognition system in order to make "smart" decisions when it comes to confirming the identity of an individual in such an application as described above. An example of this can be seen in Figure 4.2.

This same type of application can also be used for a facial recognition system. In this regard neural networks can also be used with the mathematical algorithms of the facial recognition system in order to make "intelligent" decisions confirming the identity of a particular individual. In fact, facial recognition technology is still evolving quite a bit in this area and, as described earlier in this chapter, there are a number of key constraints that can stop a facial recognition system making a 100% confirmation with regard to the identity of an individual.

One of the best examples of this is facial recognition in covert settings at very large venues, such as sporting events. Typically, a facial recognition system can be used in tandem with a closed-circuit camera television (CCTV) in order to spot people of interest. For instance, the CCTV system can take static pictures of the individuals in question, and the facial

Figure 4.3 CCTV camera being used on a large group of individuals
Source: Zynatis.com/Shutterstock.com

recognition system can then compare these pictures with the pictures that are stored in the facial-based database.

But even here at times a 100% confirmation of the individual's identity cannot be achieved because of the limiting constraints. In this regard, the use of neural networks can play a role in overcoming these particular constraints, and thus "intelligently" come to a decision with regard to the confirmation of the identity of the individual in question. An example of this type of scenario is illustrated in Figure 4.3.

In fact, the very first research conducted to prove its effectiveness with the use of facial recognition was conducted by Kohonen [7]. In his work, he demonstrated that a specific group of neurons within the brain could potentially be used in order to recognize both normalized and aligned faces of particular individuals.

Ever since then, the development and usage of neural networks have evolved greatly. For example, various other neural network topologies in facial recognition systems have come out, which include the following:

(1) The classification approach:

In this methodology, information and data from the facial-based composite image(s) are collected, and are further pre-processed and sub-sampled.

(2) The hybrid/semi-supervised approach (Intrator et al. [8]):

In these instances, the prominent features of the face are taken and analyzed, which can further reduce any errors in confirming the identity of a particular individual. In other words, those prominent features with the richest amount of unique features are taken in order to compile the facial-based enrollment and verification templates. In this approach, feed-forward neural networks (FFNN) are also used not just for classification purposes, but also for reducing the overall error rate by introducing more mathematical bias constraints, and averaging the numerical outputs that have been produced as a result.

(3) The self organizing map and convolutional approach (Lawrence et al. [9]):

With this specific methodology, self-organizing maps (also called SOMs) are called upon to illuminate the facial-based information and data into a lower-dimensional space in a Cartesian geometric plane. Also, a convoluted neural network (also known as a CNN) is utilized to partially translate any facial deformations and any statistical invariances which may be encountered when creating the facial-based enrollment and verification templates. In these aspects, self-organizing maps use much more processing power in the facial recognition system, thus the use of the convoluted neural network is highly favored.

(4) Group-based adaptive tolerance (Zhang and Fulcher [10]):

This specific type of methodology makes use of what is known as a tree model in order to deal with any of the statistical invariances which are encountered in the creation of the facial-based enrollment and verification templates. An interesting aspect here is that this kind of approach was designed for use in covert surveillance in international airports. The data inputs are the paper passport photographs themselves. A binary tree is then created and implemented where the nodes are neural-network-based. Thus, each node becomes what is known as a "complex classifier."

(5) The probabilistic-based decision approach (Lin et al. [11]):

This methodology is utilized for the sole purpose of facial-based detection. It is actually implemented in the subnets for each kind of face classification. It estimates the statistical decision range for each facial class. It also makes use of statistical-based probability level constraints in order to help lower both the false acceptance rates (FAR) and the false rejection rates (FRR).

In this chapter, we will now further examine the use of specific neural network methodologies which have been used in facial recognition systems. These are as follows:

(1) Neural networks with Gabor filters;

(2) Neural networks with hidden Markov models;

(3) Fuzzy neural networks;

(4) Convolutional neural networks.

Neural Networks with Gabor Filters

Just as much as Gabor filters have created part of the mathematical algo-rithm framework for Iris recognition, to a certain extent this can also be said about their use in facial recognition as well. In these instances, for facial recognition systems, mathematical-based propagation algorithms with multilayer perceptron structures are utilized. There are a number of key steps with this approach, and they are as follows:

(1) The pre-processing step:

In this phase, each and every facial-based composite image is normalized in order to help with the contrasting and illumination of these respective images. Also, any form of extraneous informa-tion and data is brought down by making use of what is known as a "fuzzily skewed filter." In order to accomplish this task, a median

221

value of one is assigned to each form of extraneous information and data, and reduces their respective values by calculating and applying both a statistical-based median filter and an average filter.

(2) The Gabor filter:

After the first step has been accomplished, the facial-based composite images are then processed through the Gabor filter. This is actually created by making use of what is known as a "Gaussian-based kernel function." From here, each Gabor wavelet has five individual vector orientation parameters and three spatialized frequencies. Thus in the end there are a total of 15 Gabor wavelets which have thus been created.

(3) The training of the neural network:

In this step there are certain parameters which have to be noted, and they are as follows:

- The first layer of the neural network receives the facial-based composite image(s) which have been further refined in the last step;

- The number of mathematical nodes is equal to the dimension of the eigenvector which consists of the Gabor-based features;

- The actual output of the neural network is equal to the total number of facial-based composite image(s).

- With the above parameters being taken into consideration, the training of the neural network can now start, and this follows a specific procedure:

  (a) The initialization of the various statistical weights and the respective threshold values are computed and assigned;

  (b) The calculations of the outputs of the neurons in both the hidden and the output layers are activated, assigned, and allocated making use of the sigmoid activation mathematical function.

  (c) The updated statistical weights are then assigned and allocated once again;

  (d) The iteration value is now increased in order to make the comparisons between the facial-based enrollment and verification templates.

Neural Networks with Hidden Markov Models

The use of hidden Markov models is actually a statistically based approach when it comes to their particular application to a facial recognition system. In this regard, there are two types of hidden Markov models which are thus created:

(a) The one-dimensional (1D) hidden Markov model:
Mathematically, this can be represented as follows:

$$Y = (A, B, \Pi) \tag{6}$$

where

A = the state transition probability matrix, where A_{ij} represents the statistical probability that the state i in turn becomes state j

B = $[Bj(k)]$ is also a state transition probability matrix where $Bj(k)$ is the statistical likelihood that observation k transitions over to state j

Π = the initial state distribution, whereby Π is the statistical probability that is correlated with state i.

(b) The two-dimensional (2D) hidden Markov model:
In this approach, the input values are the same as the output values of the artificial neural network (ANN) which has been created and implemented. In this regard, the inputs are the facial-based composite images that are converted over into various binary elements. From this point, the artificial neural network then extracts the unique features of the prominent parts of the face, which are subsequently stored in a 50 bit mathematical sequence. The input images are then further divided into 103 segments, of 230 pixels each. Thus, these 230 pixels represent 230 separate neurons. A hidden layer is also created by utilizing a 50 node approach. The training is accomplished by conducting a 200-iteration-based cycle for each facial-based composite image. This is then tested with input images that are similar in nature to the facial-based composite image. It is

important to note that this approach claims to have an accuracy rate of nearly 100%.

Fuzzy Neural Networks

The concept of fuzzy neural networks was also introduced in the last chapter on iris recognition. The original concept of this was initiated by the research work carried out by Bhattacharjee et al. [12]. In this work, a facial recognition system was created and implemented by making use of what is known as a "fuzzy multilayer perceptron," or "MLP" for short.

The basic premise of this for the facial recognition system is to capture the unique features of the prominent components by making use of mathematically based non-linear manifolds. One of the key theories which forms the foundation for the fuzzy neural network is once again Gabor wavelet mathematical algorithms.

The various eigenvectors are created by using the Gabor wavelet mathematical algorithms, and the hypothesis is that they must be "fuzzified."

In other words, as the eigenvector comes closer to approaching a class mean vector (from a statistical standpoint), the eigenvector will thus possess a higher fuzzy value. But, as the difference between these two vectors increases, the fuzzy value that is obtained comes close to being a zero, or null value.

However, precisely ascertaining this specific fuzzy value is calculated by the following mathematical algorithm:

$$\varphi_i = 0.5 + \frac{e^{c(d_j - d_i)/d} - e^{-c}}{2(e^c - e^{-c})} \qquad \text{Equation 4.2 [6]}$$

where:

d_i = the numerical distance of the eigenvector from the mean of the face class denoted as i

c = the constant which controls the rate at which the fuzzy value becomes a zero, a null set.

It is important to keep in mind that by using the above mathematical algorithm, any patterns whose face class is less determinate should not contribute in creating the various statistical weights to the facial prominent features in the composite image(s).

Convolutional Neural Networks

Another neural network approach which has been used in facial recognition systems is the convolutional neural network (CNN). It consists of a series layers which are actually hidden. As it relates to the physiology of the human brain, each layer consists of various types of neuron. In turn, these specific neurons are assigned a certain statistical weight factor, and thus receive an input.

In turn, each layer will then produce a certain kind of output. It should be noted that in this regard, the first input is actually the facial-based composite image(s). The output is the facial-based enrollment and verification templates that are then created.

The convolutional neural network consists of these specific layers:

(1) The convolution layer;

(2) The rectified linear units layer;

(3) The maximum pooling layer;

(4) The fully connected layer

(5) Back-propagation;

(6) Transfer learning.

The Convolution Layer

At this particular layer, each facial-based composite image is represented by a numerical distance of numbers, which can range from −1 to +1. The value of −1 can be considered to be a dark pixel-based image, and the value of +1 is a bright pixel.

The neutral value of 0 can be considered to be a gray pixel. In this range of numbers, other alphanumerical values are used, such as a backward slash, a forward slash, and a cross. It should be noted that these special characters are also used as the primary filters for the convolutional neural network.

In this process, one of these specialized filters is compared to the other two filters in a series of blocks in the facial-based composite image. This is initiated once the top left of the square is compared to another square in the facial-based composite image that is deemed to be of the same size. Once this comparison has been completed, these iterative steps will then continue throughout the entire facial-based composite image(s).

But in order to determine the exact sequence of the blocks which are to be analyzed, a concept known as the "stride" has to be taken into consideration. A stride is merely the total number of pixels that are shifted as the comparison between the blocks in the facial-based composite image(s) is carried out.

There should be no overlapping amongst the blocks as these comparisons are made. In other words, the stride should be at least as large as the total length of the special filters, as previously described. In order to help ensure that no actual overlapping takes place, the value of 0 can be added (this is also known as "padding"), thus giving the facial-based composite image(s) more of a grayscale feature to it. In turn, the final value which is derived from the convolutional neural network is also controlled to a reasonable level, so that it does not tax or overload the processing power of the facial recognition system which is using this particular neural network methodology.

This will also ensure that the byte size of the output (which is facial-based enrollment and verification templates) is the same as the input size (which is the facial-based composite image(s)).

It is also important to note that as this entire iterative process continues, only one particular value will be yielded as a result, and after all of the blocks have been compared with each other, a new square will emerge which will actually be much smaller in size than its predecessor. The size of the final square is contingent upon these specific factors:

- The actual size of the facial-based composite image(s);
- The size and kind of filter which have been used for comparing the blocks amongst one another;

- The particular value of the stride;
- The size of the padding (which would actually be the total number of 0s which have been used).

The final size of the resultant square can be computed via this mathematical algorithm:

$$O = [(w - k + 2p) / S] + 1 \qquad [6]$$

where:

O = the height and the length of the output

w = the height and the length of the input

k = the size of the filter

p = the size of the padding

s = the value of the stride.

Thus, when a filter is compared against a new block, the resulting value is stored in an eigenvector. For simple illustration purposes, assume that a particular filter is being compared to the block, and they both possess the identical value of 1. The final value of the square will also be 1, and the resulting average will also be 1. But as discussed earlier in this section, the range of the pixels can be anywhere from −1 to +1, even including decimal values.

Once this entire process of comparing filters with the various blocks have been completed, the result is what is known as the "convolutional layer." Interestingly, the output which has been yielded from one convolutional layer can be used as an input in order to initiate the next convolutional layer.

The Rectified Linear Units Layer

After every convolutional layer has been established as needed by the facial recognition system (as described in the last sub-section), the next step is to implement what is known as an "activation function." This is merely a non-linear mathematical function in which the primary goal is to incorporate non-linear properties into the overall convolutional neural network.

The primary reasoning for this is that the face is a complex feature and structure, and as a result confirming the identity of a particular individual via facial recognition is not a linear function. In general terms, an activation function provides a certain numerical value in the range between 0 and 1.

It should be noted that when the activation function is close to the numerical value of 1, it is deemed to be in an active state from within the facial recognition system. But, conversely, if the activation function is close to the numerical value of 0, then it is deemed to be in an inactive state within the facial recognition system.

Thus, the ultimate goal of the rectified linear units layer is to mitigate any activation functions with a numerical value of less than zero back to at least a state of zero.

The Maximum Pooling Layer

The primary objective of the maximum pooling layer is to condense or shrink down any inputs (which are once again the facial-based composite image(s)) that are received from the rectified linear units layer. Under the mechanisms of this layer, the facial-based composite image is split in the middle into various 2 × 2 windows, while using only a stride value of 2.

The ultimate goal of the maximum pooling layer is to reduce as much as possible the total number pf pixels which are found in the facial-based composite image(s). The advantage of this is that it will lead to shorter processing times when it comes to extracting the unique features from the prominent parts of the face.

But, if the window for some reason is less than 2 × 2, then the largest number is utilized. It should be noted that the maximum pooling layer also takes the output from the previous layer (which in this case would be the rectified units layer) and uses that as the input value. Also, these layers as just described can be used over and over again as dictated by the requirements of the environment in which the facial recognition system is being used in.

The Fully Connected Layer

Once the facial-based composite images have been processed by the above-mentioned layers in the convolutional neural network, in an iterative fashion, the information and data which can be retrieved from the maximum pooling layer are now utilized in the fully connected layer. At this level, all of the pixels that are found in the facial-based composite image(s) do not carry the same statistical weight.

In this case at this layer, the bigger a pixel is, the larger the statistical weight that it will possess. It is important to note that the each pixel in the composite-based facial image is surrounded by a series of lines. Thus the larger the statistical value is for each pixel, the thicker these particular lines will be. This entire process is actually carried out for all of the face classes which reside within the facial recognition system.

Finally, it is necessary to ascertain whether a facial-based composite image will consist of a combination of Xs and Os (these two symbols were discussed at length at the beginning of this section) in this particular level. Thus, the averages for the thickest lines in the Xs and the Os are computed, and are represented as X and O, respectively. The X or the O symbol which possesses the largest statistical average will then become the proxy value for the overall convolutional neural network.

Back-Propagation

This part of the convolutional neural network, which is called the back-propagation phase, is actually a training process for adjusting the statistical weights of the filters which have been used to parse through the facial-based composite images. This segment can be further divided into the following sub-segments:

(1) The forward pass;
(2) The loss function;
(3) The backward pass;
(4) The statistical weight update.

The Forward Pass

The primary objective here is to "pass" (as the name implies) a facial-based composite image through the entire convolutional neural network. It is important to note that the statistical weights that are assigned at this point are not completely accurate, because they have been selected at random.

The Loss Function

This mathematical function is used to ascertain what the variances are in the statistical weights that are assigned in the forward pass. In order to train the convolutional neural network in this sub-phase, only those facial-based composite images with a particular label assigned to them are utilized. This simply means that the face class being used can be easily predicted by the convolutional neural network, and shows to what degree or the level of confidence in this prediction.

In order to calculate the level of confidence, a loss function is utilized in order to ascertain if the convolutional neural network is truly reliable. The loss function is also referred to quite commonly as the mean squared error, or the MSE for short, and can be defined as follows:

$$E_{total} = \sum \tfrac{1}{2} (target - output)_2 \qquad [6]$$

where:

　target = the real result

　output = the prediction.

It should be noted that E_{total} will always be a high statistical value for training purposes, and the primary goal here is to get this as close to reality as possible (which are the statistical values that are assigned to the facial-based composite image(s)).

A convolutional neural network can never achieve a 100% reliability rate, but, once again, the primary goal is to completely minimize the total number of errors that are present in the convolutional neural network to get as close to 100% as possible. This can be accomplished by identifying those statistical weights that need to be modified or updated.

It also important to note at this point that the total number of statistical errors present in the convolutional neural network are highly correlated with the statistical weights that are being used. For example, if a statistical weight is too small or too large, then the total number of statistical errors will be deemed to be very high.

One of the goals at this stage is to correspondingly adjust the statistical weight in order to reach a weight that will translate to the smallest number of errors. In other words, the changes that will be made to the statistical weights must not be too large in variance. If this were to occur, then the optimal statistical weight will not be properly calculated.

On the converse side, if the change in the statistical weight is too small, it will take a lot of processing power on part of the facial recognition system being used to further analyze the facial-based composite image(s).

The Backward Pass

The goal in this sub-phase is to identify and ascertain those particular statistical weights which actually contribute to the greatest number of errors occurring in the convolutional neural network.

The Statistical Weight Update

The primary objective in this sub-phase is to correctly update those statistical weights that are being used in a concerted effort to reach the optimal statistical weight level. The optimal level actually refers to those particular statistical weights that give the least errors in the convolutional neural network.

Finally, it is important to note that when all of the above-mentioned steps are used in concert with another, this is also referred to as an "epoch process." In other words, an entire epoch process is used for each facial-based composite image that is captured by the facial recognition system. After going through enough epoch processes, the convolutional neural network should then be able to provide results that are valid in terms of the comparisons between the facial-based enrollment and verification templates.

One should keep in mind that face is a complex structure, and out of the total number of statistical and mathematical-based algorithms reviewed thus far in this chapter, on a theoretical level, neural networks are actually the preferred choice for implementation in a facial recognition system.

Thus, in order for a neural network system to be successful in the confirmation of the identity of a particular individual, it is imperative that the right kinds of filters are used.

In this regard, a convolutional neural network is also referred to as a "deep neural network," or "DNN" for short. As its name implies, it is very powerful when it comes to extracting the prominent features of the face.

Transfer Learning

As was described, a convolutional neural network can also be referred to as a deep neural network, because of the many layers it possesses not only to analyze the facial-based composite image(s) of the face, but also to compare the degree of correlation between the facial-based enrollment and verification templates.

But, depending upon the type of environment in which the facial recognition will be used in (and also assuming it is using a neural network system – it may not be necessarily be a convolutional neural network per se) it could be the case that there may not be enough of a population on which to actually train the neural network system.

In other words, there may not be enough existing data in order to fully train the neural network system into analyzing the facial-based composite images as well as the enrollment and verification templates of the population that is enrolling in it.

In this regard, it is then best to use a methodology known as "transfer learning." In these instances, the neural network system that is embedded into the facial recognition system can learn initially from a pre-trained model, and can then subsequently learn from the data inputs (which are really the faces of the individuals that are enrolling in the system) from the application environment that it is being currently used in.

It is also important to note that when a deep neural network is being used in a facial recognition system, the first layer is always trained on learning how to analyze the various curves and edges of the face. Then the last layer always analyzes the data inputs that are fed into it. So, it does not matter if a pre-trained model is used initially.

In this regard, one of the best-known pre-trained models to use for a deep neural network is "OpenFace," developed from Google's FaceNet project. OpenFace is actually a library of eigenfaces. This library actually contains about 500,000 eigenfaces, and it is further divided up into two separate segments. The first component actually analyzes and extracts the unique features from the prominent features of the face as they are being inputted into OpenFace.

The second component then examines multiple facial images of the same individual, using what is known as a pre-trained detector. After these two phases have been completed as just described, the raw facial images of the individuals are then converted over into eigenfaces, and then can be used to pre-train a deep neural network, such as a convolutional neural network.

It is also important to note that that the left side of the eigenface is used as a filter, and the right side of the eigenface represents the class that it belongs in the facial recognition system that is being used.

The Applications of Facial Recognition

As we have described in this chapter, and as well in our first book, there are numerous applications for facial recognition technology. It is important to keep in mind that the technology is still evolving, as is clearly evident by the sheer number of both statistical and mathematical-based algorithms that are being used for it.

But probably the biggest general application that a facial recognition system is used for is covert surveillance at large venues, especially the major international airports.

As we have described earlier in this chapter as well, facial recognition technology has also evolved to the point where it can be used to confirm the identity of particular individuals at a distance, even if they are motion.

Back in the last decade, this was an impossible feat, as the individual in question had to stand in front of a facial recognition system camera at a very short distance in order to have his or her identity confirmed. Today, we are even seeing facial recognition technology being used on smartphones, especially the iPhone X.

This section of the chapter will examine other applications of facial recognition that have also evolved as well, and include the following:

(1) The use of a facial makeup-detection system in facial recognition;

(2) Thermal face recognition for human-robot interactions;

(3) The use of facial recognition in forensics.

The Use of a Facial Makeup-Detection System in Facial Recognition – Chen et al.

The earlier part of this chapter examined some of some of the constraints that are involved in a facial recognition system. According to the research conducted by Chen et al. [13], there are other factors as well, and these include the following:

(1) The effects of plastic surgery on a face;

(2) Spoofing;

(3) Other external environmental factors.

Collectively, these constraints are also known as PIE, which is an acronym for pose, illumination and expression. It is the last one which is the point of interest in this application-based research. One of these factors is the use of makeup by the individual in question as he or she has their identity confirmed by the facial recognition system. In a recent study conducted by Dantcheva et al. [14], the use of facial makeup had a negative impact on the accuracy levels of a facial recognition system.

In their research they noted that the "use of makeup as a face alteration method poses a significant challenge to a biometric system, since it represents a simple, non-permanent and cost-effective way of confounding the system" [14]. The work of Chen et al. focuses on this unique aspect, and in it they have created and implemented a facial makeup-detection module that can be implemented in a facial recognition system.

In general, their methodology first extracts a collective set of unique features from the prominent parts of the face, which takes into consideration the shape, color and texture that have been applied by the individual in question. In return, a classifier is then utilized to help detect the presence or absence of makeup on the face of the individual.

From this point onwards, various experiments are conducted upon two particular datasets that consist of the facial images of female subjects as inputs into the makeup-detection system. The variables consist specifically of the facial-based illumination, facial expression, illumination from the external environment, and variances in the facial pose of the female subjects.

Finally, the output of the makeup-detection system is used to preprocess facial-based images against non-makeup facial-based images. Thus, the ultimate goal of this is to improve the overall matching performance of the facial recognition system that has been implemented in the application that it is supposed to serve.

An example of a female subject in the respective dataset is illustrated in Figure 4.4.

It should be noted that a very critical aspect of this proposed makeup-detection system is the utilization of the appropriate color

Figure 4.4 Makeup applied by female subject
Source: Masson/Shutterstock.com

space which will be used to process the images of the female subjects. After comparing various color schemes, which included red, green, blue (RGB), luminance/chromatic components (LAB) and hue, saturation, value (HSV), it was the latter which was ultimately selected, as it was discovered that makeup applied by a female subject can be better ascertained.

The mathematical components which constitute the HSV can be represented as follows:

$$H = \arctan (G - B) / (R - G) + (R - B)^L$$
$$S = 1 - \min (R, G, B) \qquad \qquad [14]$$

A distinguishing factor from this makeup-detection system as opposed to others developed is that this one is automated. It is believed that only one such other model was actually created, and that was in the research work conducted by Varshovi [15]. For example, their particular makeup-detection system examined a set of 120 facial-based images of 21 female subjects in both frontal and other positions.

They had accuracy rates that can be broken down as follows:

(1) 90.62% for eye shadow detection;

(2) 93.3% for lipstick detection;

(3) 52.5% for liquid foundation detection.

Examples of female subjects wearing eye shadow and lipstick for this particular dataset can be seen in Figures 4.5 and 4.6

The makeup-detection system developed in the research work by Chen et al. consists of the following four components:

(1) Face detection and landmark localization:

The Adaboost face detector (which will be subsequently reviewed in further detail) is used as a statistical-based approximator to detect and scale the face as an input image. The Gaussian mixture model (GMM) is then used to ascertain the prominent features of the face (which are the landmarks) from within the facial region. The Gaussian mixture

Figure 4.5 Eyeshadow applied by female subject
Source: Prostock-studio/Shutterstock.com

Figure 4.6 Lipstick applied by female subject
Source: Minerva Studio/Shutterstock.com

model then uses statistically based joint probability distributions to quantitatively characterize the actual locations of these prominent features of the face.

(2) Facial normalization:

In this sub-process, the facial-based composite images are cropped and aligned, focusing on three key areas:

- The regions around the left eye;
- The regions around the right eye;
- The regions around the mouth.
- From these three strategic points on the face, the shape, color, and the texture features are then extracted to create two classes of facial-based composite image(s), which are as follows:
- Makeup;
- No makeup.

(3) Region of interest (ROI) detection:

In this particular sub-process, the facial-based composite image(s) are then further normalized onto a Cartesian geometric plane, in an effort to reduce any variances that might be present from the various scales and poses that have been captured from the female subjects. The dimensions that are used for this makeup-detection system are 160 × 164 pixels. This is then further broken down into the following sub-dimensions:

- The regions around the left eye: 52 × 52 pixels;
- The regions around the right eye: 52 × 52 pixels;
- The regions around the mouth: 56 × 62 pixels.

(4) Feature extraction:

In this sub-process, for the features that constitute the makeup-detection system, which are shape, color, and texture, Gabor wavelet filters are applied in order to extract the shape and texture infor-mation/data, and local binary patters (LBP) are also used to capture color information/data.

The shape, color, and texture features are further described in more detail as follows:

(1) The color descriptor:

Color can be defined more specifically as the low-level visual feature which can be used to both quantitatively and qualitatively describe the facial-based composite image(s). In this particular makeup-detection system, each region of interest (ROI) is converted over into 5 × 5 pixel-based non-overlapping blocks. Three different mathematical algorithms can be used to extract the color-based images from the face, which are as follows:

$$P = x,y \; 1 \, / \, N \, x,y$$

$$O = N \, [1/x,y \, (Ix,y)]^2$$

$$Y = 1 \, / \, N \, x,y \, (Ix,y - p)^3 \qquad\qquad [13]$$

where:

N = the total number of pixels.

It is important to note that the above mathematical algorithms can be considered as three independent channels, which in turn yields a 225-dimensional-based eigenvector. But, in order to remove (or extract) all of the color from facial-based composite image(s), they are broken into 9 overlapping blocks of regions, thus resulting in an 81-dimensional eigen-based feature vector.

(2) The shape descriptor:

In the creation of this makeup-detection system, three types of shape descriptors were created and also used to extract any other unique features from the facial-based composite image(s) which were not detected before. These three descriptors are as follows:

• Gabor wavelets:

As noted, the use of this is quite extensive throughout both iris recognition and facial recognition. But, for the purposes of the makeup-detection system, each Gabor wavelet was applied to a 64 × 64 pixel component of the facia-based composite image(s). From here, 40 independent outputs were then created. The statistical mean, variance, and the skewness were also calculated, thus resulting in a total of 120 uncovered unique features being extracted from each facial-based composite image(s).

- GIST:

This particular descriptor is used to reduce the amount of variance that is caused by the different lighting that is used in the external environment when capturing the facial images of the female subjects. The mathematical algorithm that is used to represent GIST is as follows:

$$I^t(x,y) = [I(x,y) \times H(x,y)] / [I(x,y) \times H(x,y)]^2 \times G(x,y) \qquad [13]$$

where

$I(x,y)$ = is the input value

$G(x,y)$ = is the low-pass Gaussian filter

$H(x,y)$ = is the corresponding high-pass filter.

After the above has been calculated, a discrete Fourier transformation technique is then applied to the results of the Gabor wavelets to further refine them.

- Edge information:

Because the use of both eye and mouth makeup can further enhance the local edge structures of the face, a specific orientation histogram must be used. Thus, a canny edge detector is utilized to in order to quantitatively ascertain the true edges of the facial-based composite images(s).

(3) The texture descriptor:

This particular descriptor is utilized to ascertain as well as categorize both the micro and the macro structures of the facial-based composite image(s). This is calculated by taking the difference in the pixel intensity in the center pixel of the facial-based composite image(s) from the neighboring pixels. It should be noted that this difference is actually a binary string (a series of zeros and ones), and is then converted over to a decimal value. From this point on, uniform-based texture descriptors (in other words, those texture descriptors that that have linear-based, bitwise transitions from either one to zero or zero to one) are extracted. In this regard, maintaining a sense of uniformity in the facial-based composite image(s) is absolutely critical as it defines the micro features of the face such as the lines, edges, and the corners, where makeup tends to be applied by female subjects.

As was described earlier, two sets or classes of facial-based composite image(s) were utilized for the makeup-detection system: the makeup class or the no-makeup class. In order to segregate these two classes at a quantitative level, support vector machines and Adaboost are used (as previously discussed).

The support vector machine can be mathematically represented as follows:

$$\text{Min } w,e = ||W||^2 + C \qquad [13]$$

The premise here is that the support vector machine can ascertain a linear boundary in the facial-based composite image(s) that can maximize the margin between these two classes.

Next, the Adaboost can be mathematically represented as follows:

$$Ht(X) = Gk \ (fi,fj) = 1, \text{ if } d(fi - fj) > tk \qquad [13]$$

Once again, the basic premise behind Adaboost is to bring together or combine any weak statistical classifiers in an effort to create a single, strong statistical classifier.

With this theoretical framework established for the makeup-detection system, the actual makeup database was compiled utilizing before and after makeup images from the female subjects from various YouTube makeup tutorials (which are video-based).

A total of 151 female subjects were taken from these videos, which included four facial images for each female subject. In other words, there were two images used before the application of the makeup and two after the application of the makeup.

In the end, the dataset consisted of a total of 600 before makeup application and after makeup application facial images, with each consisting of 300 facial images.

Figure 4.7 Makeup applied by YouTube female subject
Source: kiuikson/Shutterstock.com

The second dataset consisted of a total of 154 images from a total of 125 subjects (77 total images with makeup, and 77 total images with no makeup). These images were taken from various female subjects at random from the Internet.

Collectively, these two datasets are termed the "YouTube Makeup Database" (YMU), and the "Makeup in the Wild Database" (MIW). Note that the latter refers to the images of the female subjects taken from the Internet.

Representative examples of these images collected from YouTube are illustrated in Figures 4.7 and 4.8.

Before the actual makeup-detection system was implemented in a facial recognition system, it was first tested with both the support vector machine and Adaboost. The results can be seen in Table 4.13 for the YMU dataset.

As can be seen from this table, when the support vector machine was used:

- There was a classification rate of 87.25% for the unique features from the facial images;
- The left eye and the right regions of interest had classification rates of 81.71% and 80.68%;

Figure 4.8 Makeup being applied to YouTube female subject
Source: Olena Yakobchuk/Shutterstock.com

Table 4.13 Results of the support vector machine and Adaboost

Region of interest	Support vector machine	Adaboost
The entire face	87.25 ± 1.91	88.98 ± 3.54
The left eye	81.71 ± 4.67	75.72 ± 1.99
The right eye	80.68 ± 3.08	79.89 ± 4.22
The mouth	58.94 ± 3.47	57.46 ± 5.94
The left eye + the right eye + the mouth	87.62 ± 2.01	85.83 ± 3.84
The face + the left eye + the right eye + the mouth	93.20 ± 0.56	89.94 ± 1.60

- Interestingly, the mouth region of interest had a much lower classification rate of 58.94%. This was attributed to the fact that the color of the makeup could not be extracted when lipstick was used;

- Overall, the support vector machine had an accuracy rate of 93.20%, whereas the Adaboost had an accuracy rate of 89.94%.

The makeup-detection system was then applied to the MTW dataset: the support vector machine had an accuracy rate of 95.45%, and the Adaboost had an accuracy rate of 92.21%.

With these various experiments now concluded, the next step was to actually implement the makeup-detection system in the facial recognition system. In this regard, since the support vector machine yielded the best results, this was used as the primary pattern classifier. But, there was one particular issue to be addressed, and that was increasing the level of the recognition performance between the female subjects with makeup applied and those female subjects with no makeup applied.

To counter this, a specific pre-processing routine was created by making use of what is known as a "photometric normalization routine" in order to smoothen out the edges of the face of the female subjects where makeup is usually applied the most. This is represented by the following mathematical algorithm:

$$Q = I(x,y)/I(x,y) = (Pw(x,y)\ N(x,s)^5) / Gk * [Pw(x,y)n(x,y)s] \qquad [13]$$

where:

$Pw(x,y)$ = the albedo of the facial surface in the composite image(s)

N = the surface normal

S = the reflection of the lighting in the external environment

Gk = the statistically weighted Gaussian smoothing filter.

Finally, when the makeup-detection system was incorporated in the facial recognition system, a false acceptance rate (FAR) of just 1% was realized. In all, a total of five trials were conducted on the YMU dataset. In reality, this is a huge step forward for both the development and the improvement of facial recognition technology.

As described earlier in this chapter, one of the biggest obstacles for facial recognition has been the ability to confirm the identity of a particular individual after they have added a non-natural item to their face, such as the use of makeup, glasses/sunglasses, hats, jewelry, etc. With the use of the makeup-detection system, at least on a theoretical level, the probability of rejecting a legitimate user (which is what the metric of the false acceptance rate reflects) has become much lower.

But, as Chen et al. point out, obviously more research work needs to be done in this particular area so that this makeup-detection system can be refined and used on all types of facial recognition systems.

But in this regard, it is very important to note that **the degree of makeup which is applied** by the female subjects needs to be taken into consideration as well (in other words, mathematical and/or statistical algorithms need to be created and developed) in order to avoid any instances of spoofing and/or obfuscation to the facial recognition system.

Thermal Face Recognition for Human-Robot Interactions – Hermosilla et al.

Throughout this chapter, we have described the use of facial recognition technology as the primary means by which to confirm the identity of a particular individual. There are many types of applications for this, which include physical access entry, logical access entry, the e-passport (as was reviewed in detail in our second book), and even to a certain extent single-sign-on solutions (aka SSOs; this is where an image of a face can be used in lieu of a password).

However, as was also discussed, the use of facial recognition technology is also evolving at a rapid pace, even to the point where it can confirm the identity of individuals at a distance. This even holds true application-wise. The work conducted by Hermosilla et al. examined the use of facial recognition technology for human-robot interactions (aka HRI applications).

This is where facial analysis can be used to so that robots can actually interact with human beings, and vice versa, but in a **natural way**, as opposed to a **machine-based way**. In other words, the primary goal here is to try to make robots much more personalized in the way of services and particular behaviors.

In this regard, it is important to note that human-robot interactions making use of facial recognition technology have their own set of requirements, which are as follows:

(1) Variations in lighting in the external environment when the images of the individual in question are being captured cannot be an influence;

(2) Any variable expressions in the face cannot be taken into consideration;

(3) Only facial-based composite images can be captured per individual.

As a result of these specific constraints, the use of thermal-based methodologies in facial recognition has been called upon. Thus, the primary goal of the research by Hermosilla et al. is to introduce the usage of thermal-based methodologies for establishing human-robot interactions with facial recognition technology. But, another component that is being added here is also the use of vascular-based networks.

By incorporating the latter, both the variations in the lighting from the external environment as well as the variable expressions in the face of the individual can be captured.

The overall approach to developing this new application involved making use of various SIFT descriptors to confirm the geometrical face of the individual in question as well as transforming those faces into the various vascular networks. In turn, the latter was performed using statistical-based skin segmentation and morphological operators. This process is illustrated in Figure 4.A.

The sub-phases of the above model are described in further detail as follows:

(1) Face segmentation:

In this sub-phase, a skin detection model is actually created in the thermal spectrum by statistically modeling the intensity of the skin pixels, their corresponding distributions, as well as their non skin-based distributions utilizing the concepts from the mixtures of Gaussian (MoG).

The skin intensity model can mathematically represented as:

$$P_{skin}{}^x = \sum 1/ \text{ square root } 2\pi\sigma_s \exp{[-1/2 \ X \ 1(x-Ux)2/O^{2x}]} \qquad [16]$$

The non-skin intensity model can mathematically represented as:

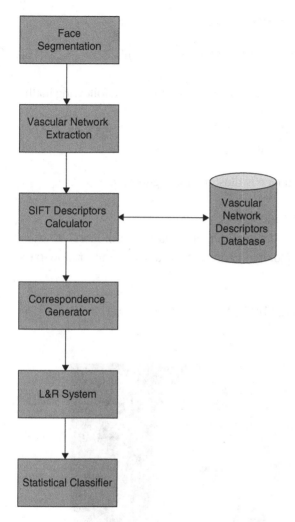

Figure 4.A Development of thermal system

$$P_{\text{non-skin}}{}^{x} = \sum 1/ \text{ square root } 2\pi\sigma_N \exp\ [-1/2\ X\ 1(x-Ux)2/O^{2x}] \qquad [16]$$

It should be noted that a specific pixel is actually detected when its intensity has a much higher statistical probability of belonging to a particular skin class versus a non-skin class. From here, the skin mask of the face can be calculated as follows:

$$I_{mask}(j,i) = [1 \text{ if } P_{skin} I(I,j) > P_{non\text{-}skin} J(I,j)]$$

$$I_{mask}(j,i) = [0 \text{ if } P_{skin} I(I,j) < P_{non\text{-}skin} J(I,j)] \qquad [16]$$

The actual skin image of the face is calculated by the following mathematical algorithm:

$$I_{skin} (I,i) = I_{mask} (I,j) I (I,j) \qquad [16]$$

A thermal image of a face is illustrated in Figure 4.9.

(2) Vascular network recognition:

The resultant skin image from the last sub-process is then "smoothened" by actually filtering it from a 3 × 3 uniform low-pass statistical filter:

$$I_{smooth} = I_{skin} * 1/9 [1,1,1,] \times [1,1,1] \times [1,1,1] \qquad [16]$$

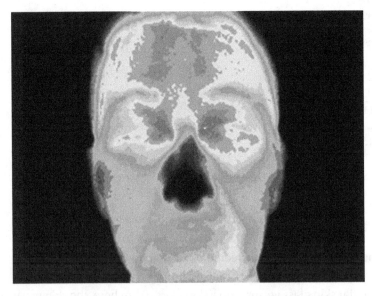

Figure 4.9 Thermal image of face
Source: Anita van den Broek/Shutterstock.com

From this point, the "smoothened" skin image is dilated by the following mathematical algorithm:

$$I_{opened} = I_{smooth}\ f(x)\ [1,0,1,] \times [0,1,0] \times [1,0,1]\ XOR\ [1,0,1,] \\ \times [0,1,0] \times [1,0,1]\ [16]$$

The vascular network image is then calculated as follows:

$$I_{vascular} = I_{smooth} - I_{opened} \qquad\qquad [16]$$

A vascular image of a face can be seen in Figure 4.10.

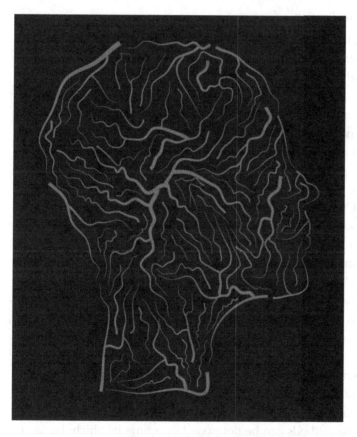

Figure 4.10 Vascular image of face
Source: newelle/Shutterstock.com

(3) Wide baseline matching using local interest points:

The various SIFT descriptors (as described previously) were actually obtained from the vascular image network by using a specific approach known as Lowe's methodology. Each of the SIFT descriptors represents a small portion of the facial-based composite image. The SIFT descriptor consists of the following components:

- A geometrical position (Xo, Yo)
- An orientation (O)
- A scale (o)
- Vector-based characteristics (V1 ... V128)

(4) Face classification:

In this last sub-process, the identity of the individual is confirmed by examining the statistical closeness between the vascular image of the face and the thermal image of the face.

It should be noted that the datasets for this scientific study came from the UXXX Thermal Faces Databases. This database consists of 156 thermal-based facial images. There are a total of 26 individuals in this database, with a corresponding six images each.

In order to capture the specific facial images that were needed, a Cedip Jade UC infrared camera was utilized. This type of camera was specifically chosen because it has a spectral image range of 8–12 µm, and a resolution of 320 × 240 pixels.

Interestingly enough, in addition to capturing the raw, facial images, videos were also captured of all of the 26 subjects. Their faces were in a fixed position, and they had to recite vowels (up to 2000 vowels were captured), as well as mimic happy, sad and angry facial expressions (up to 100 video frames were captured in these instances for each of the subjects).

The overall results of this scientific study indicate that using the vascular components of the face actually helps to preserve important features of the thermal-based face images. Because of this, more specialized and highly precise methods can be developed over time in which the use of facial recognition technology can greatly enhance the human-robot interaction environment.

The Use of Facial Recognition in Forensics – Ali et al.

There is no doubt that the field of forensics science has garnered much intrigue amongst the public. It is actually a very complex field, which requires much painstaking work and research in order to collect the needed evidence in order to bring a case to trial, and to have a successful outcome in a court of law. Forensics science is primarily involved in collecting the latent evidence at a crime scene. This simply refers to data which are clearly not visible to the naked eye, but still actually does exist.

In this regard, forensic examiners have many tools they can use in order to garner this unseen evidence. Very often in the past forensic investigations, it was the fingerprints left behind which were of prime interest (and to this day, still are). But now, the field of biometric technology continues to evolve, especially in iris recognition and facial recognition.

These two specific modalities are now being called upon to aid the forensic investigators in their investigative work. With respect to the use of facial recognition, the forensic investigator often needs to examine any video (which is made available from the CCTV cameras) and the respective images that are available at the crime scene.

In these particular instances, the forensic investigator has to perform a manual search in these videos or images in order to find the suspect or individuals of interest that they are looking for in particular. There is no doubt that this can be very much a time-consuming as well as a laborious process. On top of this, these images then have to be compared against a database of mugshots in order to confirm that the right individual is being investigated.

Thus, this is where the use of facial recognition technology will come into critical play. For instance, it will help to automate the process when comparing the images of the individuals in question against the mugshots which are in existence in the database, but it will also greatly improve both the efficiencies and the standardization in these comparison processes.

But so far there is no current facial recognition system on hand which has been developed specifically for forensic investigation applications. Because of the extremely stringent requirements that are required to make forensic evidence admissible in a court of law, the same holds true for a facial recognition system. In other words, it has to be thoroughly evaluated and completely verified (and perhaps even certified) before it can be used in forensic investigation cases. There are numerous reasons for this, which include the following:

(1) The repercussions of an invalid decision made by a forensic investigator by using a facial recognition system are far more severe than an invalid decision made in a commercial application environment. The primary reason for this is that forensic evidence is judged by a court of law on a "black or white" basis. This means that the evidence either can be accepted or not accepted in a court of law – there are no gray areas that can be established.

(2) As mentioned, although facial recognition technology has advanced, it is still very much prone to variability issues such as the facial expressions of the individuals in question, changes in the pose of the face, changes in lighting from the external environment etc. These are factors which have to be literally 100% eliminated if the forensic evidence collected by a facial recognition system can be admissible in a court of law.

(3) Although the statistical and mathematical algorithms in facial recognition are constantly evolving (as can be seen by the sheer amount covered in this chapter), confirming the identity of an individual in question still comes down to examining the statistical closeness between facial-based enrollment and verification templates. At the present time, there is no legal precedence where this kind of statistical comparison can be accepted in a court of law. Thus, any forensic evidence collected based on these kinds of comparison cannot be made admissible.

(4) As described earlier in this chapter, Facial recognition technology is now very often used in conjunction with CCTV-based technology. Although the images and the videos that are produced from the CCTV are of both high quality and caliber, they still do not completely meet the demanding requirements of possessing the so-called forensic-grade quality requirements so that the respective images and videos can be used in a court of law as evidence.

But, despite these above-mentioned obstacles, there is an approach that is currently being developed which holds great promise for the evidence collected by a facial recognition system to be of forensic grade, which would thus increase its probability of being admitted as evidence in a court of law. The model that is currently being developed is known as the "Bayesian framework for forensic face recognition," and is reviewed in detail in the next sub-section.

The Bayesian Framework for Forensic Face Recognition

As described in the last sub-section, the way that biometric systems work in order to confirm the identity of an individual, the enrollment and verification templates are compared with each another, and the statistical correlation is examined.

If there is enough closeness between the two according to the parameters which have been set forth, then the individual in question will have their identity confirmed. If it is deemed that there is not enough statistical closeness between the enrollment and the verification templates, then the identity of that particular individual cannot be confirmed, and thus he or she will then have to go through the entire process again.

While this is a proven and acceptable way in which to confirm the identity of a particular individual in commercial applications, this would not be acceptable in the field of Forensics, because any evidence collected in this manner would not be accepted by a court of law. The primary reason for this is that it is a **threshold measure which is being used as a form of evidence**.

At the present time the only way that forensic evidence (that is collected by a facial recognition system) can be admitted by a court of law is if a **score-based system is actually utilized**. In this regard, one of the best techniques to use is known as the "Bayesian framework." In it, a likelihood ratio is computed from the threshold measure which was calculated from the comparison of the enrollment and the verification templates.

It is important to note that the key differentiating factor between the likelihood ratio and the threshold value is that a final degree or a final value is calculated. In other words, with the former, the value is absolute, whereas with the latter the value is subjective, because it can be variable each time that it is used. But in order to first calculate the likelihood ratio the posterior probabilities must be first computed. Note that the mathematical algorithm below has been designed specifically for a facial recognition system being used in a forensics application. Further, it is assumed that the evidence gathered will be admissible in a court of law.

This algorithm can be described as follows:

$$Pr(Hp|E,I) / Pr(Hd|E,I) = [Pr(E|Hp,I) / Pr(E|Hd,I)] \times [Pr(Hp|I) / Pr(Hd|I)] \quad [17]$$

where:

Hp = the prosecution statistical hypothesis (this is where the suspect is the source of the questioned face)

Hd = the defense statistical hypothesis (this is where the non-suspect is the source of the questioned face)

E = the forensic evidence that is available

I = the background information (or changes in the external environment that the facial recognition system will encounter).

From the quantitative measure that is ascertained by the above-described equation, the likelihood ratio can be computed by the mathematical algorithm:

$$Pr (E|Hp \, I) / Pr (E|Hd, I) \quad [17]$$

The likelihood ratio now gives a quantitative measure for the degree of support for one hypothesis (where the suspect is the source of the questioned face) versus the other hypothesis (where the non-suspect is the source of the questioned face).

It is also important to note that the likelihood ratio also takes into consideration the statistical probability of a particular piece of forensic evidence being taken into consideration against these two competing statistical hypotheses, as well as the circumstances of the case and the analysis of the face in question (which was conducted by the facial recognition system).

Once the likelihood ratio has been computed by the above mathematical algorithm, it then must be evaluated by a forensic investigator in order to determine if it can be admissible in a court of law. This is accomplished with the following process:

(1) The value of E is compared against a questioned face versus the suspect's from the respective databases;

(2) The questioned face is then compared against the suspect's face under similar conditions (this is known as a comparison under a control situation). The derived value from here is known as the "wide source variability" (WSV);

(3) The questioned face is then compared against a database of various suspects' faces (this is known as a comparison under a variable situation). The derived value from here is known as the "between source variability" (BSV).

These computations are illustrated in Figures 4.B, 4.C and 4.D.

Although the Bayesian framework does provide a solid theoretical foundation for a forensic face recognition system, it is very important to stress once again that such a system must be able to produce evidence in a court of law. For example, if the identity of an individual cannot be confirmed the first time in a commercial-based application, then a second or even third chance can be afforded to get the identity confirmed.

But in the case of forensic applications, there is no second chance. The facial recognition system has to not only **produce evidence that is admissible in a court of law, but that particular piece of evidence must also be accurate**. In fact, it is the latter which is of utmost importance. For example, if the forensic evidence as collected by the facial recognition system is not accurate, then there is a strong probability that the wrong person could be convicted. In other words, it could very well be that an innocent person will be found guilty.

Also, one must keep in mind that with a forensic facial recognition system, human intervention will always be required in order to confirm the validity and the authenticity of the forensic evidence that has been collected. In other words, there will be a manual approach that will

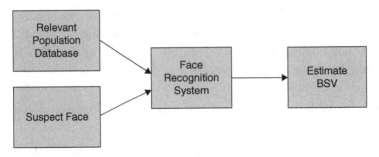

Figure 4.B Questioned face vs. suspect's face

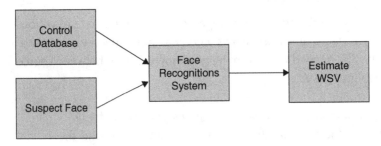

Figure 4.C Comparison of faces in controlled situations

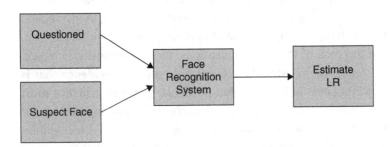

Figure 4.D Comparison of faces in variable situations

be required as well. But the goal is to also standardize the evidence-collection process with a forensic facial recognition system.

Just as there are limitations with a facial recognition system in a commercial applications, there will also be limitations to a forensics-based one, assuming that the Bayesian framework is specifically utilized. These are as follows:

(1) The sheer number of facial-based composite image(s) that are used as a variable to compute both the BSV and the WSV values;

(2) The database must be able to account for:

- The variations of lighting in the external environment;

- Any changes in facial expression of the individual in question.

(3) The BSV and the WSV values are also statistical probability density functions, and therefore the respective estimations are sensitive to the type of mathematical algorithm that is being used to compute them. It is important to note that the mathematical algorithms as presented in this sub-section are most optimal ones to be used when computing the values for both BSV and WSV, but other types of mathematical algorithms can be developed and utilized as well. But using different types of mathematical algorithms will lead to different values, thus affecting the validity and the authenticity of the forensic evidence.

But apart from these quantitative measures just described, there are also qualitative measures which have to be taken into consideration in order to determine if forensic evidence that is collected by a facial recognition system can indeed be admissible and used in a court of law. The guiding principle for this is known in the legal world as the "Frye rule."

This legal precedence states that the judge in any case must be the so-called gatekeeper in the instances where such forensic evidence is used. In other words, the judge must determine if the forensic facial recognition system is also deemed to be acceptable for use by the scientific community. In other words, in addition to a technological validation, it must have a scientific validation as well.

But recently, an extension of the Frye rule was initiated known as the "Daubert rule." In addition to the judge being the gatekeeper, the forensic recognition system that is being used must be peer-reviewed by the biometrics industry as well (in addition to the scientific community), and the likelihood ratios that are calculated and any standards and controls that exist in the forensic facial recognition system must be peer-reviewed and challenged as well.

Figure 4.11 Facial recognition forensics
Source: Zoka74/Shutterstock.com

It is interesting to note that in European countries this level of scrutiny is not required. Rather, it is entirely up to the judge presiding over the specific case to determine the admissibility of the forensic evidence that is collected by the facial recognition system.

An image of facial recognition forensics is shown in Figure 4.11.

The Limitations of Facial Recognition

Our first book reviewed the major biometric modalities that are being used today. While there is no doubt that each modality has its certain set of advantages, they possess their fair share of disadvantages as well. In other words, while one modality may work well for one particular application, there is no guarantee that it will work equally well in a different application environment.

The same holds true for both iris recognition and facial recognition. For example, while both may work well for large-scale applications, they are not optimized for extremely low-level applications. In this book, Chapter 3 extensively reviewed iris recognition, as well as its disadvantages. The disadvantages with facial recognition were also reviewed, but in this sub-section we review them in more detail.

In particular, these limitations are as follows:

(1) Illumination;

(2) Pose;

(3) Occlusion;

(4) Optical technology;

(5) Expression;

(6) Mathematical/statistical algorithmic evaluations.

Illumination

When it comes to illumination, the statistical and the mathematical algorithms which were reviewed at length in this chapter almost exclusively rely upon color in order to recognize the facial-based composite image(s) of the individuals in question. It is from here the unique features are extracted by these particular algorithms, and some can make use of grayscale images as well.

For instance, when we see a color on a certain object, that color is a function both of the surface of the object in question, as well as of the kind of light that is being reflected upon it. When it comes to the eye, the color interpretation of the object actually comes from the light receptors in our eyes. The information that is gathered here is then sent to the brain for further processing.

The color that we actually perceive (from the color spectrum) is also a function of light energy and the light wavelength. This phenomenon also applies to facial recognition systems, and is known specifically as "chromacity." In other words, the color intensity of a certain pixel in a facial-based composite image(s) depends to a large extent on the lighting that is available in the external environment.

But, keep in mind that it is not just the statistical value that is assigned to a pixel that can change when the lighting in the external environment changes. The intensity value which is assigned to the particular pixel in the facial-based composite image(s) can fluctuate greatly as well.

Another obstacle that is encountered is known as "solarization." This specifically occurs when the face region of the individual in question can be obscured by shadow effects. This can greatly impede unique feature extraction from the facial composite image(s). In fact, solarization may be more pronounced when comparing the raw images of the same individual versus the comparison of raw images of two different individuals.

The facial recognition systems of today are adapting better to the illumination obstacle in that they can confirm the identity of an individual in certain radical conditions, but the direction from which the illumination is coming onto the face of the individual is still a hurdle that needs to be overcome.

Pose

After illumination, this is the next major limitation for facial recognition systems. For example, consider the scenario when an individual presents the frontal part of their face for raw image acquisition. Assume that they are not wearing any external objects on their face, such as jewelry, glasses/contact lenses, hats, etc. The facial recognition system will thus take "plain-based" raw images of that particular individual.

Now consider the fact when this same individual comes back again to have a second raw images taken, wearing a combination of the above-mentioned external objects or even all of them. In this time around, the facial recognition will have a much more difficult time in confirming the identity of this particular individual.

In order to counter this obstacle, three different approaches have been utilized, which are as follows.

Multispectral-based approaches

With this particular approach, there are multiple facial-based composite images that are required to help train the facial recognition system. The basic premise here is to allow for the capture of **all the poses** that are available in these particular images. The end result is that these facial-based composite images must be classified according to some sort of scheme by the facial recognition system. It is important to keep in mind that this entire process must be repeated for **each and every pose that is available, for each and every facial-based composite image** that is presented to the system. Because of this, there are obviously restrictions to using this kind of approach. First, many facial-based composite images are needed for each and every individual who is going to be scanned by the facial recognition system. Second, this method only does pure texture mapping, thus, any forms of expression and changes in lighting in the external environment cannot be taken into consideration. Third, because so many iterations are required for just one particular individual, much more processing power is required on the part of the facial recognition system.

Single-model-based approaches

With this methodology, several data points from the facial-based composite image(s) are required. One of the primary advantages with this approach is that the data of the individual can actually be collected from various different sources such as different scanners, different camera makes, different lenses, etc. Unlike the above-mentioned approach, the objective here is to include each and every possible pose combination in one facial-based composite image. Thus, this image would then become a three-dimensional (3D) model. But this has its set of limitations as well. First, although the data points can be collected from differing sources as just described, it may be the case as well that there may not be enough data points. Second, most facial recognition systems of today do not allow for data to be used from multiple sources. Rather, the data have to be directly inputted from the camera and the extraction mechanism that the facial recognition system is using. To alleviate these problems, the scientific community has come up with a hybrid approach known as the "active appearance model," or AAM for short. With this, only a few data points are used and the iterative process as described with the last model is modeled, so that a number of poses can be combined into just one huge "superpose" which would be placed onto just one frontal photo and a secondary profile image.

Geometric approaches

With these techniques, a special sub-layer of the various poses is created, and from here a specialized graph is then created which can the link notes from within the sub-layer in order to model the transformation that is required in order to ascertain the various rotations of the individual in question. In this regard, elastic bunch graph matching (EGBM) has been widely utilized.

Occlusion

The term occlusion literally means being "obstructed." As applied to facial recognition, this simply means that some part parts of the face are covered for some reason or another, and thus cannot be readily captured by the facial recognition system. This is where one of main drawbacks is with facial recognition. Although it can now take images of people at a distance in groups, **a full facial image is still required** by the facial recognition system in order to confirm the identity of an individual. An alterative to this to use a facial recognition system which just requires parts of the face in order to carry out the necessary verification and/or identification scenarios.

Optical Technology

When a facial recognition system makes use of optical-based technologies, it is important to keep in mind that different output files will be created. Also, there is no set of best standards or practices yet in existence to mandate the use of optical technology in facial recognition systems, thus there are different cameras that can be used with their own sets of weaknesses and disadvantages.

Expression

Any inconsistent changes in facial expression can also be an obstacle in the identification of a particular individual. But it should be noted that it isn't as much of an impediment as is the lighting in the external environment or the pose of the individual in question. But when you add all of these three together obstacles together, then a facial recognition system will not be able to confirm the identity of an individual.

Mathematical/Statistical Algorithmic Evaluations

The bulk of this chapter has reviewed the statistical and the mathematical algorithms which so far have been used in facial recognition. All of their strengths and weaknesses were discussed as well in detail, but in general they are as follows:

(1) Inconsistencies in the error rates (most notable the false acceptance rate, the false rejection rate and the ability to verify rate).

(2) Specialized mathematical and statistical algorithms take extra processing power on the part of the facial recognition system.

(3) Extra memory usage and consumption.

(4) They are not scalable or portable – in other words, if the database size of the population increases, the mathematical and/or the statistical algorithms will also have to be redesigned from scratch. Also, each vendor has their own proprietary algorithms, meaning they are specific to only one type of facial recognition system and cannot be used in another one.

The Applications of Facial Recognition

Given the covert nature and the ability to deploy facial recognition easily in other non-biometric systems and technologies, it is no wonder that it has a wide range of market applications it can serve.

Probably the biggest application for facial recognition has been that for the e-passport, and to a certain degree the national ID card system, for those nations who have adopted it.

For example, the International Civil Aviation Organization (also known as the ICAO) has made facial recognition templates the de facto standard for machine-readable travel documents.

Also, along with iris recognition, facial recognition is being used quite heavily at the major international airports, primarily for covert surveillance purposes, in an effort to scan for individuals on the terrorist watch lists.

Also, contrary to public support of it, facial recognition can be used very covertly at venues where large crowds gather, such as sporting events, concerts, etc. Facial recognition systems can also be used in conjunction with CCTV cameras, and strategically placed in large metropolitan areas.

For example, the city of London is a perfect example of this. At just about every street corner there is a facial recognition/CCTV camera system deployed.

Because of this vast network of security, the London police were able to quickly apprehend and bring to justice the terrorist suspects who were involved in the train bombings which took place.

Another popular application for facial recognition is for border protection and control, especially widely used in the European countries.

Facial recognition is also heavily used in conducting real-time market research studies. For instance, it can be used to gauge a potential customer's reaction to certain advertising stimuli by merely recording that individual's facial movements.

Casinos are also a highly favored venue for facial recognition, as a means to identify and verify the welcomed guests versus the unwelcomed guests.

Facial recognition has also been used in both physical access entry as well as time and attendance scenarios, but nowhere near to the degree that hand geometry recognition and fingerprint recognition are currently being used in these types of market applications.

Case Study: Razko Security Adds Face Recognition Technology to Video Surveillance Systems

Older-generation video technology includes such tools as multiplex/time lapse cameras, digital video recorders (DVRs), as well as network video recorders (NVRs).

While these traditional technologies have proved their worth over time, the expense of maintaining them over time has proliferated, for many businesses, no matter how large or how small.

A very strong, inherent disadvantage of this traditional security technology is that these are primarily sophisticated archiving mechanisms, meaning that potential criminals and suspects can only be seen after the particular footage is recorded, thus they cannot be identified in real time and apprehended immediately.

In other words, the potential criminal or suspect could very well leave the crime scene far behind and elude law enforcement officials long after the video footage has been carefully examined by security personnel.

Also, depending upon the size of the business, it is a huge expense to maintain a staff of security guards to identify the literally thousands of individuals who enter and exit the premises on a daily basis.

But, with the addition of facial recognition technology to current CCTV technology, the identification of potential suspects and criminals can now occur in real time, and thus apprehension can occur very quickly on the scene, just seconds after the crime has occurred.

Although it sounds complex, the idea behind all of this is quite simple. A facial recognition database of all potential criminals and suspects is created, and implemented in the CCTV technology.

As the particular individual walks by the CCTV cameras, the facial images are then instantaneously compared to the database, and thus, a potential positive match can be made.

And through the facial recognition technology developed by Cognitec, an alarm is sounded in real time, once a positive match is made between the facial recognition databases and the CCTV camera footage. This is perfectly illustrated by Razko Security.

Its president, Mr. Ted Eliraz, was approached by an individual known as Mr. Mike Kavanaugh, a Canadian Tire business owner, based in Oakville, Ontario.

Their business requirements were as follows:

(1) To have multiple CCTV cameras with facial recognition technology implemented at various places of businesses;
(2) To have a central facial recognition database for ease of administration;
(3) The most important: a reasonable cost.

With the facial recognition technology provided by Cognitec, the streaming video is displayed in real time, and when a positive match is made, the face of the potential criminal or suspect is then displayed, along with any appropriate law enforcement details and information about the individual in question. When installing this biometrics-based system, some big hurdles had to be overcome, in particular:

(1) Determining the exact locations of the CCTV/facial recognition cameras at the place of business;
(2) The various lighting conditions encountered from the external environment.

After conducting a thorough systems analysis and design, the cameras were located at the main entrance, the exteriors, and the glass doors at the various Canadian Tire locations.

In the end, Canadian Tire had this technology implemented in more locations throughout Canada, and the results proved to be very successful.

For instance, within the first six months of operation, four suspects were apprehended, and with further implementation of this technology at other Canadian Tire dealership locations, the facial recognition databases of potential suspects and criminals has grown, thus resulting in a much higher apprehension and capture rate.

NOTE: Case Study provided by Cognitec Systems, GmbH.

References

[1] V. Blanz and T. Vetter, Face Recognition Based On a 3D Morphable Model. *IEEE Transactions on Pattern Analysis and Machine Intelligence* 25:9 (2003), 1063–1074.

[2] I. Marqués, Face Recognition Algorithms. Proyecto Fin de Carrera (June 16, 2010).

[3] A. Javed, Face Recognition Based On Principal Component Analysis. The *International Journal of Image, Graphics, and Signal Processing* 2 (2013), 38–44.

[4] X. He and P. Nigoyi, Locality Preserving Projections. *The Proceedings of Conference On Advances in Neural Information Processing Systems*, 2003.

[5] B. Scholkopf and K.R. Müller, *Nonlinear Component Analysis as a Kernel Eigenvalue Problem*. Technical Report 44. Max-Planck Institut for biologische Kybernetik, 1996.

[6] N. Delbiaggio, A Comparison of Facial Recognition's Algorithms. Bachelor's Thesis Degree Programme in BIT (2017).

[7] T. Kohonen, *Self-Organization and Associated Memory* (Berlin: Springer, 1989).

[8] N. Intrator, D. Reisfeld and Y. Yeshurum, Face Recognition Using a Hybrid Supervised/Unsupervised Neural Network. *Pattern Recognition Letters* 17 (1995), 67–76.

[9] S. Lawrence, C.L. Giles, A.C. Tsoi and A.D. Black, Face Recognition: A Convolutional Neural Network Approach. *IEEE Transactions on Neural Networks* 8 (1997), 98–113.

[10] M. Zhang and J. Fulcher, Face Recognition Using Artificial Neural Network Group Based Adaptive Tolerance (Gat) Trees. *IEEE Transactions on Neural Networks* 7:3 (1996), 555–567.

[11] S.-H. Lin, S.-Y. Kung and L.-J. Lin, Face Recognition /Detection By Probabilistic Decision Based Neural Networks. *IEEE Transactions on Neural Networks* 8 (1997), 114–132.

[12] D. Bhattacharjee, D.K. Basu, M. Nasiouri and M. Kundu, Human Face Recognition System Using Fuzzy Multilayer Perceptron. *Soft Computing – A Fusion of Foundations, Methodologies, and Applications* 14:6 (2009), 559–570.

[13] C. Chen, A. Dantcheva and A. Ross, Automatic Facial Makeup Detection With Application in Face Recognition. *Proceedings - 2013 International Conference on Biometrics, ICB* (2013), 1–8. 10.1109/ICB.2013.6612994.

[14] A. Dantcheva, C. Chen and A. Ross, Can Facial Cosmetics Affect the Matching Accuracy of Face Recognition Systems? In *Biometrics: Theory, Applications and Systems (BTAS), 2012 IEEE Fifth International Conference*.

[15] S. Varshovi, Facial Makeup Detection Using HSV Colorspace and Texture Analysis. Master's Thesis, Concordia University (2012).

[16] G. Hermosilla, P. Loncomilla and J. Ruiz-del-Solar, *Thermal Face Recognition Using Local Interest Points and Descriptors for HRI Applications*. Department of Electrical Engineering, Universidad de Chile, Center For Technology.

[17] T. Ali, R. Veldhuis and L. Spreeuwers, *Forensic Face Recognition: A Survey*. Signals and Systems Group, FEMCS. The University of Twente, Enschede, The Netherlands.

5 | **Final Conclusions**

Thus far, our first two books were entitled:

* *Biometric Technology: Authentication, Biocryptography, and Cloud-Based Architecture*
* *Adopting Biometric Technology: Challenges and Solutions*

The first book covered the use of biometric technology from a wide variety of perspectives. These topics were covered in some detail in Chapter 1 and Chapter 2 of this book, but, to recap, the first book provided an overview of what biometric technology is all about.

For instance, it covered topics such as the difference between physiological and behavioral biometrics, providing for a formal definition of what biometrics is all about, what a biometric template is, reviewing the major key performance indicators (KPIs), as well as reviewing the biometric sensors.

It is important to reiterate the importance of the latter, as this can be considered to be the heart of the biometric technology in question. After all, without it, no raw images or recordings can be captured in order to extract unique features to confirm the identity of the individual in question.

Also, the major biometric modalities that are in use today were examined as well. These technologies, from both a physiological and behavioral standpoint, were reviewed in detail. To summarize, the physiological-based biometrics are those which take an actual snapshot of your physical and biological selves. These include the eyes, the face, the hand, the finger, and the voice.

In this regard, the modalities here include hand geometry recognition, fingerprint recognition, retinal and iris recognition, vein pattern recognition, facial recognition, and voice recognition (in this particular instance an image is not actually captured; rather a recording of the voice is captured).

In a manner similar to voice recognition, the behavioral biometrics collect a recording of our unique mannerisms when we type on a computer keyboard and the way we sign our name. The former is known as keystroke recognition, and the latter is known as signature recognition (in this instance, it is not the signature itself that is unique, but rather **the way in which we sign** our name is unique).

Biometric technology is also a rapidly evolving field, thus there are other types of modalities that are currently under research and development. This includes the likes of DNA recognition, earlobe recognition and gait recognition (this is the unique mannerisms in the way we walk). If any of these come to fruition, it will be DNA recognition that will prove to be the "ultimate biometric technology of all."

The primary reason for this is that the DNA consists of very rich and unique information and data which can confirm the identity of a particular without question. Currently, it is retinal recognition which holds this title.

Although the other physical and behavioral-based biometric modalities are extremely reliable when it comes to confirming the identity of a particular individual, there is always the small margin for some error as it is the degree of statistical correlation that is examined (any deviations are measured specifically by the failure to accept rate and the failure to reject rate). As was also discussed, the distinction of being the most controversial biometric modality belongs to facial recognition.

Also, the first book was designed for the C-level executive of a business or a corporation who is considering implementing a particular biometric system. Therefore, in this regard, a comprehensive project management guide was also provided which will guide the chief executive officer, the chief information officer, and even the chief information security officer towards a very successful implementation.

Apart from the development of newer modalities, the field of biometrics is expanding into other areas of technological development as well. One such example of this is in Biocryptography. As reviewed in the first book, the biometric template is nothing but a mathematical file, or representation of the physiological or behavioral traits that have been collected.

Therefore, the chance of an identity theft occurring if any of these templates is stolen or hijacked is actually quite minimal. Also, the statistical probabilities of reengineering a biometric template to the actual raw image is almost nil.

But just like anything else technology-related, a biometric template is also prone to a cyber attack. Thus, it also becomes very important to further protect a biometric template.

In these instance, cryptography is often used as an added layer of protection to the biometric template. In the simplest terms, cryptography is the science of scrambling and descrambling messages, so that they will be rendered useless if they were to be intercepted by a third party.

In these circumstances, it would be the biometric template that be scrambled at the point of origination and then descrambled in order to confirm the identity of the individual.

The various networking infrastructures in which the principles of biocryptography could work very well were also examined, and these include the use of a client server network, public key infrastructure, and the virtual private network.

In the world of information technology, the use of the cloud is an ever-growing need by businesses and corporations of all kinds and sizes. Because of this, biometric technology could work in a cloud infrastructure as well as from a security standpoint. It is important to keep in mind that for a small organization, implementing a full-blown biometrics system can be quite cost-prohibitive.

For example, not only does hardware (the actual biometric devices themselves) have to be purchased, but other accessories will probably have to be included such as the servers, databases, any software development that is needed, etc. Thus, the idea here is to create the use of biometric technology as a hosted offering, which would thus become known as "biometrics as a service," or "BaaS" for short.

The basic premise here is that the entire biometrics infrastructure (such as the servers, databases, software applications, etc.) would be outsourced to a trusted third party, such as an Internet service provider.

Thus, in order to implement a complete biometrics system, all a business owner would have to do is purchase the requisite biometric device, open up and purchase a BaaS account, and connect their devices to their account so that they would be interlinked with the biometrics infrastructure.

Of course, the benefits to the business owner would be fixed, monthly pricing which would be very affordable, as well as scalability so that the business owner could decrease or increase the size of their biometrics infrastructure as their business contracted or expanded, respectively.

One of the common themes of biometric technology is the implications it has not only from the technological perspective, but also from the social aspect. One may ask at this point why biometric technology has such a strong impact upon societies in general, and why it remains so controversial.

Well, consider this point for a moment. When other security tools are implemented at a place of business or organization, such as firewalls, routers, network intrusion devices, other machine learning security tools, etc., not too much thought is given. They are deployed and implemented as when and where needed in the organization, and not much thought is given after that (other than they should be doing the job that they should be doing – which is fortifying the defense perimeters of the business).

But when biometric technology is implemented in the same regard for the same kind of security applications, questions of the invasion of privacy rights and civil liberties violations often take effect. Why is this so? Well, the primary reason for this is that biometric technology often works as a "black box phenomenon."

In other words, garbage in, garbage out. The same holds true of the other security technologies as well, but with biometric technology it is a physiological or behavioral piece of ourselves that is being captured. We have no control over this, especially when the raw images or recordings are being recorded and captured to create the requisite enrollment and verification templates.

Because of this we experience a complete sense of the lack of control on a psychological level. Because of this, we then find ourselves claiming that the biometric technology that is being used (for the purposes of this book, such as iris recognition and facial recognition) is invading our personal privacy and space, when in actuality it is really not. The technology is simply doing what it is asked to do – which is to confirm our identity based upon our unique physiological and/or behavioral traits.

Our second book explored this topic in very extensive detail. This book was divided into three distinct sections. The first part provided a brief overview of the major biometric modalities, on both the physical and behavioral sides. A brief summary of them was provided, as well as some of the major societal issues that was impacting each and every one of them.

Examples of such issues included the following:

(1) Can I contract an ailment from direct interface with a biometric modality (examples of this are hand geometry recognition and fingerprint recognition)?

(2) Is the covert theft and/or hijacking of a biometric template(s) the same thing as credit card theft? Will the same kinds of repercussions occur as well?

(3) Can a biometric template be reverse engineered back to the original raw image and/or raw recordings?

(4) Is the United States Federal Government (for that matter, even other governments around the world) keeping covert tabs on me and my whereabouts with the use of facial recognition technology? This type of issue is also referred to as "Big Brother watching."

(5) Can I go blind from having my eyes scanned by an iris scanner?

(6) The misuse of miniature biometric modalities (such as those of portable Fingerprint readers) by both law enforcement agencies and officers.

(7) Can a hijacked and/or a stolen biometric template be used to launch a subsequent identity theft attack on me?

(8) Can a biometric template from a deceased individual be used to spoof a biometric device?

(9) Can my biometric templates be used by a third party for other kinds of gain?

(10) What if I refuse to submit myself to a biometric screening? Will I be forced to do it, or lose my rights as a citizen?

The above-mentioned issues are only a sampling, there are many others that the second book has reviewed, but these are some of the top ones. Apart from these top 10 issues, there are other social barriers that can impede both the adoption and the use of biometric technology. It should be noted that in this regard, there is an interesting trend.

For example, in the developing nations, biometric technologies are actually greatly accepted and widely used. The primary reason for this is that the use of biometrics gives the ability for these citizens to be counted as individuals in the eyes of their own government – because there is now an irrefutable electronic trail that confirms their identity versus a disposable paper trail.

But in the developed nations such as the United States and those in Europe, the adoption rate and usage of Biometric Technology is actually much lower, and there is in fact resistance to using it.

Again, the primary reason for this is that at least here in the United States, we have the Constitution (the European nations probably have a similar document as well) that guarantees our fundamental rights to be counted as individuals in the eyes of the Federal Government. If we are not, then there are other legal recourses one can take. Therefore, we have the right to choose not to use a biometric system if we feel that it impedes upon our constitutional rights.

In this regard, the second book examined this in close detail as well, focusing on the following sub-topics:

(1) The specific privacy rights that are associated with this trend;

(2) The legal aspects that are associated with storing latent information and data by a particular biometric system;

(3) The impact of time upon the biometric templates that are stored in the various databases worldwide;

(4) More psychological errors being introduced due to increasing the speed of processing times in a particular biometric system;

(5) The specific perceptions of biometric technology in the United States and the European nations versus the developing nations;

(6) The ergonomic design of the various biometric modalities;

(7) Function creep (this is in regard to the lack of a standards and best practices in the biometrics industry worldwide);

(8) The legal implications of creating and storing a biometric template from both a physical and behavioral perspective.

Once this extensive framework was provided, two new, major applications of biometric technologies were examined as well, namely the e-passport and the e-voting machine. The former replaces the traditional paper passport by containing a smart-card-like chip that can actually store numerous Biometric templates that have been created by the various biometric modalities (in this regard, the most commonly used templates are fingerprint recognition, iris recognition, and even facial recognition).

With the latter, biometric technology is actually being used to confirm the identity of a particular voter rather than using the traditional means (such as the driver's license, state ID, etc.) before they cast their ballot. Also, through the use of biometric technology, individual votes can now have an audit trail that is associated with them, to provide proof that an individual has actually voted. This, of course, is also causing a huge storm of controversy,

From the perspective of the e-passport, the following topics were covered:

(1) The mechanics and the engineering aspects of the e-passport, covering both the hardware and the software angles;

(2) The major Security vulnerabilities of the e-passport;

(3) The societal impacts of an e-passport infrastructure, such as the following:

- Privacy;
- Usability and accessibility;
- Health and safety;
- Social and cultural considerations.

From the standpoint of the e-voting infrastructure, the following topics were covered:

(1) The transition to an e-voting infrastructure;
(2) The security vulnerabilities that are present;
(3) The specific places where biometric technology can be used and implemented throughout the entire e-voting process;
(4) The examination of various case studies, including the adoption and usage of an e-voting infrastructure in Mozambique.

Finally, at the end of the second book, various strategies were also discussed as to how the acceptance rate of biometric technology could be greatly improved, focusing on the United States. General strategies were reviewed, and specific ones as well, focusing on the following applications:

(1) Time and attendance;
(2) Mobile and wireless devices;
(3) Single-sign-on solutions.

Our third book, which is this one, has continued with the theme of biometric technology. But rather than taking an overall and general approach to the topic matter, it was decided to focus upon two of the main biometric modalities, which are iris recognition and facial recognition.

The primary reasons why these were picked were that the technological advances in both are occurring rapidly, and both of these particular modalities can capture the respective iris and facial images of individuals at a distance, and even in groups. Just a decade ago, this was a totally inconceivable thought. For instance, the end-user had to stand in very close proximity in order to have their iris scanned or an image of their face captured.

Because of these rapid developments, so too have the mathematical algorithms which are used in these particular biometric systems been developed. As was eluded to at the beginning of this chapter, the biometric sensor can be considered to be at the heart of the any modality. After all, these are where the raw images are captured from.

But the mathematical (and even the statistical) algorithms are just as important as well. After all, once the raw images are captured it is these specific algorithms that will extract the unique features from them and from there create the needed enrollment and verification templates that will confirm the identity of the individual in question.

Also, it is these particular mathematical and statistical algorithms that will examine the degree of closeness between the enrollment and the verification templates. Of course, if the degree is deemed to be close enough, the identity of the individual will then be confirmed. But, if this degree is too far apart or not close enough, then the identity of the individual cannot be confirmed and the entire process will have to be repeated.

So, as one can see, the mathematical and statistical algorithms that are used in both iris recognition and facial recognition are just as much of a crucial component as the sensor themselves. But rather than being in a central location like the sensor and being visible, the mathematical and the statistical algorithms are not seen (in fact, they are proprietary to each biometric vendor, therefore the public can never really see the specifics as to what goes into them or even how they are created) and are used at various stages throughout the biometric system as the enrollment and verification processes take place.

Chapter 3 of this book is devoted primarily to iris recognition. When one thinks of this particular biometric modality, there is often confusion between the iris and the retina. The beginning of the chapter reviewed the differences between the two, as well as the primary functions they serve when processing the information and data that allow to have vision.

It is important to note that while retinal recognition has proven itself to be a viable biometric technology, it is not widely used or deployed, primarily because it has been deemed too user-invasive. Chapter 3 then transitioned over to the iris, first examining the actual physiological structure of the iris. Then, the mathematical algorithms which are used today in iris recognition were examined. The breakdown of these algorithms is as follows:

(1) The "Father" of iris recognition – Dr. John Daugman:

Dr. John Daugman has been deemed to be literally the inventor of the mathematical algorithms behind iris recognition. His work primarily covers the use of Gabor wavelet mathematics, and the creation of various kinds of "iris codes."

(2) The theoretical framework of iris recognition – Tarawneh and Thunibat:

This particular scientific study took a unique approach that examined the mathematical algorithms that are currently being used at each phase of the enrollment and the verification process. The phases that were examined include the following:

- Image acquisition – capturing the actual raw image of the iris;
- Segmentation – breaking down the raw image of the iris into various components;
- Feature encoding – capturing of the unique features from the raw image(s) of the iris, and from there creating the enrollment and the verification templates;
- Feature matching – the statistical closeness of the enrollment and the verification templates are compared and ascertained.

(3) Reducing the effects of pupil dilation and constriction – Proenca and Neves:

One of the biggest obstacles in iris recognition today is in dealing with the effects of pupil dilation and constriction. In order to counter this, Proenca and Neves created a newer set of mathematical algorithms known as "IRINA," which will thus result in much more robust iris-based composite image(s) being made available. The result of their work showed that IRINA was effective in all of the datasets it was provided; in other words, it proved useful in countering the effects of pupil dilation and constriction.

(4) Reducing the effects of eyelids and eyelashes – Lin et al. and Zhou and Sun:

Another obstacle in iris recognition is the eyelids and the eyelashes. It is important to note that the iris-based composite image(s) can only contain the actual image of the iris, and nothing else. At times, the eyelids and the eyelashes of the particular individual being studied can come into view, thus obstructing the image of the iris. The work of Lin et al. and Zhou and Sun examined this more closely, not only by using the theoretical framework established by Dr. John Daugman, but also by using a newer mathematical algorithm known as canny edge operators.

(5) Reducing the signal noise in the eye image – Shivani and Sharma:

This particular research work introduced yet another new mathematical algorithm known as reverse biorthogonal wavelet. The primary objective here is to improve the unique feature extraction process, in an effort to create more robust and optimal based enrollment and verification templates. Their work showed that by using this newer type of mathematical algorithm, the comparison time between the enrollment and the verification templates is drastically shortened.

Once the specific frameworks of these mathematical algorithms were established, Chapter 3 then segued into examining some of the specific applications of iris recognition, apart from those in which it is being used primarily today. The market applications which were examined include the following:

(1) Spoofing – print attacks: Gupta et al.:

In the world of biometric technology, one of the common questions that often gets asked is if a particular modality can get spoofed or not. In other words, can an impostor fool an iris recognition system into accepting him or her as a legitimate user? This is what the work of Gupta et al. primarily focused upon. But this study examined how an impostor can fool an iris recognition system by **using a printed image of an iris, not using an actual live scan**. Two different kinds of optical sensors were used, and one of them was very much prone to this kind of spoofing. In order to counter this, two types of statistical measures can be employed, which are known as the local binary pattern (LBP) descriptor and the histogram of oriented gradients descriptor (HOGS).

(2) Wireless networks – Ibrahim et al.:

There is no doubt that wireless systems will dominate all sorts of information technology applications, even that of iris recognition.

This is what the work of Ibrahim et al. focused upon. They also proposed the development and the use of two newer mathematical algorithms, known as the Libor Masek algorithm and the genetic algorithm optimization. They also proposed the development and the deployment of a brand new kind of wireless system. Overall, Ibrahim et al. concluded that the use of a wireless component in an iris recognition system is effective in the case of those applications where remote connectivity is required, and that the genetic algorithm is far more accurate than the Libor Masek Algorithm.

(3) Fuzzy neural networks – Karthikeyan:

There is much work currently being done in biometrics around neural networks. This is an area of research that focuses on replicating the various processes of the brain and implementing them in a biometric system in order to reach more "intelligent" conclusions. For example, rather than using a statistical approach to compare the enrollment and the verification templates, neural networks can be used to serve this purpose. But rather than taking a "yes or no" approach like the statistical approach does, neural networks can make their decisions as well by taking into consideration the "gray" or more subjective areas when the enrollment and the verification templates are compared with each another. Karthikeyan focused upon a subset of neural network technology known as "fuzzy neural networks." Overall, he concluded that the use of fuzzy neural networks can help to speed up the processing time for the comparison of the enrollment and the verification templates.

(4) Biocryptography:

As was discussed at the beginning of this chapter, one of the questions that often gets asked is whether, if a biometric template is hacked into or hijacked, it can be reverse-engineered back into the raw image format. This actually has never really happened before but, in theory, some scientific studies have demonstrated that this is possible. Thus, biometric templates need an extra layer of protection, and this is where the principles of cryptography can come into use. In very simplistic terms, it is the science of scrambling and descrambling a virtual object (such as a biometric template) while it is in transit from the point of origination to the point of destination. In this regard, this sub-section of Chapter 3 focused upon the following topics:

- The cipher biometric template;
- Biocryptography keys;
- Biocryptography in a single biometric system;
- Biocryptography in a client server biometric system;
- Biocryptography in a hosted biometrics environment;
- Biocryptography and virtual private networks.

Finally, Chapter 3 concluded with a case study that examined the famous *National Geographic* picture of the Afghan girl known as Sharbat Gula.

Chapter 4 of this book then transitioned to facial recognition technology. Out of all of the biometric technologies that are available today from both a physical and behavioral standpoint, it is facial recognition that is deemed to be the "most controversial" biometric modality of all. There is no distinct reason or logic for this, other than to many people it symbolizes covert surveillance by law enforcement agencies at all levels (federal, state, and local).

As was discussed in the first book, facial recognition received a lot of hype and attention just right after the terrorist incidents of "9/11." For example, it was deemed that it would be the "ultimate" biometric technology when it came to fighting the war on terrorism. But when it failed to live to this hype, both the public and the media totally downgraded the technology.

The primary reason why this happened is that, at the time, facial recognition was still (and continues to be) an evolving biometric technology. For instance, end-users had to stand very close to the camera in order to allow the required raw images to be captured. Also, many of the extraneous variables (which are also discussed in Chapter 4) still greatly impeded facial recognition technology.

Chapter 4 first started out with the question: which is a better Biometric modality to use ... iris recognition or facial recognition? Although we provided some answers, we will come to some conclusions on this at the end of this chapter.

When compared to the chapter on iris recognition, there was a much heavier emphasis placed upon the statistical and mathematical algorithms of facial recognition. The primary reason for this is that when compared to iris recognition, facial recognition, although it is deployed worldwide, is still under much research and development.

There is still more work that needs to be accomplished before facial recognition can come to the level of acceptance of the older biometric modalities such as fingerprint recognition and hand geometry recognition. The result of more research and development taking place in facial recognition is of course the creation of more mathematical and statistical algorithms.

The following sub-topics were covered in Chapter 4:

(1) An overview of how facial recognition actually works;
(2) Defining the effectiveness of a facial recognition system;
(3) The two macro approaches used in facial recognition (the appearance and the model-based approaches);
(4) The advantages and disadvantages of facial recognition technology.

After these sub-topics were examined, Chapter 4 then transitioned to the mathematical and statistical algorithms that are currently being explored in facial recognition technology. Although the two macro approaches were also reviewed, from within that particular group, there are five other sub-approaches, which are as follows:

(1) The geometry-based approach;
(2) The template-based approach;
(3) The bit by bit approach;
(4) The appearance/model-based approach;
(5) The neural network approach.

The first four sub-approaches can be viewed as being more traditional; but it is the latter which is capturing great interest amongst the scientific community. For example, neural networks can be used for enrollment and template matching. In this regard, the prominent features of the face can be represented as sophisticated models. Neural networks can also be used for deep levels of statistical analysis of the face, using various discriminant functionalities.

The following statistical algorithms currently being used or being explored in facial recognition technology were reviewed:

(1) Principal component analysis;
(2) Discrete cosine transforms;
(3) Linear discriminant analysis;
(4) Locality-preserving projections;
(5) Gabor wavelets;
(6) Independent component analysis;
(7) The kernel PCA.

It is interesting to note that Gabor wavelets, which have been so widely used in iris recognition, are also being used in facial recognition. But, out of all these statistical algorithms, it is principal component analysis that is receiving the most attention. In this regard, it is independent component analysis that is viewed by the scientific community as an alternative to principal component analysis.

The mathematical algorithms that are currently being used in facial recognition systems are as follows:

(1) Eigenfaces;
(2) Fisherfaces;
(3) Local binary pattern histograms;
(4) Neural networks.

Out of the first three, it is eigenfaces that is being the most widely used at the present time. Essentially with this particular technique, various facial-based models are created from actual raw images. These models are then superimposed over the actual facial-based composite image(s) in order to confirm the identity of a particular individual.

We once again visit the use of neural networks, but this time with respect to how they are being incorporated from a mathematical-based algorithm approach. In this instance, there are five major groupings of neural networks that are under research and development. These are as follows:

(1) The classification approach;
(2) The hybrid/semi-supervised approach (Intrator et al.).;
(3) The self-organizing map and convolutional approach (Lawrence et al.);
(4) The group-based adaptive tolerance approach (Zhang et al.);
(5) The probabilistic-based decision approach (Lin et al.).

From these five groupings, there are four sub-groupings from which specific mathematical algorithms have actually evolved. These are as follows:

(1) Neural networks with Gabor filters;
(2) Neural networks with hidden Markov models;
(3) Fuzzy neural networks;
(4) Convolutional neural networks.

In this regard, it is the first two sub-groupings that are being used the most. The primary reason for this is that these are much more established approaches. For instance, the use of Gabor filters has been established via their development in iris recognition, and hidden Markov models are a proven statistical modeling approach that is utilized heavily in both key-stroke recognition and signature recognition.

In the same manner as in Chapter 3 with iris recognition, once the theories and concepts of both the statistical and mathematical algorithms were established, various applications of facial recognition were then reviewed in detail. These are as follows:

(1) The use of a facial makeup-detection system in facial recognition – Chen et al.:

As was discussed in detail not only in our first book but in Chapter 4 as well, facial recognition is vulnerable not only to changes in the external environment (with the prime example of that being the lighting conditions), but also to changes to the face of the individual in question. In these instances, even the use and absence of makeup can be an obstacle for a facial recognition system. The work of Chen et al. focused primarily on this particular aspect. They developed a makeup-detection system, which in theory could be implemented in a facial recognition system. Their system actually improved the probabilities of an individual being identified correctly by a facial recognition system in the absence or the presence of makeup. But, Chen et al. also mentioned that **the degree of makeup that is applied to an individual** in question is as important to take into consideration as the presence or absence of makeup.

(2) Thermal face recognition for human-robot interactions – Hermosilla et al.:

As has been described at length, trying to make both iris recognition and facial recognition systems more "intelligent" via the use of neural networks continues to be one of the primary objectives of the biometrics industry. In this regard, there is also strong interest in designing facial recognition systems to actually interact with robots for security-related applications. This emerging field is known as human-robot interactions (HRI). Also, another goal here is to understand how to make robots more personable and human-like through the concepts of HRI. This is what the work of Hermosilla et al. focused upon. To do this, they added another component known as "vascular networks" that can be applied to the thermal regions of the face in order to preserve them. Although there is still much work that needs to be done in this area, overall, Hermosilla et al. concluded that the preliminary results of their study indicated that facial recognition systems could potentially interact with robots, but that many precise techniques would have to be further developed and refined.

(3) The use of facial recognition in forensics:

As was discussed, the field of forensics, in a very broad sense, involves collecting what is known as "latent data" at a crime scene.

285

This is essentially evidence that is left behind, and cannot be easily seen by the naked eye. There is now strong interest in using facial recognition technology in order to help automate the process of the examination and analysis of facial images that have been collected by a CCTV system or any other type of surveillance tool. But as was noted, the requirements for forensic evidence to be admissible in a court of law are very stringent. This even holds true for any evidence that is collected by a facial recognition system. At the present time, Facial recognition technology makes use of a **threshold system** in order to evaluate information and data presented to it (for example, comparing the facial-based enrollment and verification templates). This cannot be used in forensic investigations, and as a result facial recognition Technology has to make use of a **score-based system** in order for any evidence that is collected to be admissible in a court of law. This what the research work of Ali et al. focused upon. They created what is known as a "likelihood ratio" in order to establish a score-based system. They proved that this method could theoretically create forensic evidence that could be admissible in a court of law, but that there were limitations that need to be overcome, which were reviewed in detail as well. They also concluded that such a system will never be 100% automated; some sort of human intervention will also be required in order to make sure that the evidence that is collected by a facial recognition system is both forensically sound and accurate.

Finally Chapter 4 ended by reviewing some of the limitations of facial recognition technology as whole, and a case study. The specific limitations can be summarized as follows:

(1) Illumination;

(2) Pose;

(3) Occlusion;

(4) Optical technology;

(5) Expression;

(6) Mathematical/statistical algorithmic evaluations.

Finally, this book concludes our series on biometric technology. As reviewed at the beginning of the this chapter, the first book provided an overview of the technology of biometrics, with a focus upon its usage in the cloud, and the principles of cryptography.

Also, other key facets were reviewed such as the key performance indicators (KPIs) and other forms of performance-based metrics. A portion of the first book was also devoted to examining the biometric sensor – which can be considered to be at the heart of any biometric system.

Our second book examined the social implications of biometric technology, and why in certain parts of the word it is accepted quite readily (such as the developing nations) versus other geographic regions (such as the developed nations, with the United States and the countries in Europe being the prime examples).

One of the key takeaways here is that when compared to the other forms of security technologies, it is biometric technology that is the most prone to any claims of violations of privacy rights and civil liberties. Two major applications of biometrics were examined as well, namely the e-passport and the e-voting infrastructures.

The third book has taken a different angle, in that we examined much more of the scientific aspects of biometric technology, by focusing on the mathematical and the statistical algorithms that have been used or are currently being explored in both iris recognition and facial recognition. At this point, one may ask why these two specific biometric modalities were chosen for this book.

There are a number of key reasons for this, one of them being primarily that when compared to other biometric modalities (not including those that are currently under research and development, and thus have not been proven viable yet) is that these two particular modalities are seeing a growth in application development and use.

In particular, these two technologies have evolved to the point that they are now very miniature, and the actual sensor or camera can actually be used on a wireless device or tablet. This is especially true of the recent launch of the iPhone X, where facial recognition is now being used as a primary means of login versus the "touch ID" technology that was used on earlier versions of the iPhone.

In fact, iris recognition is now even being used as a means of replacing the traditional username and password combination. With just one scan of the eye, an individual can be logged into their workstation in just a matter of a few seconds, versus the minutes (or even longer) it can take by entering in your password, and perhaps even having it reset.

Second, as also has been pointed out at numerous times throughout this book, in the last decade an individual would literally have to stand in front of a camera in order to have their iris or face scanned in order to compile the needed raw image(s).

But now, the technology has evolved to the point that it can take these particular images from a distance, and even as individuals are walking in groups. Thus, both iris recognition and facial recognition have evolved as one of the security tools of choice at major international airports worldwide.

Third, these two biometric modalities are of the contactless type. This simply means that the individual does not have to directly touch or even interface with the technology, as opposed to fingerprint recognition or hand geometry recognition.

Because of this distinct advantage, the adoption rate will probably grow over time for both iris recognition and facial recognition, especially for the former. There is still some hesitancy amongst the public about having direct, physical contact with a biometric modality.

Fourth, both of these biometric modalities will have a significant impact upon the current war on terrorism, as they can be used covertly in order to confirm the identity of any terror suspects. Also, they have been used extensively in Afghanistan in order to confirm the identity of refugees, so that they can be relocated back to their homes after they have been displaced by military operations.

Also in this regard, both iris recognition and facial recognition are being used to ensure that these displaced individuals are indeed receiving their fair share of government aid and assistance to which they are entitled.

Fifth, with both iris recognition and facial recognition, there is a much shallower training curve for an individual to use these particular systems. For instance, either he or she will be required to be in a front of a camera in order to have the raw image(s) of the iris or face captured, or the images will collected by a much more covert means.

This is in stark contrast to other physical and behavioral modalities where some level of direct training is required. Because of this low learning curve that is involved, this will only help to increase the adoption rate of both iris recognition and facial recognition.

Sixth, these two biometric modalities can easily be integrated into the legacy security infrastructure of any business or corporation as an add-on. This simply means that there is no exhaustive study that will be required in order to determine how iris recognition or facial recognition can be intertwined into a layer of security that is already in place.

For example, as was eluded to before, if an organization wishes to eradicate the use of the username/password combination, all that is needed is to simply fit the needed iris recognition scanners in the workstations via a simple USB connection. With regard to facial recognition, if a law enforcement agency wishes to keep tabs on people entering and exiting a gathering at a large venue, all that is needed is to implement the facial recognition system in conjunction with the CCTV technology that is currently being used.

It is also important to keep in mind that, as these two particular biometric modalities continue to evolve over time in terms of both sophistication and size, the retail cost of them will also further come down, thus making them very affordable to any size or kind of organization.

In the end, if one really thinks about it, there is nothing that is magical or mysterious about biometric technology. It is just like any other type of security tool, just like a firewall, a network intrusion device, or a router, that can be used to fortify the lines of defense for either an individual (such as their smartphone) or a business or a corporation (such as protecting their IT infrastructure, as well as other tangible assets, whether they are physical or virtual).

Biometric Technology is prone to failure and cyber-based attacks just like any type of technological tool. As has been mentioned in great detail throughout these three books, the only difference between biometric technology and other forms of technology (even non-security-based ones) is that it is a piece of our physiological or behavioral selves that is being captured – nothing more, and nothing less.

In this regard, it is the author's view that the biometrics industry has done a poor job of actually explaining to the public at large what is exactly being done to their physiological samples or behavioral recordings after they have been collected. Thus, this has led to the "black box" stereotype of biometric technology, which has thus only heightened the fear and angst amongst the public, especially here in the United States and the countries in Europe.

Thus, it is imperative, as a business or a corporation readies itself for a biometrics implementation, that it also gives serious thought to training its employees and temporary workers not only into its proper use, but how the biometric modality that is going to be implemented works as well, from a non-technical standpoint. It is also imperative that enough time is given for these individuals to absorb what they are being taught, and how it will impact their day on the job, and even their personal lives as well.

Remember, biometric technology is also being deployed in products that are available to consumers, such as smartphones and other forms of wireless device. Therefore, the time that a business or corporation takes for this particular training will only mean in the end that the acceptance rate of the biometric modality that is going to be implemented will be greater in the end, and there will be less resistance to its use.

But it is also important to keep in mind that the use of a particular biometric modality cannot be mandatory. For example, if there are employees who refuse to use the system in question, then an alternative means must be provided to confirm their identity. This also holds true for the public at large as they try to access government-related services. If biometric technology becomes a mandatory security tool to be utilized by individuals, this will only decrease its subsequent adoption rate, and cause even more distrust or even hatred of the technology.

It is also important to note that biometric technology should not be used solely by a business or a corporation as the primary line of defense. Rather, it works best when it is used in conjunction with other biometric and even non-biometric security technologies. The use of biometrics in this regard is also known as a "multimodal security solution."

This simply means that there is more than one layer of defense in the perimeter; so for example if a cyber attacker were to break through one line, the chances that he or she will be caught are much greater as they try to break through the second lines of defense.

But ideally, a business or a corporation should use more than just two layers of defense; rather they should use as many layers as they can afford and reasonably implement. The concept of multimodal security solutions was reviewed in great length in our first book.

On this note, it is also very important to keep in mind that the use of security technology in general (whether it is biometric or non-biometric) should not be relied on exclusively to keep any type of cyber threat and risk at bay. It also takes a great deal of human vigilance, thus creating a proactive mindset.

In fact, achieving a high level of security takes both security technology and the proactive mindset amongst not only employees but the public as well. A simple diagram of this is as follows:

High level of security = multiple layers of security + a proactive mindset

So, in the end, which biometric technology is better to use, iris recognition or facial recognition? In the author's view, at the present time, it would have to be Iris recognition. For example, it has evolved to the point that it could soon prove itself to be a mature biometric technology, and it has evolved greatly over a short period of time. As mentioned, it is a contactless type of technology, so therefore its adoption rate will be far greater in the end.

Iris recognition in fact is deployed in many more applications than is facial recognition, and its impacts, both positive and negative, will be felt worldwide. It even currently dominates those particular market applications where fingerprint recognition and hand geometry recognition have been used the most.

The technology has proven itself over the last decade and well into this one, and there are not nearly as many issues with it, from both a technical and a social impact standpoint when compared to facial recognition.

This is not to say that facial recognition won't experience a greater adoption rate at a future point in time, but there are still some technical hurdles and obstacles that it must overcome first, most notably how it can handle variable changes in the external environment from which the raw image(s) are captured. Most importantly, even if these technical obstacles are overcome and resolved, it still must also cross all of the social stigmas and barriers that are currently facing it.

Index

Ali, T. 251–8, 285–6
anonymity 14
Apple Corporation: fingerprint
    recognition 39, 75
Apple Pay 75
Authentec 75

behavioral biometrics 4, 78–9, 270;
    acceptance 35–6; definition 90;
    differences from physical-based
    biometrics 55–8, 90–2; *see also*
    keystroke recognition; signature
    recognition
Bhattacharjee, D.K. 224
biocryptography 153–4, 164–74,
    271, 280–1; cloud computing
    170–1; iris templates, protection
    of 167–74, 280–1; keys 166,
    281; meaning 164–5; virtual
    private networks (VPNs) 171–4
biometric databases: security 20
biometric modalities: contactless
    devices, advantages of 288;
    ergonomic design 17–18, 35;

facial recognition devices 82–3;
    fingerprint recognition devices
    85–7; hand geometry recognition
    38, 48, 49–50, 79–81; iris
    recognition devices 84–5; key
    performance indicators 66–70;
    keystroke recognition devices 79,
    88; logical access control 73–4;
    mobile devices 74–5; networked
    50–2; physical access control
    71–2; signature recognition
    devices 79, 87–8; surveillance
    devices 76–8; terrorist
    identification, impact on 288;
    time and attendance devices
    72–3; vein pattern scanners
    81–2; voice recognition
    devices 83–4
biometric process 63–4; facial
    recognition 182–4; iris
    recognition 104–28; retinal
    recognition 95–7
biometric technology:
    acceptance 5–6, 10–12, 33–6,

274–5; apprehensiveness in acceptance 4–6, 43–4, 272–4, 290; best practices and standards 32; definition 54–5; e-voting using 31–3; hardware 39, 48–9; legal framework 19–21; mandatory system, issues for 20–1, 290; market application 70–8; networked modalities 50–2; overview 1–40; perception of 15–17; social issues 43–8; software 39–40, 51–2; technical issues 42, 52–88; training employees 290; United States Federal Government 18–20, 34
biometric template: biocryptography 164–74, 280–1; evidence in court proceedings 21, 252–8; hacking 15, 65–6, 131–9, 154, 280–1; iris 104; legal status 19–20; mathematical files 64–6, 113, 153–4; meaning 63–4; storage 20, 25; see also enrollment template; verification template
biometrics: definition 52–5; market research tool 53–4; medicine, role in 53; overview 1–40; see also behavioral biometrics; physiological biometrics
biometrics as a service (BaaS) 171, 271–2; virtual private networks (VPNs) 171–4

Blanz, V. 196
Burch, Frank 104

case studies: facial recognition 265–7; iris recognition 174–7
CCTV (closed-circuit camera television) 76, 83, 183, 218–19, 264–7; case study 265–7; images as evidence in court of law 252, 286
Chen, C. 234–45, 284–5
ciphertexts 157–8
closed-circuit camera television see CCTV
cloud computing 271; biocryptography 170–1
Cognitec Systems: case study 265–7
color: illumination obstacle for facial recognition 259–60
contactless biometric modalities 288; see also facial recognition; iris recognition
convolutional neural networks (CNNs) 225–33; deep neural networks 232–3
court of law: biometric templates as evidence 21, 252–8; CCTV images 252, 286; forensic evidence 252–8, 286
covert surveillance 76–8, 288; see also CCTV
cryptography 271; asymmetric key systems 159–64; ciphertexts 157–8; decryption 156–7; definition 156; e-voting process, application to 30–1; encryption

156–7; mathematical algorithms 158–9, 162–4; meaning 155–6; symmetric key systems 158–9, 161–2; *see also* biocryptography

cyber attacks 271; iris spoofing 131–9, 279; print attacks 132–9, 279

Dantcheva, A. 234
Daugman, John 100, 104, 105, 114, 120, 277–8
decryption 156–7
developed nations: biometric technology, acceptance of 6, 10–12, 33, 274–5; e-passports 22–3; e-voting 22–3; *see also* United States
developing nations: biometric technology, acceptance of 5–6, 10–12, 33, 274–5; e-passports 21–2, 26; e-voting 21–2, 26–7
devkit *see* software development kit
Diffie-Hellman algorithm 162–4
dilation 109; mathematical algorithms 115–19, 278
DNA recognition 36, 270
drivers' licences: security vulnerability 10

e-commerce: mobile 75
e-passports 21–2, 23–6, 275; computer infrastructure 24; developed nations 22–3; developing nations 21–2, 26; evolution 23–4;

facial recognition 264; iris recognition 131; process 24; security threats 24–5; social implications 25–6
e-voting 21–3, 26–33, 275, 276; biometrics, use of 31–3; cryptography, application of 30–1; developed nations 22–3; developing nations 21–2, 26–7; infrastructure 29–33; public key infrastructure 31; security vulnerabilities 30–1; transition to 29–31; United States 22–3, 27, 29–33
earlobe recognition 36
eigenfaces 186–7, 193–4, 207–13, 283; OpenFace 233
embedded encoding 149–50
encryption 156–7
enrollment template: iris recognition 113–15; wireless-based iris recognition 139–47
ergonomic design: biometric modalities 17–18, 35
European Union: biometric templates 19–20
evidence: Bayesian framework for forensic face recognition 253–8; biometric templates in court proceedings 21, 252–8; CCTV images 252, 286; forensic 252–8, 286
expression: facial recognition 263
eye 92–5: *see also* iris; retina
EyeDentify Inc. 94, 95

eyelashes 108; mathematical
algorithms 120–4, 278–9
eyelids 107–8; mathematical
algorithms 120–4, 278–9
EZW encoder 149–50

facial makeup: facial recognition
detection system 234–45, 284–5
facial recognition 179–267,
281–6; acceptance 35;
advantages and disadvantages
181–2, 188–90, 258–63;
advantages over other
technologies 287–9;
appearance based approach
186, 193–4; applications
233–58, 264–7, 284–6;
Bayesian framework for use
in forensics 253–8; bit by bit
approach 193; case study
174–7, 265–7; choice between
iris and facial recognition
179–81, 291–2; contactless,
advantages of being 288;
convolutional neural networks
(CNNs) 225–33; deep neural
networks 232–3; devices 82–3;
e-passports 264; effectiveness
criteria for the system 184–6;
eigenfaces 186–7, 193–4,
207–13, 233, 283; evaluation
of mathematical/statistical
algorithms 263; evidence
in court of law 252–8, 286;
expression 263; facial makeup-
detection system 234–45,
284–5; false acceptance rate
(FAR) 189; false rejection rate
(FRR) 189; fisherfaces 187,
213–15; forensic use 251–8,
285–6; fuzzy neural networks
224–5; geometry-based
approach 191–2; human-
robot interactions 245–50,
285; illumination obstacle
259–60; limitations 258–63,
286; mathematical algorithms
190–5, 206–33, 277, 282–4;
mathematical files 65,
113–14; model based approach
186–8, 193–4; neural network
approach 194–5, 217–33,
284; occlusion 262; OpenFace
233; optical technology 262–3;
pose limitation 260–2;
privacy rights issues 181;
process 182–4; smartphone
39; statistical algorithms
190–206, 223–4, 283;
techniques 186–8;
technological advances
276, 287–8; template-based
approach 192; thermal images
245–50, 285; three-dimensional
imaging 183–4; transfer
learning 232–3; unique physical
features used in 61; vascular-
based 246, 248–50, 285
fingerprint recognition 15;
acceptance 35; devices 85–7;
education on advantages of 45;
market application 37–8,

46–7; mathematical files 65, 113; smartphone 39, 74–5; unique physical features used in 60, 86–7

fisherfaces 187, 213–15

forensics: Bayesian framework for face recognition 253–8; facial recognition, application of 251–8, 285–6

Fulcher, J. 220

function creep: multi-modal security devices 18–19

fuzzy neural networks 147–53, 280; facial recognition 224–5; image 150; iris recognition 151–3; mathematical algorithm 151–3, 224–5

Gabor wavelets: facial recognition 204–5, 221–2, 224; iris recognition 105, 111–12; neural networks with Gabor filters 221–2

gait recognition 36

Goldstein, Isadore 94

Google FaceNet project 233

Gupta, Priyanshu 131–9, 279

Haar wavelets 148–9

hacking: biometric templates 15, 65–6, 131–9, 154, 280–1

Hamming distance model 114–15, 127–8

hand geometry recognition: acceptance 35; market application 38, 48, 49–50, 79–81; mathematical files 65,

113; unique physical features used in 60

He, X. 203

Hermosilla, G. 245–50, 285

Hough transform technique 107

human-robot interactions (HRI) 245–50, 285

Ibrahim, Ali Abdulhafidh 139–47, 279–80

identification 62; fingerprint recognition 85

identity theft: fear of 14–15

illumination obstacle: facial recognition 259–60

International Committee for Information Technology Standards (INCITS) 184

Intrator, N. 220

Iridian Technologies Inc. 100, 129

iris 100–1; physiology 101–3, 124

iris recognition 90–177, 277–81; acceptance 35, 129; advantages over other technologies 287–9; biocryptography to protect templates 167–74, 280–1; case study 174–7; choice between facial and iris recognition 179–81, 291–2; contactless, advantages of being 288; development 100–1, 128–9; devices 84–5; e-passports 131; enrollment template 113–15; false acceptance rate (FAR) 144–6; false rejection rate (FRR) 116, 144–6; feature encoding

111–12; feature matching
113–15; fuzzy neural networks
147–53, 280; image acquisition
106–7; logical access security
130; market applications 38,
128–53, 279–81; mathematical
algorithms 104–28, 277–9;
mathematical files 65, 114;
normalization 108–11;
physical access security 130;
process 104–28; segmentation
107–8; single-sign-on solutions
(SSOs) 130; smartphone 39,
75; spoofing 131–9, 279;
technological advances 276,
287–8; theoretical framework
106–15, 278; timekeeping 130;
unique physical features used
in 60, 85, 102–3; verification
template 113–15; wireless
networks 139–47, 279–80
IrisCode 104

K-D tree mathematical
algorithm 123–4
Karthikeyan, T. 147–53, 280
key performance indicators (KPIs):
ability to verify rate metric
69–70; biometric modalities
66–70; equal error rate 69;
failure to enroll rate 70; false
acceptance rate (FAR) 68–9,
144–6, 189; false rejection
rate (FRR) 69, 97, 116,
144–6, 189; retinal scanning
devices 97–100

keystroke recognition: acceptance
35–6; devices 78–9, 88;
statistical profiles 65, 88, 92,
113–14; unique behavioral traits
used in 61, 88, 270
Kohonen, T. 219

law: biometric technology 19–21
Lawrence, S. 220
Lin, Ma 120–1, 278–9
Lin, S.-H. 221
logical access security 7, 55–8,
113; biometric devices 73–4;
iris recognition 130

McCurry, Steve 174–7
makeup see facial makeup
market applications: biometric
technologies 70–8; facial
makeup-detection system
234–45, 284–5; facial
recognition 233–58, 264–7,
284–6; fingerprint recognition
37–8, 46–7; forensic use of
facial recognition 251–8,
285–6; hand geometry
recognition 38, 48, 49–50,
79–81; human-robot interactions
245–50, 285; iris recognition 38,
128–53, 279–81; logical access
security 73–4; mobile devices
74–5; physical access security
71–2; retinal recognition 98–9,
100; surveillance 76–8; time and
attendance devices 72–3;
see also biometric modalities

market research: biometrics, use of 53–4

mathematical algorithms: asymmetric cryptography 162–4; Bayesian framework for forensic face recognition 253–8; convolutional neural networks (CNNs) 225–33; Diffie-Hellman algorithm 162–3; eigenfaces 207–13; evaluation for facial recognition 263; eyelashes 120–4, 278–9; eyelids 120–4, 278–9; facial recognition 190–5, 206–33, 277, 282–4; fisherfaces 213–15; fuzzy neural networks 151–3, 224–5; Gabor wavelets 105, 111–12, 204–5, 221–2, 224; Haar wavelets 148–9; iris recognition 104–28, 277–9; K-D tree 123–4; local binary pattern histograms (LBPH) 215–17; Morlet wavelets 120; Needham-Schroder algorithm 159; neural networks 217–33, 284; pupil dilation and constriction 115–19, 278; reverse biorthogonal wavelet 124–8, 279; RSA algorithm 162–3; symmetric cryptography 158–9; wireless-based iris recognition 141–7

mathematical files: biometric templates 64–6, 113, 153–4

mobile technology: biometric devices 74–5; e-commerce 75; see also smartphone

Morlet wavelets 120

Müller, K.R. 206

multi-modal security devices 291; function creep 18–19

National Geographic 174–7

near field communications (NFC) 8, 10

Needham-Schroder algorithm 159

neural network technology 91; convolutional neural networks (CNNs) 225–33; definition 150; facial recognition 194–5, 217–33, 284; fuzzy neural networks 150–3, 224–5, 280; iris recognition 147–53, 280; mathematical algorithms 217–33, 284

Neves, Joao C. 115–19, 278

Niyogi, P. 203

occlusion: facial recognition 262

OpenFace 233

optical technology: facial recognition 262–3

passports: paper 23, 131; security vulnerability 10, 131; see also e-passports

passwords 7; smartphone 38–9; vulnerability 37, 38–9, 73–4

physical access security 7–9, 55–8, 113; biometric devices 71–2; iris recognition 130, see also fingerprint recognition; hand geometry recognition

physiological biometrics 4,
78, 269–70; definition 90;
differences from behavioral-based
biometrics 55–8, 90–2; see also
facial recognition; fingerprint
recognition; hand geometry
recognition; iris recognition;
retinal recognition; vein pattern
recognition; voice recognition
plastic surgery: facial makeup-
detection system 234–45
pose limitation: facial
recognition 260–2
print attack: iris recognition
132–9, 279
privacy rights: facial recognition
181; impediment to adoption
of biometric technology
13–14, 272–3
Proenca, Hugo 115–19, 278
profiling 14
public key infrastructure: e-voting
process 31
pupil dilation see dilation

radio frequency identification
(RFID) technology 75
Razko Security: case study 265–7
recognition: identification 62;
meaning 58–63; verification
61–2; see also facial
recognition; fingerprint
recognition; hand geometry
recognition; iris recognition;
keystroke recognition;
retinal recognition; signature

recognition; vein pattern
recognition; voice recognition
retina 92–5; physiology 94–5
retinal recognition: acceptance 35;
advantages and disadvantages
97–100; criteria for evaluation
99–100; devices 93, 94–5; false
rejection rate (FRR) 97; process
95–7; research and development
47–8; unique physical features
used in 60, 94; usage 98–9, 100
reverse biorthogonal wavelet
124–8, 279
robots: human-robot interactions
245–50, 285
RSA algorithm 162–3

Scholkopf, B. 206
SDK see software development kit
security: biometric databases
20; biometric technology as
mandatory system 20–1, 290;
e-passports, threats to 24–5;
e-voting, risks for 30–1; multi-
modal security devices 18–19,
291; passwords 37, 38–9, 73–4;
smartphone 38–9; timecards
9–10, 37–8, 73; usernames
37, 73–4
Sharma, Yuvraj 124–8, 279
Shivani, Pooja Kaushik 124–8, 279
signature recognition: acceptance
35–6; devices 79, 87–8; statistical
profiles 65, 113–14; unique
behavioral traits used in 61, 270
Simon, Carleton 94

single-sign-on solutions (SSOs) 37, 45, 74; iris recognition 130

smart cards 7–9, 131; legal issues 20; security weaknesses 8

smartphone: facial recognition 39; fingerprint recognition 39, 74–5; iris recognition 39, 75; security issues 38–9

society: biometric technology, acceptance of 5–6, 33–6, 43–8, 274–5; United States adoption of biometric technology 13–21, 34–6

software as a service (SaaS) 171

software development kit (SDK) 40, 52

spillover: multi-modal security devices 18–19

spoofing: facial makeup-detection system 234–45; iris recognition 131–9, 279

statistical algorithms 65, 88, 92, 113–14; discrete cosine transform (DCT-II) 202–3; evaluation for facial recognition 263; facial recognition 190–206, 223–4, 283; Gabor wavelets 204–5; independent component analysis 205; kernel PCA 206; linear discriminant analysis 203; locality-preserving projections 203–4; principal component analysis 197–202

Sun, Junping 121–4, 278–9

surveillance 14; biometric devices 76–8; types 76–7

Tarawneh, Rasha 106–15, 278

terrorist identification: biometric modalities, impact of 288

thermal facial images 245–50, 285

Thunibat, Omamah 106–15, 278

timecards: buddy punching 9–10, 37–8, 73; security weaknesses 9–10, 37–8, 73

timekeeping: biometric devices 72–3; iris recognition 130

Tower, Paul 94

tracking 14, 76

transfer learning 232–3

United States: biometric technology, acceptance of 6, 10–27, 29–40, 274–5; e-passports 22–3; e-voting 22–3, 27, 29–33; Federal Government use of biometric technology 18–20, 34; history of voting system 27–9; social impediments to adoption of biometric technology 13–21, 34–6

usernames 7; vulnerability 37, 73–4

Varshovi, S. 236

vein pattern recognition (VPR): scanner 81–2; unique physical features used in 61

verification 61–2; fingerprint recognition 85

verification template: iris recognition 113–15; wireless-based iris recognition 139–47

Vetter, T. 196
virtual private networks
(VPNs): biocryptography
171–4
voice recognition: devices 83–4;
unique physical pitch used in
61, 83–4
voting system: history in United
States 27–9

wireless technology: EZW
encoding 149–50; iris
recognition 139–47, 279–80;
near field communications
(NFC) 8, 10; *see also*
smartphone

Zhang, M. 220
Zhou, Steve 121–4, 278–9

Printed in the United States
by Baker & Taylor Publisher Services